Indian Asia

The Making of the Past

Indian Asia

by Philip Rawson

ELSEVIER · PHAIDON

Frontispiece: a *mithuna*, man and woman together; such couples punctuated the decorative and narrative sculptured reliefs on the Buddhist stupa of Nagarjunakonda, now destroyed. 2nd century AD, Krishna delta region. They epitomize the atmosphere of Indian art.

ISBN 0 7290 0046 X

Elsevier–Phaidon, an imprint of Phaidon Press Ltd,
Littlegate House, St Ebbe's Street, Oxford

Origination by Art Color Offset, Rome, Italy

Filmset by Keyspools Ltd, Golborne, Lancashire, England

Printed and bound by Brepols, Turnhout, Belgium

Contents

Maps

Preface to the series

This book is a volume in the Making of the Past, a series describing the early history of the world as revealed by archaeology and related disciplines. The series is written by experts under the guidance of a distinguished panel of advisers and is designed for the layman, for young people, the student, the armchair traveler and the tourist. Its subject is a new history – the making of a new past, uncovered and reconstructed in recent years by skilled specialists. Since many of the authors of these volumes are themselves practicing archaeologists, leaders in a rapidly changing field, the series is completely authoritative and up-to-date. Each volume covers a specific period and region of the world and combines a detailed survey of the modern archaeology and sites of the area with an account of the early explorers, travelers, and archaeologists concerned with it. Later chapters of each book are devoted to a reconstruction in text and pictures of the newly revealed cultures and civilizations that make up the new history of the area.

Titles already published

The Egyptian Kingdoms
The Aegean Civilizations
The Spread of Islam
The Emergence of Greece
The Rise of Civilization
The First Empires
Rome and Byzantium
The Iranian Revival

Biblical Lands
The New World
Man before History
The Greek World
Barbarian Europe
The Roman World
Ancient Japan

Future titles
Ancient China
The Kingdoms of Africa

Prehistoric Europe
Archaeology Today

Introduction

Indian civilization, between about 500 BC and 1200 AD, was perhaps the most glorious and influential the world has ever seen. Amazingly, the Indian achievement is still not properly recognized; India's present problems may obscure it to some extent. But there is no longer any reason why the western world should remain blind to the special importance and value of India's contribution to world history and culture.

The subcontinent of India, which includes modern Pakistan and Bangladesh, is roughly the size of Europe. Westerners may find it hard to believe, but in fact her culture, literary and artistic, has produced more major works of art and intellect than the whole of the European tradition; and that despite the extraordinarily destructive tropical climate which has consumed untold quantities of sculpture, painting and manuscript. If the art and culture of Indianized Southeast Asia are reckoned in, the wealth of the integrated civilization appears so vast as to defeat the grasp of the imagination.

The creative potential of Indian culture made itself felt far beyond the borders even of the Indianized kingdoms of Southeast Asia. Cultural realizations of fertile Indian conceptions took place in China, Japan, Tibet, inner Asia and the Mediterranean world. Their genuine influence in the west is still growing. There can no longer be any real doubt that both Islam and Christianity owe the foundations of both their mystical and their scientific achievements to Indian initiatives. It is also surprising that western historians, when they discuss Asia, leave almost completely out of account the Indian tradition of maritime trade which was already over a millennium old before the Arabs came onto the stage of history, and which continued right through the Middle Ages. India's merchant adventurers were exploring the coasts of Asia, and developing international commerce over thousands of miles of sea in large cargo and passenger ships while the Romans were still developing the Mediterranean.

What we know of material culture in Indian Asia is tiny in relation to what once existed. But an enormous amount certainly waits to be unearthed, and archaeology has in that sense only begun. There could be stupendous discoveries yet to be made. We know, for example, that somewhere adjacent to the Kabul region of modern Afghanistan there was in the 4th century AD a reclining sculpture of the dying Buddha 1,000 feet long, carved into a cliff face. It is no longer visible. It is scarcely conceivable that it should have been destroyed. It is probably still lying in position, buried perhaps under fallen rock.

To define the character of an entire civilization which extended at least two thousand years and many thousands of miles is a daunting task. But for Indian Asia there is a clear unifying root. This is a complex of ancient symbolic ideas which was fixed and condensed into two bodies of text that were treated as sacred, and so preserved unchanged over more than two and a half millennia. The first is the Hindu Veda, a collection of ancient hymns with their associated Sanskrit literature and famous appendix called the *Upanishads*. The second is the literature of Buddhism. Certainly in their modern forms scattered throughout this vast area of the world the various expressions of Hindu and Buddhist ideas may seem outwardly different from one another, each being intimately woven into the fabric of its specific society. But through the visual arts their intrinsic unity as branches from the same root becomes clearly apparent.

This root spread out from India to strike deep into the soil of those disparate regions of Asia, with their widely various populations and totally dissimilar physical environments. Buddhism in particular naturalized itself in the freezing wastes of Mongolia among a population of horse-breeding nomads living in tents, in the cultivated heartland of China, and among tropical forest on the vast river plains of Southeast Asia. Hinduism established itself for varying lengths of time on the plains of Indochina and in the volcanic southeastern islands; there on Bali it still flourishes.

The art which survives to testify to the greatness of the culture of Indian Asia represents a totally unique manifestation of the human creative spirit. It has taken many decades for it to win appropriate recognition in the west; that process will be charted in this book. Among the surviving monuments, fortunately, are many that have been reclaimed from the grip of very hostile environments – rocky desert or tropical jungle – and restored to surprisingly good condition; their sculpture and ornament, if not their surface painting, may be relatively well preserved, and give a good idea of their original magnificence. The way some monuments are still used can give vital clues to the meaning and usage of comparable ancient works now abandoned. But when political and financial circumstances finally permit we can look forward to a considerable increase in our knowledge and appreciation of the splendid civilization that was Indian Asia.

Chronological Table

	NORTHERN INDIA	SOUTHERN INDIA	MALAYA AND BURMA	THAILAND	INDOCHINA	INDONESIA
BC	c. 2000 Aryans enter India c. 1300 Aryans settle in Punjab c. 900 Compilation of Veda complete c. 800 Sage Kapila c. 600 *Upanishads* crystallize c. 527 Death of Mahavira c. 489 Death of Buddha c. 450 Foundation of Pataliputra 327 Alexander enters India 323 Alexander dies Greek Kingdoms of northwest 321 Mauryan dynasty founded 272–232 Ashoka Maurya stupas	Neolithic Colonization of Ceylon First caves cut in Western Ghats under Shakas Shatavahanas in Deccan	Neolithic Indian trading stations	Bronze Age coastal culture on Neolithic base	Bronze Age coastal culture on Neolithic base	Bronze Age coastal culture on Neolithic base
	c. 200 *Kamasutra* begun 187–75 Shungas in Magadha c. 120 Eudoxos sails direct to India					
100	75–30 Kanva dynasty Shakas in Ujjain Buddhist texts written Trade with west flourishes		Buddhist centers			
AD	Kushans control northwest Mathura sculpture flourishes Great Kushan king Kanishka			Buddhist centers	Kingdom of Funan founded by a Brahman on the Mekong river	75 Shaka prince colonizes Java Buddhist centers
100	c. 120 Kushans open overland route to Mediterranean Buddhism in China Gandharan art flourishes	Shatavahanas patronize great southeast stupas Second wave of cave cutting in Western Ghats			192 First royal foundation in Champa	
200		Apogee of southeastern Shatavahana art	Buddhist art in Malaya		Mi Son the Cham capital in north	
300	Rise of Gupta dynasty Creation of Hindu temple art begins *Natyashastra* composed	Major painting at Ajanta	Buddhist bronzes	Buddhist bronzes	Funan Buddhist art	
400		c. 360 Hindu Pallavas take control of southeast	c. 470 Great Pyu city at Prome in Burma		Chen-la founded	
500	c. 440 Great dramatist Kalidasa Great mathematician Aryabhatta	Great series of Chalukyan temples at Aivalli and then Badami (7thC)	Flourishing kingdoms in Malaya		Major icons made	
600	606–47 King Harsha of Kanauj Decline of Buddhism Great era of Hindu temple building		Mon kingdoms of southern Burma and Thailand		616 Khmer kingdom founded Rise of Hinduism	
700	Earliest Orissan temples Rise of Pala dynasty in northeast, patronizing Vajrayana Buddhism, which flourishes in Tibet	Last painting at Ajanta Pallava architecture begins in southeast Mamallapuram	Great kingdom of Burmese Pyu Great kingdom of Malaya		Cham oppress Khmer Decline of Chen-la	Pallava script adopted in central Java Emergence of Shailendra dynasty of central Java Hindu temples
800	Rise of Chandellas and beginning of Khajurahs	Chalukyas control west, build much art Elephanta cave temple Ellora rock-cut shrines Shankaracharya, greatest Hindu philosopher Cholas oust Pallavas in southeast, also Shaivas	Bodhisattva bronze from Chaiya	Khmer rule S Thailand	Khmer recover c. 880 Founding of Angkor Bakong built	Borobudur built Lara Jonggrang, Prambanan
900	Major northern and western dynasties build Hindu shrines Incursions of Islam Rajarani temple, Orissa	Cholas build huge temples, cast bronzes	Infiltration of racial Burmese		961 Pre Rup, Angkor Cham retreat to south	927 Kingdom of east Java rises, building and sculpting
1000	Lingaraja temple, Orissa Rise of Hindu Senas in northeast, competing with Palas Temples of Jagannatha, Puri, Orissa	1005 King of Shrivijaya dedicates a temple in Chola domain	1056 King Anawrahta's decree in Burma Pagan begun, much building		Baphuon, Angkor	
1100	Gradual conquest of north by Islam 1196 Palas extinguished, end of Buddhism in India	Rise of Hoyshalas in Mysore Eclipse of Chalukyas in west			Angkor Wat 1177 Angkor sacked by Cham	
1200	c. 1230 Konarak temple, Orissa		1287 Pagan sacked by Mongols	Racial Thai occupy all country	1181 Cham defeated 1215 Angkor Thom and Bayon complete	
1300			Buddhist work continues in Mandalay, Rangoon		Cham shrines at Binh Dinh	1268 East Javanese Chandi Jago
1400		1386 Eclipse of Hoyshalas				Islam infiltrates

1. India and her Culture

The land of India. India is a subcontinent some 2,000 miles from north to south. But geographically it is a unit, cut off as effectively by natural features from the land mass of Asia, as by the sea around its coasts. In the north, through the great 1,600-mile-long mountain chain of the Himalaya ("the resting place of snows") only a few high and difficult passes give onto the tableland of Tibet. Along the southern Himalayan foothills runs a band of high, steep and forested terrain still inhabited by hardy mountain peoples such as the Gurkhas and Sherpas. To the northeast, dense tropical jungle stretches unbroken for hundreds of miles into China and Burma, clothing innumerable high ridges and precipitous gorges; it has been impassable throughout history. This jungle was inhabited by tough tribal populations, chief survivors of whom are the Nagas, with their own culture and affinities to ethnic groups of mountaineers in southwest China and Burma, but virtually no contact at all until recently with India. In the west, what is now the arid mountainous upland of Baluchistan, beyond the Indus valley, has been, if not impassable, certainly inhospitable. Invaders and fugitives have passed this way to and from southeastern Iran. The Bolan pass, near Quetta, has carried a trickle of trade. But the northwestern corner of the subcontinent, now shared between Afghanistan and Pakistan, has been of cardinal importance. For through the corridor which runs in along the valley of the Kabul river over the Khyber pass, down towards the basin of the Indus with its tributaries, has flowed an immense volume of India's trade. Invading peoples and armies have entered by this route, the first of them the Aryans in the second millennium BC. For this reason the northwestern corner has always been ethnically the most mixed in population, and the most disturbed.

The geographical armature of India, defining the shape of settlement, the distribution of the old major cities and the patterns of political structure, has been conditioned by two features: first, the truly enormous rivers, which

Previous page: itinerant musicians in the Karakoram mountains near Gilgit. The landscape typifies the northern terrain which isolates India from Central Asia.

Left: landscape near the Bolan pass, in modern Pakistan, a desiccated river valley, typical of the western terrain which the monsoon has deserted.

Opposite: map of India and Southeast Asia, showing principal sites in the diffusion of Indian culture.

Below: bathers in the holy river Ganga; to all Hindus this great river is a goddess whose water will wash away their evil deeds.

provide long-range communications as well as water; and second, the stretches of difficult mountainous terrain, once densely forested, which establish natural barriers. The Indus to the west was especially important during periods of Indian prehistory, when it flowed into the sea far to the east of its present delta, through the shallows of what is now the Rann of Kutch. It actually rises 1,000 miles beyond the plains, far to the north of the Himalaya. The region of its upper tributaries, called "the Five Rivers" (Panch-ap = Punjab), was the cradle of India's most ancient literary culture, the Veda, produced by the immigrant Aryans. Around its lower reaches major kingdoms flourished between the 2nd century BC and the 2nd–3rd centuries AD. But with the gradual desiccation of the northwestern corner, the area became, by the 6th century AD, a region of uncertain economic status, its earlier, relatively wealthy kingdoms taking on the character of buffer zones.

By far the most important of the other great rivers of India is the Ganga, and her chief tributary, the Yamuna. Both are adored by Hindus as goddesses. Ganga rises in the Himalaya; her source is a great natural ice formation in a cave, which is still worshiped as a phallic emblem (*lingam*) of the god Shiva. The cave, sacred to Amarnath, is a holy pilgrimage place. The Ganga alluvial river plain, running over 1,000 miles roughly from west to east, between 90 and 300 miles wide, has been the economic and political heartland of the subcontinent, watered by many lesser rivers. Especially its middle reach in an area of Bihar, called in ancient times Magadha, has nourished the greatest empires of northern India. Its delta mouths opening into the Bay of Bengal are also fed by the Brahmaputra, which runs in from that virtually impenetrable jungle-clad barrier of hills to the northeast. It, too, rises far to the north of the Himalaya.

Some 100 to 300 miles south of the Ganga runs a broken series of ranges of hills from east to west, ending to the west in the Vindhya mountains. These, although not high,

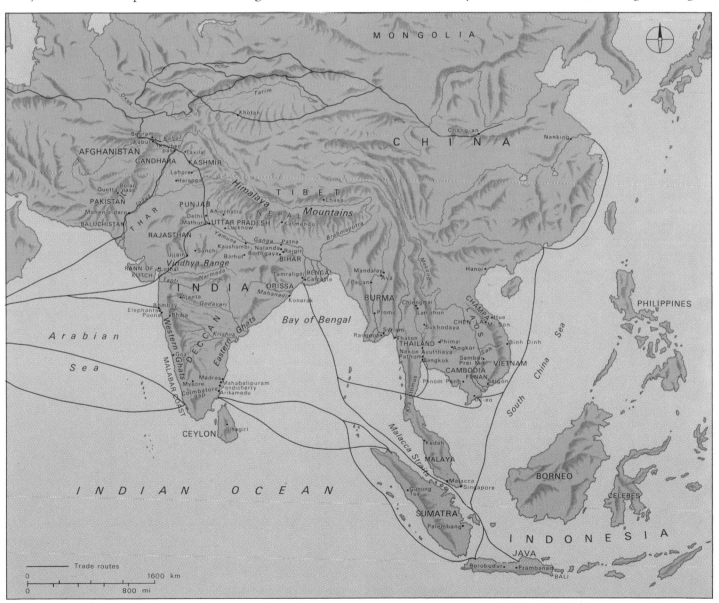

were nevertheless a barrier, pierced by a major gap running between the valleys of the Son and Narmada rivers. The main arteries of trade and conquest passed either through that gap from the upper Ganga plain to the northwestern Deccan, or around the western end of the Vindhyas. The western coastal region around and to the south of the mouth of the Narmada was, especially during the centuries immediately before and after the opening of the Christian era, a major trading region, with ports and cities feeding western trade up to the Punjab and the Ganga valley.

Parallel with and close to the western coast of the Deccan runs a ridge of high mountains, broken by gorges, called the Western Ghats. Their steep-sided tables have long provided powerful fortresses. The ports along the

A boat on a lagoon in Kerala. This landscape, with its tall coconut palms, is typical of the far south of the Deccan where Dravidian languages are spoken.

coast tended to be related directly with routes running inland through the Ghats, across the plateau that slopes away towards the east. But by far the most important of these routes was that provided by the valley of the Tapti river, whose mouth lies close by the Narmada, but whose course opens a passage to the southeast. It links with the valley of the Godavari, the most important of the rivers of the Deccan, which runs away to the southeast, cutting through a far less significant range of hills called the Eastern Ghats. To the north of the Godavari delta on the Bay of Bengal lies the state of Orissa. But the whole region north of the main Godavari valley and south of the eastern end of the main east-west mountain barrier south of the Ganga plain, was always difficult and dangerous terrain. Even along the eastern coast there was relatively little contact between southern Bengal, with the adjacent mouths of the Mahanadi river, and the delta of the Godavari.

Away to the south of that delta stretches for some 800 miles the long tropical coastal plain of southeastern India, a land of palm trees inhabited mainly by Tamil-speaking population, ethnically distinct from the peoples of the north. They developed their own great dynastic kingdoms on the economic basis of that fertile plain, which is watered principally by eastward-flowing rivers, notably the Krishna. In the southernmost point of the triangle of the Deccan another small spine of mountains is broken by the Coimbatore gap, which has given since at least the 1st century BC an easy crossing for trade goods from one coast to the other, avoiding the sea journey either around Ceylon or through the shallow straits between Ceylon and the Indian coast.

Trade and communications. The sea and the rivers have provided the major arteries for transporting goods from one part of India to another. The roads, which branched off from the main armature just described, provided another. The great advantage of water transport was that it was relatively free, if dangerous. Overland transport was often far more dangerous, at risk from war and civil disturbance; and kingdoms that could command the roads were able to enrich themselves by tolls. Many of the wars and dynastic movements in Indian history took place for the sake of capturing and controlling trade. The development of seagoing trade with the west took place initially in the last three centuries BC. In the days of the Indus valley civilization regular commerce with the Arabian Gulf had existed. At Lothal (Ahmadabad district) a harbor with a tide-sill and a basin for quite large boats has been discovered and excavated. No doubt some coastal commerce continued until regular trading began between the eastern colonial states of the Roman Empire and the area around the mouth of the Indus. A sailor Eudoxos is the first in Classical sources said to have made the direct journey from Egypt to India in 120 BC. The early prosperity of the city of Mathura (2nd century BC–5th century AD) was probably connected with trade passing up the Indus from, among other places, Ptolemaic and Roman Egypt. Certainly Egyptian and Romano–Egyptian art motifs were assimilated there, though the influence was reinforced by more direct overland trade in the 2nd century AD. It was from coastal trade that west-coast ports around the mouth of the Narmada river were designed to benefit.

An important site has been excavated on the southeast coast of India, in the Tamil plains, called Arikamedu. It was a lagoon-side port, and can be dated to near the beginning of the Christian era. It produced Roman pottery and trade goods of about that date. Its existence tallies very well with the achievements of a legendary Greek sailor, Hippalos, who is said, in 5 AD, to have discovered the skill of sailing on the monsoon direct from the Gulf of Aden across the Arabian Sea, to make landfall well south on the Malabar coast. Arikamedu could have served as entrepot for goods then taken around the coast of the peninsula or overland via the Coimbatore gap. They could then pass up into the Ganga valley by way of the delta, on which lay a large, ancient port-city called Tamralipti.

The development of the Indianized kingdoms along the coasts of Southeast Asia was a direct function of the setting up of regular sailing patterns around the coasts, as well as road links overland. There can be little doubt that the Indians and their Southeast Asian counterparts became great sailors. We have one or two representations of substantial ships with sails and banks of oars from between the 7th and 12th centuries AD (e.g. the paintings at Ajanta; a memorial stone at Eksar, western India, 9th century; and reliefs on Borbudur, Java, c. 800, which show outrigger vessels). We read in literary sources of ships which could carry as well as cargo upwards of 200 passengers.

Our knowledge of the distribution of Indian ports and associated petty kingdoms throughout Southeast Asia is still far from complete. But it is already clear that they were all functions of the coincidence between practical sea routes and available areas of relatively hospitable fertile terrain. To the south, the routes which passed through the Malacca Straits generated kingdoms in southern Sumatra (Palembang) down into Java, and on into Borneo, Celebes and the Philippines. To the north, the major trade route probably crossed the neck of the Malay peninsula at the isthmus of Kra, where an entrepot kingdom flourished called Suvarnabhumi ("land of gold"). Sea routes reached from there to parts of the southern coast of Thailand, where the eastern Mon kingdom was founded, and to Indochina, where Funan, Chen-la and the kingdoms of the Khmer and Cham flourished. Goods of the early seaborne trade in Indochina that have been excavated include Ptolemaic, Roman and Sasanian objects. The sea connection was fortified by at least one major land route running between lower Burma and the Thai plain. The seasonal monsoons made it possible to sail on fairly

Above: stone carved relief from Borobudur, Java, c. 800 AD, illustrating the type of boat with tripod mast and heavy outrigger which carried trade through the islands.

Below: lower panels of a 9th-century memorial stone at Eksar, southern India, which illustrates ships with banks of oars which would have carried India's seaborne trade with the rest of Asia.

predictable winds in both directions across the Bay of Bengal between the southeast coast of India and Malaya and the Malacca Straits.

Climate. The monsoons are the dominant climatic features of the whole of this tropical region. India particularly relies for its fertility upon the southwest monsoon, which blows from June for about three months. The rest of the year is dry, save in a few areas of the far south. This wind blows as a consequence of the lower atmosphere over the Asian landmass warming up during the summer, and rising. Moist air then flows in across the Indian Ocean to take its place, and as it reaches the coastal mountains – the Western Ghats – and then approaches the Himalaya, it deposits torrential rain upon the land. The Deccan plateau, lying in the "rain shadow" of the Ghats, is relatively ill watered. The plains to the south of the Himalaya receive the greatest share of the rain. The monsoon clouds, as they advance and build up over a countryside parched by months of baking heat, are welcomed by the people with relief, hope and pleasure. Seeds germinate, trees blossom and the land changes almost overnight from brown to green. Much Indian poetry hymns the first thunderstorms and the breaking of the rains, as heralds and metaphors of the delights of consummated human love. Water is sacred; it represents life. If the monsoon fails, as occasionally it does, starvation and famine follow. Very frequently, on the other hand, it produces vast floods in the areas it reaches, which cause widespread destruction and loss of life, as well as spreading fertile alluvial silt. Rivers may even change their courses by tens of miles in one season. India is truly a land of extremes.

Such a climate has been devastating to material culture. Its extremes of heat and humidity, and its tropical insect population, have destroyed untold quantities of art. Under these conditions the people's most urgent need has always been to contain and control the monsoon floods, holding as much of the water as they possibly can for use later in the year, as the country once again dries up. The water needs to be distributed through complex irrigation systems among the fields. Even the great rivers are subject to wide seasonal fluctuations of level. The Ganga itself may fall by early June some 80 feet below its flood level.

Tank or reservoir near Madras in south India. Such tanks retain the monsoon water for use in the dry season, and the fertility of much of India depends upon them.

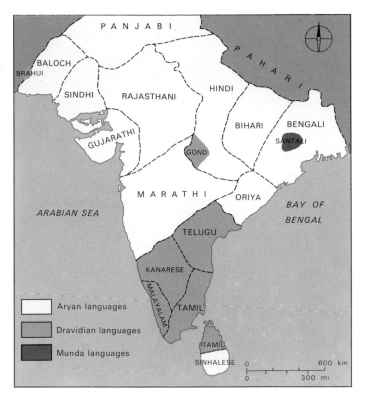

Map illustrating the language distribution of India; in the north are the languages based on Sanskrit, in the far south languages of the Dravidian group.

Generally speaking, the greatest cities of India have flourished on the banks of the major rivers whose waters can be continually tapped by various mechanical aids to irrigate a hinterland from which the cities are fed. But many cities, especially dynastic capitals, have flourished away from the rivers. All these have depended upon huge reservoirs, or tanks, which the monsoon fills. The building of these tanks, and the repairing of their often enormous dams, was one of the chief functions of rulers and governments, a function interpreted in Indian religion as an essential part of the mediation between heaven and earth implied by royal status. Cities, with their temples and gardens, would be laid out around the water systems. And to breach a dam was considered one of the most dreadful crimes.

But India is fundamentally a land of villages. The countryside is patterned with villages linked to one another by a network of paths; they lie from half a mile to a mile or two apart, according to the land's capacity to support the population. Each of these villages needs its own water supply. On the lower ground wells may reach down to the water table. Wherever possible the village has its own spring, tank or pond. In parts of the uplands every little fold in the ground has its small dam, which holds for as long as possible the runoff from last year's monsoon. It is thus not surprising that a symbolism of luxuriant foliage provides one of the principal elements in the decoration of religious–dynastic architecture, and that divine creative energy is interpreted in India as a kind of juice or sap of the

universe. It was also natural that Indian hydraulic engineering skills, fortified by religious doctrines, should have provided a strong economic foundation for their overseas kingdoms. Local customs reflecting these ideas on a small scale survive to the present day. It is still possible, for example, to watch a Thai Buddhist monk spend all day repeatedly raising a small golden vessel in the shape of a goose to the summit of a stupa, full of water which he has blessed, and pouring it onto the dome using a trip cord; or to witness small figures that represent the fertilizing god and fertile goddess in sexual intercourse being carried around the sown rice nurseries of Indochina.

It is generally accepted that the track of the monsoon shifted in historical times. Documentation is uncertain; but it seems that by the 7th century AD the monsoon had moved east, and ceased to water the belt of land lying to the west of Rajasthan. The lower valley of the Indus, once well watered and forested, is so no longer. The Thar is a desert. The exact historical relationship of climate and forest in India is still little understood. But it is certain that most of India was once densely forested, and that the forests were inhabited by populations whose relics are the present Adivasis (aboriginals). The epic *Mahabharata* (c. 400 BC) describes the great forests of central India. And there are many references in literature, up to and right through the medieval period, to hermits retiring to live in remote forest.

Language distribution. Precisely how and when the various ethnic and linguistic groups in the Indian population established themselves we have little certain knowledge. Our best information concerns the Aryan, Sanskritic-speaking invaders into the northwest; for they have carefully preserved the memory of many details of their own past, when they were actually in the process of settling in India, in their vast body of ancient sacred literature centered on the Veda. Before them at least three, possibly more, successive ethnic groups who left no literature had entered and colonized the subcontinent, probably fairly sparsely. The present language distribution has, however, a great deal to do with historical patterns. In the north there are a few isolated pockets of older tongues: Santali in Bengal, which is probably related to the Mon language originally spoken in lower Burma, Thailand and Cambodia; and Brahui and Gond, related to the modern south Indian group. The overwhelming preponderance in the north is of Sanskritic languages, each a regional derivative from the archaic Aryan tongue.

Sanskrit, in its earliest form a highly inflected and complex language, definitely seems to have asserted itself as the root language over the whole of the north by about 800 BC. As time went on, Sanskrit speakers evolved a simplified form of Sanskrit; then, as their geographical distribution widened, a group of simplified variants called Prakrits evolved. These were the spoken languages of the different cultural regions of the north; and a vast quantity of literature – which is read by scarcely any westerners – was written in the regional Prakrits, which prevailed throughout the period with which this book is concerned. One of these simplified languages is Pali, which is still the sacred language of the vast Buddhist Theravada literature of Ceylon, Burma, Thailand and Vietnam. It was most probably the Prakrit of the region of western India around Ujjain and Sanchi in the 3rd and 2nd centuries BC. Magadhi was probably the Prakrit spoken by the Buddha, who lived in Magadha. The extensive literature of the Jains was composed in it. The modern languages descended from the Prakrits are mostly called by the modern names of the regions in which they are spoken. Discounting variants which exist even within them, these are now 13: Rajasthani, Punjabi, Pahari-Newari, Hindi, Bihari, Bengali, Oriya, Marathi, Gujarati and Sinhalese in Ceylon. Baloch and Pashtu are spoken in modern Pakistan and Afghanistan. Persian, itself a language of Aryan type, used by the Muslim Mughal dynasty in the 16th to 18th centuries AD, has blended with Sanskritic vernaculars to produce modern Hindustani.

The southern group of languages have an ancestry quite different from the Sanskritic. They are sometimes called Dravidian, and one opinion is that they may be descended from the speech of the inhabitants of the Indus valley civilization of c. 2800 BC–1350 BC, who were gradually pushed southwards by the invading Aryans from the north. Ethnically, however, the Dravidian speakers have no clear-cut characteristics. For, of course, language has no essential connection with race. All the Dravidian languages produced large and vital literatures. They are Tamil, Telugu, Kanarese and Malayalam. But since all of southern India came to subscribe to the literary culture of the Aryan Brahmans, all these languages have many Sanskritic loan-words and idioms.

Material culture. The material culture of early historical India is little known. Excavation has brought the plans of several settlements and cities to light, and, no doubt, will bring many more. We know from literature that the earliest Aryan settlements (before 1000 BC) in the Punjab consisted of round and square huts built of bamboo, having perhaps more than one story. Huts and cattle pens were surrounded with palisades and earth walls. The chiefs were buried under mounds of earth heaped over a wooden chamber built around a central post – a kind of tumulus. As time went on, and Aryan settlement advanced into the Ganga plain, becoming richer, the wooden houses became larger, with several rooms, including one for the sacred fire, all thatched. The Sanskrit *Grihya Sutras* (c. 700 BC), part of the sacred literature, mention still larger houses with their own ponds and walls, containing assembly rooms, stores and latrines and surrounded by gardens. Public squares were laid out, along with roads and bridges. There were plates, cups, spoons and mirrors of precious metals, elaborate clothes and jewelry, fine wooden beds

The Jarasandha-ka-Baithak at old Rajgir, the base of a wooden watch tower which once stood by the city gate.

and furniture. Images of deities were also made, but we have no idea what they were like. For to testify to all this opulence described in words, only a few isolated and banal objects remain: the Fort Munro sword, an ax or two, and coarse gray-ware potsherds.

Of the early city period following 600 BC in the north we also have some remains, notably at old Rajgir, not far from modern Patna, in Magadha. The town lay in a valley; on the surrounding hilltops a 25-mile girdle of Cyclopean stone walls protected it. Fragments of other such walls also survive elsewhere. The opening of the valley was protected by a moat and an earthwork: we know earth-bank fortifications elsewhere, for example at Ahicchatra (north Orissa), where they are faced with baked brick. This latter city had a central temple on which the main streets converged. By the gate at old Rajgir stands a huge stone platform, called the "Jarasandha-ka-Baithak" ("the throne of Jarasandha," a mythical king). In fact it seems to be the base of a great wooden watch tower; and similar smaller platforms in the town were also probably the bases of other wooden buildings. All of these are gone, beyond recovery. And this brings us to a most important point concerning the whole of Indian material culture.

What remains to us, with a few exceptions only, consists of stone, fired clay (terracotta) and stucco, though only a fraction of work even in these more durable materials survives. From the earliest times to the latest, millions upon millions of houses and palaces, large and small, have been made of mud brick and timber from the extensive forest. The texts tell us that many of them were richly carved, containing wall paintings and painted panels, and superbly worked furnishings. Of all of these virtually nothing survives. The terrible climate of India has destroyed them. Where chance has preserved some early terracottas, a few ivory panels, a handful of early

wall paintings on plaster, we are obliged to use our imaginations to reconstruct the widely flourishing arts we know once existed. Of all the pictures and illuminated books we know to have been produced in India, on palm leaf, birch bark or cotton cloth, nothing survives that is older than c. 1000 AD, apart from fragmentary Buddhist manuscripts preserved in the dry sands of Central Asia.

There is no such thing as a consistent history of early Indian art. For it is impossible to construct anything but a conjectural picture of Indian material culture from the scraps that remain. Some of the first representational relief sculptures at the stupas of Sanchi and Barhut (1st century BC), however, illustrate splendid wooden buildings, many stories high. Early Buddhist caves in the Western Ghats (e.g. Bhaja) are stonecut transcriptions of huge wooden halls, with even the joist-ends carefully imitated. We know, therefore, to some extent what some of the vanished buildings looked like. They all share two principal features: a tunnel-vault made with curved transverse wooden ribs, probably thatched; and an arched window framed by a hood-molding of ogival outline, called the *chaitya* arch, which was usually filled with a wooden lattice to admit cooling air and keep out bright

Facade of the Buddhist preaching cave at Bhaja, 2nd century BC. Its features imitate the wooden architecture of the millions of houses which once existed all over India, but have now totally vanished.

sunlight. This arch is an Indian thematic form, adopted in brick and stone architecture all over Southeast Asia, modified in the regions.

What survives does so because it was executed in more permanent materials. There is a relative abundance of early pottery and small figurative terracottas, which tell us a good deal about the appearance and pleasures of at least the more fashionable citizens. Any abandoned brick and stone structures which nature had not destroyed, or ancient mounds containing them, have usually been systematically dismantled and plundered by local people for reusable building material. And it seems likely that it was considered necessary or appropriate during our period for only religious buildings to be executed in stone or baked brick, though even today there are parts of India where temples are still made of wood, notably the Himalayan regions and parts of the far south. At old Taxila, on high northwestern terrain, it is true that there are relics of masonry covering the period c. 300 BC–300 AD. In the ancient fortified city-mound at Kaushambi the collapsed remains of the only masonry vault (c. 400 BC) known in pre-Muslim India have been found. But apart from such isolated instances all the relics of Indian material culture are religious.

It may well be that archaeology will turn up the plans of towns and palaces, and decipher medieval cities, for a mass of excavation waits to be done. In Ceylon, at Sihagiri (Sigiriya), for example, the foundations of a huge late 5th-century AD palace complex and surrounding city have been revealed. It could be said that to some extent Indian archaeology may have been biased in favor of discovery and conservation of religious structures, ignoring other avenues of search; but that was very largely due to the fact that they still survived in relative abundance above ground, and were made of stone. Stone sculptures on religious buildings are the chief remaining testament to the artistic glory of ancient India, with a minute number of wall paintings. But they indicate the existence of schools of

Right: section of wall by the path ascending Sihagiri in Ceylon, painted with figures of celestial girls, c. 500 AD.

Below right: one of the celestial girls painted on plaster at Sihagiri.

Below: the lion rock at Sihagiri, 600 feet high. At the top was a palace, inhabited c. 500 AD; at the foot lay a palace and city recently excavated.

secular arts flourishing wherever wealth and patronage would have encouraged them.

Indeed the character of many surviving religious works is distinctly secular; some of the wall paintings, for example at the Buddhist rock-cut monastery of Ajanta, are extremely sensual in style, and highly inappropriate to the environment of a body of ascetic monks. And this suggests that such paintings were done not by painter-monks, but by secular artists, accustomed to decorating private houses, who turned their skills when required to the representation of Buddhist themes. It is therefore a question worth considering, to what extent the art of India actually was so uniformly religious as it appears to be. This issue will be discussed in the final chapter. But what has come down to us as Indian material culture is unequivocally religious; and so this book will discuss that culture in terms of the two great religions which generated it, by tracing the evolution of the Buddhist shrine and the Hindu temple.

Literary sources. In a special sense the roots of Indian civilization are linguistic and literary. It was through particular types of literature that it developed and spread, maintaining its vitality for millennia. The different regions of India and Southeast Asia had, of course, secular poems, plays and stories like any other culture. But in addition they shared a vast body of ancient text, Hindu and Buddhist, which was looked on as sacred, and was a constant source of ideas and cultural inspiration. This literature has survived when material culture has vanished, passed on in the memories of special social groups, and copied from manuscript to manuscript. The Sanskrit language was the vehicle of much of this text, as we have seen, with one of its derivatives, Pali, being the vehicle for the Theravada Buddhist texts, and another, Magadhi, used for Jain text.

Most important has been the role of a relatively simplified Sanskrit as a lingua franca for the educated. The development of this literary Sanskrit has its own history. It represents a survival from the first stage of the simplification of archaic and complex Sanskrit, perhaps kept alive

in the west of India – an issue to be discussed later. But a great upsurge of courtly poetry, drama and prose took place in the chief cities of northern India in the centuries just before and then after the birth of Christ, which adopted this classical Sanskrit as its medium. At the hands of a host of sophisticated writers it became capable of a subtlety and complexity of sound and meaning unparalleled in any other language. As used by philosophers and logicians it was able to intensify and condense thought to an extraordinary degree; and some of the Indian texts best known to the English-speaking world are such condensations.

This Sanskrit was acquired and cultivated by writers all over India, whose spoken mother tongues had become mutually unintelligible. It still is. Through this medium they were able to communicate with each other; and vast libraries of Sanskrit literature were built up in every region of India, as well as in the Hindu kingdoms of Southeast Asia. There were slight regional variations. The Sanskrit used by Mahayana Buddhists was idiosyncratic, with a specialized vocabulary, but even so it remained perfectly intelligible to non-Buddhists. It was the language of the great Buddhist Mahayana texts which were translated into Chinese, Tibetan, Mongolian, Korean and Japanese, as well as into Old Javanese and Mon. Some form of Sanskrit and its literature was the agent in the spread of Indian culture into the regions of Southeast Asia, where the fundamentally tribal populations in Neolithic or Bronze Age stages of civilization had no written literature or technical scholarship of their own. To the present day the Sanskrit epic *Ramayana* remains the chief source of legend and drama in many parts of Southeast Asia, albeit much modified by local mythology.

This Sanskrit language has given Indian culture its coherence and force. Sanskrit is the world's most ancient tongue to survive intact, because the priestly caste of originally Aryan Brahmans regarded it as their religious duty to preserve unchanged the mass of Sanskrit text

Palm-leaf page of Buddhist Wisdom text, written in Nagari script in Sanskrit. Dated 1112 AD. Victoria and Albert Museum, London.

known as the Veda, which is centered on four collections of hymns. This text, and its vehicle the word, they held to be sacred, an audible manifestation of Supreme Principle, the Brahman. All canonical manifestations of sacred word were similarly treasured. The Veda was too holy to be written down; so it was learned by rote, and passed on from generation to generation of teachers in lines of descent from masters to pupils, chanted from mouth to ear. The hymns themselves go back at least into the second millennium BC. Their archaic and grammatically elaborate Sanskrit is a relation of the lost archaic forms of Greek and other European tongues – the group called by linguists "Indo–European." The hymns invoke and praise a pantheon of deities, and were meant to be chanted during sacrificial ceremonies. Over the millennia the meanings hidden in the hymns, and in their beautiful linguistic structure, were explored and deepened by Brahmans who spent years of their lives in meditating on this focus of their religion. By the 4th century BC a mass of explanatory text, including phonetic, metaphysical, mythical and logical speculation, had gathered around the hymns, even though no one any longer actually spoke their language. Perhaps no one ever did speak it in its strictest and most elaborate form. About the 5th century BC two great epic poems, the first versions of the immense *Mahabharata*, which is the more archaic, and the *Ramayana*, the more sophisticated, were composed in the relatively simplified but beautiful Sanskrit. They consolidated the classical form of the language.

The beginnings of literacy. The question of when Sanskrit texts were first written down has not yet been fully solved. Many scholars believe that Sanskrit and its derivatives must have been written at least by the 5th century BC. For it is virtually certain that the administration of the large cities and kingdoms then in existence would have been impossible without some form of script. Libraries must also have existed by the 2nd century BC. But the earliest actual writing known to us from historical times is a set of inscriptions cut on rocks and on stone columns all over India by order of the emperor Ashoka, in the third quarter of the 3rd century BC. Their languages are local Prakrits. The script used is called Brahmi (in the northwest another called Kharoshthi was used, derived from Achaemenid Aramaic). Brahmi is fully capable of notating classical Sanskrit. It follows the careful phonetic system developed by the Brahmans to enable them to understand their archaic sacred Vedic Sanskrit; and all the later Indian scripts are derived from Brahmi. (Kharoshthi remained in occasional use only in the northwest and in Central Asia into the early Middle Ages.)

It must always be remembered, however, that our sole evidence for the earliest writing is in the form of official inscriptions on stone, or on coins; and these materials tend to distort lettering in specific ways. We know nothing of the cursive lettering that would have been needed for

Sculpture of a goddess in Nepal, 10th century. A dedicatory inscription detailing her virtues is cut on the surrounding rock in a version of Nagari script.

manuscripts. We can only be sure that it must have existed. For even the Brahmans would have needed to write out the vast bulk of less sacred literature they themselves produced; and the character of the earliest secular Sanskrit literature, including the epics, seems to be that of written, not of purely memorized text. In the north, Brahmi gradually acquired flourishes and a transverse line across the top of each letter, to become the beautiful and often aesthetically elaborate Devanagari, the "divine-city" script of the early Middle Ages, which is now standard for all Sanskrit and most vernacular publications. This in turn developed variants, notably the Bengali after the 11th century, and the Tibetan after Indian culture was established in Tibet in the 8th century. In the Deccan and Ceylon Brahmi became more and more rounded, ending up as a looped script. It is still used to record their Pali texts also in these countries of Southeast Asia which adhere to Theravada Buddhism. In central India and in the Tamil plains more angular versions of Brahmi gradually evolved. The earliest Southeast Asian inscriptions known, dating to the 4th and 5th centuries in Malaya and Borneo, are in fair Sanskrit, written in an early form of southeast Indian script. Some later inscriptions, for example those of the Khmer, are in both fine Sanskrit and superb lettering.

There are regions of southern India where non-Sanskritic languages have flourished, with their own scripts and literature, notably Tamil, in the southeastern plains. Tamil poetic literature was recorded from the earliest centuries AD, when the first anthologies were collected of poems composed by wandering bards. These remained almost unknown until the late 19th century, when the rare manuscripts were brought out from old libraries and edited. But first the Buddhists, and then the Brahmans, "colonized" the southeastern part of India under the patronage of royal dynasties. They were thus in a position to dominate the Indian commercial and cultural expansion overseas which originated in the Tamil regions. Brahmans and Buddhists constituted two rival specialized social groups, each preserving their own body of sacred literature, one or both of which provided a cultural and social nucleus wherever Indian colonies were established. They are the chief key to the long continuing vitality and immense geographical spread of Indian culture.

The Brahmans claimed the most ancient status. Since each Brahman had the faculty of preserving in his own memory the huge body of sacred text, he was looked on by the rest of society as a vessel of all kinds of knowledge, and supported by the community. Brahmans were thus free to develop intellectual and conceptual skills to an extent almost unknown in any other early culture. As well as preserving the religious and philosophical literature upon which their status rested, they acted as ministers of state and administrators; they were lawyers and moral philosophers. They evolved sciences of logic, mathematics, astronomy, engineering (especially hydraulic), medicine (complete with a large pharmacopoeia of drugs) and metallurgy. They were responsible for developing and recording the vast heritage of ancient Indian thought and literature not only in Sanskrit, but in Prakrits too. Even today huge libraries of manuscripts exist which are by no means fully explored. Chiefly because of their millennia-long intellectual labors far more of the literature and scholarship of India has been preserved than of almost any other civilization. And it must be remembered that for every scholar whose name is mentioned in modern studies of Indian culture, there are dozens scarcely less important who contributed to the development of every school of thought. When Hinduism traveled overseas it was the Brahmans' learning that supported a theory of kingship and a ceremonial state organization upon which the success of the overseas kingdoms was founded.

The importance of Sanskrit. Far too few people in the west understand clearly the immense historical and cultural role Sanskrit still plays in the world. Intellectual discoveries made in India are now accepted as a fundamental ingredient in the consciousness of modern man. Major examples are the decimal system of numerals used in modern place-mathematics, including the zero without which whole reaches of science would be impossible. We call them Arabic; but the Arabs only transmitted them to the west from India, and themselves called the numerals "Indian." Their earliest recorded appearance in India is in an inscription dated 695 AD, but they were certainly used in calculation by mathematicians some centuries earlier. Along with the numerals themselves went a concept of number as potentially infinite, which was reflected in cosmologies with "universes numberless as the sands of the Ganges" that were already familiar by the 2nd century AD.

From the 7th to the 12th century Indian mathematicians developed many techniques and concepts far in advance of those of the west. Among them were the use of plus and minus quantities, the extraction of square and cube roots, the solution of certain quadratic equations, a clear insight into the implications of zero and infinity, into trigonometry, spherical geometry and calculus, chiefly as applied to astronomy. In the 5th century the astronomer Aryabhatta proposed a heliocentric theory of the planets, together with the notion that the earth rotated on its own axis. Such mathematical ideas were abstracts from the fertile matrix of Brahmin introspection and observation, nourished by an intense interest in logic. This last Brahmin interest has not yet been fully investigated, since few

South Indian bronze of a royal devotee, 15th century; his hands are joined in devotion. Images like this were dedicated at shrines all over India, and kings often ended their lives as ascetics. Delhi Museum.

Sanskritists, western or eastern, are capable of following out the extreme conceptual refinements especially of the later schools of Navya-Nyaya.

Another science early developed in India was linguistics. This evolved from the study of grammar and meaning, initially because the archaic Sanskrit in which the Veda was composed gradually became unintelligible to the Brahmans whose task was to memorize it and use it in ritual. The two greatest grammarians were Panini (5th century BC) and Patanjali (2nd century BC) and perhaps the greatest theoretician of meaning was Bhartrihari (5th century AD). It was their discovery of Panini that prompted the brothers Grimm in Germany to initiate the comparative study of linguistic structure upon which our modern understanding of language is based. Also in Germany during the earlier 19th century, the Schlegels and the philosopher Schopenhauer, among others, recognized the seminal importance of the Sanskrit language, its literature and philosophy, and incorporated what they could into the German idealist tradition. This, though temporarily at a disadvantage in the west, is beginning to reassert its once great influence on western thought.

Hinduism. The Brahmans are, of course, identified with Hinduism. But historical Hinduism is by no means a direct reflection of ancient Aryan Vedic thought. In practice it is an amalgam of the Aryan social system with popular worship of gods, and with a theory of kingship based upon a functional relationship between the human king and his deity. In the Aryan social system, which evolved to become the caste system, the role of the Brahmans was cardinal. Local gods of the people were gradually assimilated to a group of major deities; their various local myths were collected and synthesized by the Brahmans in their medieval encyclopedias of legend, the *Puranas*, so that in the end Shiva, Vishnu, the goddess under various names, Surya the sun god, Ganesha god of wealth, and Brahma the creator, became the principal figures in the Hindu pantheon. They were not major Vedic deities, although the other gods of the Veda were kept alive in the Brahmans' own texts, and were sometimes consciously introduced into Hindu iconography in the later Middle Ages. The great gods of historical Hinduism, however, were sponsored by the Brahmans, who generally took charge of their temples, and who ensured that they were identified by a wealth of mythology as personifications of the Supreme Principle. It was these gods whom Hindu kings took as their metaphysical sponsors. Within Hinduism sects grew up, principally on the basis of the individual's choice of one or other of the deities as personal lord. Needless to say, the sects themselves produced considerable quantities of devotional and theological literature.

The life of an Aryan after childhood was codified into four stages. He became successively student, householder, forest dweller and finally a homeless ascetic who had renounced the world, even the calm of the forest, to seek an ultimate spiritual realization in total asceticism. During the last stage he might pursue the extremes of knowledge by one of the many different techniques of meditation, including the yogas, far more intensively than would have been possible at any earlier stage. Most ordinary Aryans never got beyond the stage of householder. But many Brahmans took their responsibilities seriously, and thus generated a whole class of wandering ascetics, who were looked on by the people as especially holy, and invited imitation. By the 6th century BC, when the Buddha, founder of Buddhism, and Mahavira, founder of Jainism, were living, it had become customary even for non-Brahmans who felt the call to become ascetics and follow various teachings. The Ashokan inscriptions (third quarter of the 3rd century BC) call on the populace to respect "Brahmanas and Shramanas" – the latter being, no doubt, such non-Brahmanical ascetics. Among these people history knows of several different orthodox and unorthodox sects.

Icon of the dynastic deity Vishnu, holding his discus and conch shell, in the style of northeast India of the 12th century. Delhi Museum.

Buddhism. Buddhist literature describes the Buddha as trying several such teachings before discovering his own way. When he achieved his ultimate enlightenment under the pipal tree at Bodhgaya, he realized four holy truths: life is suffering; the cause of suffering is desire; the way to the release from suffering is to abandon desire; the way to abandon desire is the noble eightfold path of the Buddha's discipline. After his enlightenment, until his death and passing into Nirvana, the Buddha continued to preach, converting many laymen, and building up his order of ascetic monks, which remained thereafter the kernel of Buddhism. They preserved his teaching, and as time went on, elaborated a huge body of doctrine.

View of a ruined stupa at the great ancient city of Ayutthaya in Thailand, which lay at the focus of trade routes, and produced art and architecture in a distinctive style during the Middle Ages.

The Buddhist tradition was preserved in three basic forms. First was the Theravada ("way of elders"), or Hinayana ("lesser vehicle"). This was a "fundamentalist" school, whose texts are preserved in Pali, and believed itself to be closest to the original teachings of the Buddha. It survives especially in Ceylon, Burma and Thailand. The Mahayana ("great vehicle"), whose texts are in Sanskrit, shared a great body of disciplinary text with the Hinayana; but it developed a series of doctrines and metaphysical texts which go far beyond the narrow scope of Hinayana. Where the latter limits itself to teaching methods for each individual's own salvation, the Mahayana emphasizes universal compassion as a cardinal principle, and implies that Hinayana is vitiated by self-interest. The third school, Vajrayana ("thunderbolt vehicle," post 550 AD), accepts Mahayana principles, but adds a whole armory of older, magical and meditative techniques, many of them adopted from Hindu sects.

During the diffusion of Buddhism throughout India and Southeast Asia, the Buddhist order of literate monks played a role comparable to that of the Brahmans in Hinduism. Indeed it seems that by the medieval period the distinction between Hinduism and Buddhism in Southeast Asia had become blurred; for to this day Brahmans from India are employed to conduct certain court ceremonials in Bangkok, the capital of Thailand, where Buddhism is still the state religion. At the center of Buddhism, however, was a theory of total renunciation. While Brahman theory allotted places and times of life to ordinary human desires and ambitions, even though these

View of the great Buddhist monument at Borobudur through the lush landscape of central Java; built c. 800 AD.

were held to be in the last resort obstructions to ultimate spiritual achievement, Buddhism taught that all forms and customs save the Eightfold Path were absolute barriers to any advance whatever. Buddhist monks were supposed in theory to discipline and dedicate themselves, entirely abandoning any ordinary human purpose. In practice they may not have done so. For once Buddhism had developed its own powerful institutions, based usually upon monasteries under dynastic patronage, monks did come to play political and economic roles.

They also developed powerful schools of logic and psychology. But it was characteristic of Buddhism that its lack of commitment to any specific outward system enabled it to adapt to the social systems of many different populations, and to present itself as a spiritual ultimate against the background of almost any alien religion. It taught, in principle, that no system of society, thought or knowledge was of any final value; hence it never set out to impose an alternative social or doctrinal system of its own in any area into which it penetrated. In this it was unlike Hinduism, to which a substratum of caste theory was essential. Buddhism in its various forms was thus able to survive and prosper in many countries of the east: China, Korea, Japan, Mongolia, Tibet, Burma, Thailand, Ceylon, Cambodia, Vietnam and parts of the great archipelago from Malaya and Sumatra to Celebes. Hinduism penetrated into continental Southeast Asia and Java; but after great initial success it lost its hold on the populace, who came to accept Buddhism. In India proper, on the other hand, Buddhism, after a millennium and a half of existence, surrendered its hold upon the people, leaving the field to Hinduism with its entrenched social system. For vast numbers of non-Indian peoples in Asia, however, Buddhism is still both the basis of true morality and the way to ultimate release.

Jainism. There remains to be mentioned one religion very important in parts of India, but not known to have flourished outside until well after the period covered by this book. It is that of the Jains, founded by Mahavira, the older contemporary of the Buddha. Jainism teaches that the way to the spirit's release from the bondage of matter lies in total abstinence from injuring any living creature. Few people are able to carry this doctrine to its ultimate conclusion, which is, of course, motionless suicide by starvation and thirst. For neither animal nor plant may be eaten as food, trodden on or breathed in, nor water, even with its insects filtered out, drunk; for it was held to contain a living spirit. The heroic saints of Jainism are thus those who deliberately attain suicide by abstinence. They are represented in art as Jinas, immobile, radiant beings. Their spiritual triumph was often commemorated by the erection of a pillar; and many Indian kings abdicated to end their lives in this way. Jain temples closely resemble Hindu, save that an icon of the Jina, the spiritual victor, occupies the central place.

The Dance as Hindu Ritual

This Chola bronze of the early 12th century from south India epitomizes the connection between dance and ritual in India. This very posture is used by modern dancers in the living Kuchipudi tradition. Shiva's dance here symbolizes the activity of creation, the divine act which continually weaves with its patterns the world of phenomena, and then obliterates it. He dances thus in the heart of his faithful worshipers. Dance became in the Middle Ages one of the standard elements of ritual in Hindu temples, though it was also a secular, courtly entertainment. But with the assimilation of the imagery of court and heaven, the distinction between secular and religious dance, which both relied on the same legends for their subject matter, ceased to have any significance. Indian dance traditions were adopted and developed all over southeast Asia.

Left: wall painting of the 6th century AD in Cave 1 at Ajanta, showing a female dancer and musicians, courtly performers of the time, a surprising subject for a Buddhist monastery.

Opposite: dancers in the Manipuri tradition, one of the four ancient Hindu traditions surviving in Assam, belonging to the Triveni company.

Below: Kamala performing Bharatnatyam, the south Indian version of ancient temple and courtly tradition. Indian dance comprises an elaborate language of mime.

Far left: frieze of dancers on the late medieval temple of Chidambaram. The dancers here wear elaborate skirts closer to the modern Manipuri costume than Bharatnatyam of southern India.

Left: this sculpture of a celestial musician playing a flute was cut on a temple at Bhuvaneshvara, Orissa, in the 11th century. It illustrates music as the heavenly art intimately related to the dance. All the arts are believed to originate in, and connect humanity with, the celestial regions. The modes of music are essentially divine, and to play them well depends upon transcendent inspiration. Victoria and Albert Museum.

Right: portion of a frieze from a 13th-century temple in Bombay state on the Shatrunjaya hill, illustrating celestial beauties and male musicians and dancers. These demonstrate the image of the temple to be a kind of celestial royal court.

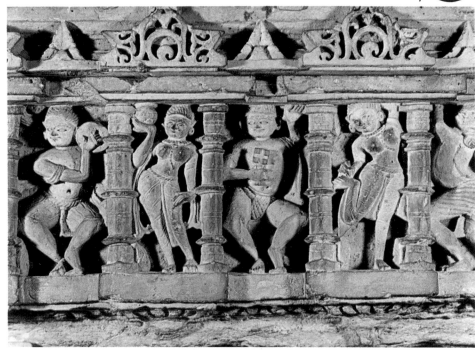

Above: a Paccha character in the Kerala Kathakali dance tradition.

Above left: the Ketjak, a modern Balinese dance in which the rhythmically chanting and swaying chorus of monkeys plays the major part. The dancers enter trance.

Left: an *Apsaras*, celestial girl, sculptured on the Bayon, Angkor, Cambodia, c. 1200 AD, a heavenly prototype of the earthly female dancer in Lakon style.

Below: Cambodian dancer of the modern court troupe performing in the 11th-century court of Angkor Wat. She wears a crown like the sculptured dancers, and her fingers curve like lotus petals.

Above: Thai dancer performing a modern version of palace dance in Bangkok.
Above right: relief carving on the Buddhist monument of Borobudur, c. 800 AD, representing a female court dancer entertaining a prince and his consort.
Right: female dancer executing a sword dance, acting a role in the Indian *Ramayana* story, carved on a frieze in the Prambanam Shiva temple, c. 900 AD.
Below: Khmer sculpture of a celestial girl dancer of the 12th century AD; another image of the heavenly prototypes of earthly dancers. Musée Guimet, Paris.

Left: the modern Ramayana Ballet Company of Jogjakarta enact the episode of the Demon Ravana, who has carried off Rama's wife Sita, killing the eagle who is Rama's helper. Traditional Javanese dance styles keep alive a tradition originating long ago in India.

Left: one group of Balinese dancers features the Barong, a benevolent monster characterized by a mask based upon the Kala monster of older art. Here Barong confronts the evil Rangda witch in a ritual danced in trance.

Below: the Balinese solo dance, the Baris, expresses the profoundly inspired character of the epic hero.

2. Western Knowledge of Indian Asia

India and the west. India has been known to the west in two different ways: first, as a contemporary culture; second, as the object of antiquarian and archaeological scholarship. She was known by the contemporary Greeks and Romans, who had some admiration for what they could grasp of her culture. Then during the Middle Ages India became a remote region of fantasy. Only at the Renaissance were a few direct contacts established by Europeans, though the fantasy died hard. In the 17th century western travelers, especially the Frenchman Bernier, wrote excellent firsthand accounts of what they saw when they visited the east. Thereafter growing trade and the accompanying warfare brought Europeans into closer and closer contact with Indian reality. Trading stations were opened, and European merchants came into direct confrontation with alien ways of life. By the end of the 18th century European powers had begun effectively to rule different regions of India and Southeast Asia, and their civil and military administrators began seriously to take account of native customs, laws, geography and economics. All these people, however, were concerned with present realities, not with understanding or appreciating the achievements of the past with which this book is concerned.

Serious interest in India's past developed through the 18th century. Banks's illustrated publication of Captain Cook's voyages had a tremendous influence upon people's interest in exotic regions. European scholars living in India, who had been trained in Greek and Latin Classical literature, began under the guidance of Indian pandits to investigate the Sanskrit tradition, and apply the methods of Classical scholarship to native material. Their work made a great impact upon western culture. During the 19th century this movement gained force. In addition, officers of the East India Company, and later, after 1859, of the Indian Civil Service and Indian Army, many of whom were men of lively intelligence, devoted themselves to exploring India's cultural heritage. Their incentives were mixed. They needed to know about the people they were administering; so they published first-rate gazetteers of the Indian districts. But at the same time they were often men brought up in the European tradition of the "curiosus," the amateur who pursued knowledge for its own sake, collecting and codifying strange natural objects, rare artifacts and unconventional information. Only gradually did it dawn upon most of them that what they were dealing with was the tail end of a glorious civilization several thousand years old.

It was by no means unusual right through the 19th century for European Christians to believe that the world was created in 4004 BC, according to the calculations of Bishop Ussher which were based on Biblical genealogies. But as the sciences of archaeology and Darwinian evolution developed in Europe, European perspectives broadened. Engineer officers and district magistrates plunged into the search for documents bearing on the

Above: foreign soldier sculpted on the Barhut railing, 2nd century BC He has a Greek sword and diadem. Indian Museum, Calcutta.

Previous page: an English merchant in Bengal in 1760, portrayed by Dip Chand, smoking his hookah attended by Indians. Victoria and Albert Museum, London.

roots of Indian civilization and the origins of man in India, giving to Indian studies the bias towards antiquity which they still have. It is significant that even today virtually no research has been or is being done by western scholars into medieval Indian material culture and archaeology. This book must, of necessity, reflect this bias. Furthermore, very few Indian scholars have made it their business to integrate their study of their own culture with that of Southeast Asia. In the whole of India and Southeast Asia, despite their undeniable achievements, archaeology and scholarship are still in their infancy. Westerners are, however, beginning to take it for granted that any genuine understanding of human history must include a decent knowledge of Indian culture, art and history. Philology and comparative religion in particular are inconceivable without much study of Indian sources.

The relationship between Indian and early eastern Mediterranean civilizations is very scantily documented; but certain speculations are generally accepted as valid. The original seaborne trade connections set up during the third and second millennia BC between western Asia and the Indus valley culture seem to have survived at least intermittently into Classical times. In 975 BC Hiram, king of Tyre, is known to have imported exotic animals – apes and peacocks – as well as ivory, almost certainly from western India.

The Greeks in India. The Greeks had more than casual connections with India. To begin with they shared a great deal of culture as well as common linguistic elements with the Aryans; both worshiped a sky father (Greek Zeus Pater, Sanskrit Dyaus Pitar) inhabiting the vault of heaven (Greek Ouranos, Sanskrit Varuna), an earth mother and the sun. The warriors of both peoples would have understood each other very well. And one must remember that the term "Greeks" refers not only to the inhabitants of Athens and Sparta, but also to city peoples of Asia Minor and of Hellenized Egypt. The armies of the Persian empire which invaded Greece in 480 BC included Asiatic Greeks, many of whose kin also lived and worked in Iran. It included Indian troops too. For that same empire invaded and claimed sovereignty over the Indian region of Gandhara (510 BC), which was later one of the most important parts, culturally and politically, of India's early historical empires. It is thus by no means unreasonable to assume that some Greeks and Indians had at least outline knowledge of each other, even if it was not committed to writing. When Alexander the Great marched into the Punjab and down the Indus (326 BC) he was probably at once testing the limits of the Persian empire which he had just conquered, and pursuing a natural interest in a legendary region. At the great city of Taxila, in Gandhara, he and his entourage would have encountered early Indian civilization at its most sophisticated.

Darius the Great of Persia had sent, about 510 BC, a Greek mercenary named Scylax to sail down the Indus. He had returned to Arsinoe in Egypt after a two-year journey. The information he gathered seems to have been the source of Herodotus' account of India (5th century BC) which would have been familiar to all post-Renaissance western Europeans with a Classical education. Herodotus knew of the "two races," "white" Aryans and "dark" aboriginals; of the crocodiles in the Indus, and of the cotton from which the Indians made their clothing, and which was "better than sheep's wool." He also knew of a religious sect who ate nothing that had life, and lived on millet. This must be the Jains, whose religion had been founded about a century before by Mahavira. Herodotus' account also contains some "marvels," one being the long-popular story of giant ants which guard Indian gold. Another Greek writer on India about 100 years later was Ctesias, who lived for 20 years at Susa in southern Iran. His account of India, however, contains far too many such "marvels," and these were the sort of stories which became current during the European Middle Ages, obscuring more accurate knowledge.

Perhaps the most important probable contact between Indian and Greek culture was in the field of philosophy. This contact is not documented; but then that was no era of documentation. Many European scholars, including Colebrook, Garbe, Winternitz and Rawlinson, accept the validity of the contact. Indeed one Greek writer whose works have been much quoted, Megasthenes, himself commented on the likeness between many aspects of Greek and Indian philosophy. He was in an excellent position to judge. For he was sent about 300 BC by Seleucus, one of the Greek officers left as rulers of the colonies set up by Alexander, as ambassador to the capital of Chandragupta Maurya at Pataliputra, in Magadha. Philosophical ideas owing a debt to India seem to have been imported into Greek philosophy especially by the Pythagoreans (6th century BC), who greatly influenced the thought of Plato (5th century BC) and of the Neo-platonists. Chief of these last was Plotinus (3rd century AD) who himself traveled in Persia, and whose influence,

Plotinus, the 3rd-century Neoplatonist, who probably introduced elements of Indian speculation into the west. Museo Ostiense.

added to that of Plato, upon the whole European mystical tradition has been profound and all-pervasive. In this respect, it seems, the west has owed an unacknowledged debt to India for over 2,000 years. Another major Neo-platonist, Iamblichus, wrote the biography of Pythagoras, describing his travels throughout western Asia in the pursuit of philosophical teachings; and this reinforces the likelihood of the contact being genuine. The two ideas specially credited to Indian influence are, first, the theory of reincarnation, which had been developed in India in the *Brahmanas* and major *Upanishads* by about 900 BC; and second, the idea of deliverance or release from the contingent world by illumination. In addition, literally hundreds of parallels between Greek and Indian philosophical expressions have been listed by scholars in the field. Elsewhere in this book references will be found to direct trade contacts between the Classical Mediterranean world and India which can be documented by archaeology. They tend strongly to support the likelihood of the philosophical connection being real.

A knowledge of Indian philosophy was recorded by many other Classical writers. The sage Apollonius of Tyana (c. 50 AD) went to Taxila, and studied with Brahman teachers. A Gnostic called Bardasanes learned much from an Indian embassy that visited Syria c. 220 AD. He knew about Brahmans and Buddhists, and how they lived. His account of life in a Buddhist monastery is quite accurate; and his description of a cave temple in western India containing an image of a deity half-male, half-female, is startling; for no such temple or icon of that date is known today, though it could well have existed and would be quite orthodox. The Christian Father Clement (150–218 AD) met Buddhists in his home city of Alexandria in Egypt, and is the first western writer to mention Buddha by name, calling him Boutta. He knew that Buddhists "worshiped a kind of pyramid beneath which they think the bones of some divinity lie buried" – a tendentious but fairly clear description of the Buddhist

Sailors shipwrecked in India repair their ship and repel giant crabs; a typical fantasy about India, from *India Orientalis* (1598). Victoria and Albert Museum, London.

Terracotta panel from Harwan, western India, 5th century AD, showing western influence in the heads of conversing monks. In the middle are three ascetics; at the bottom geese. Museo Nazionale d'Arte Orientale, Rome.

stupa. The collection of fables attributed to the Greek Aesop, who lived in Lydia, contains many stories which also appear in Indian legend, and seem to have originated in India. For the animal fable is one of the most popular kinds of Indian literature.

There is further ample documentation of the continuous contact between eastern Christian traders and Buddhist communities in western Asia, until the coming of Islam in the 7th century put an immediate stop to all such intercourse. However, the Muslim Arabs themselves maintained relations with India, and, for example, the scholar al-Biruni (born 973 AD) actually learned Sanskrit to read the Hindu classics when he accompanied the invader, Mahmud of Ghazni, on his campaigns of looting and destruction across northern India. It was, as we have seen, such Muslims who transmitted Indian mathematical and astronomical knowledge to the west through their own lingua franca of Arabic. But it is also likely that the Indians themselves learned far earlier of the achievements of Greek mathematics, and developed their own ideas with their help.

European rediscovery of India. Europe can be said to have rediscovered India in the physical sense in 1498. In this year the Portuguese crowned the success of a series of exploratory expeditions they had been pushing further around the coasts of Africa, by reaching Calicut on the southwest coast of India. They were helped by an Indian sailor (not, as is often said, an Arab). By 1511 Albuquerque had captured Malacca, so gaining control of the sea routes to the Indies, and Portuguese soldiers of fortune then reached Burma, Thailand, Vietnam and Indonesia. What they were seeking was twofold: first, to discover the semimythical Christian community founded by the legendary "Prester John"; and second, far more important, to outflank the Turkish and Arab Muslims who obstructed European access to "the Indies," fabled lands of treasure, spices and all delights. Unquestionably they were in search of plunder or, alternatively, trade; but their motives, as well as those of the other Europeans who followed them, contained a strong element of crusade against Islam. For Portuguese memory of the North African Muslim occupation of the Iberian peninsula was still very much alive. After the establishment of their colony in Goa (mid-16th century) they systematically set about the slaughter not only of Muslims, but also of Hindus. Saint Francis Xavier from Navarre, who is buried in Macao, became one of the Scourges of the East converting masses of Asian people to Catholicism under threat of torture and death. An account of the Hindu kingdoms was left by the Portuguese travelers Paes and Nuniz; while Jesuit missionaries who had learned Persian appeared late in the 16th century at the court of the Mughal Akbar, briefly and unsuccessfully to engage in debate there. Portuguese translations of a few Indian classics were made; and Portugal's greatest epic poet Camoëns sailed to the east with one of these expeditions. He was shipwrecked in 1560 at the mouth of the Mekong river in Cambodia. In his *Os Lusiadas* he gives a heroic account of hardships and triumphs in those fabulous and dangerous lands and seas.

The Portuguese pushed their discoveries on through Southeast Asia, into the Philippines – a Spanish possession after 1565 – up to China, and on to Japan. Albuquerque sent an embassy to Thailand in 1511–12, which there heard of Cambodia. Several missionaries traveled in these regions, and one, Antonio de la Magdalena, even visited Angkor, though his account remained unpublished. The first published account was by G. de Santantonio in Valladolid, Spain, in 1604. One Portuguese, Philip de Brito, made himself king at Syriam from 1602 to 1613. In 1596 the Dutchman J. H. van Linschoten published a book which clearly revealed to Europe for the first time the full details of the Portuguese discoveries in the east, which had been till then a closely guarded secret. Partly because the Catholic terrorism of the Portuguese had made their presence unwelcome, their power then rapidly faded, and two Protestant countries, Holland and England, who had been themselves fighting wars against the Catholic powers in Europe, began to oust them from the eastern trade. In this they were specifically resisting papal bulls which had divided the "colonial world," allotting the west – the Americas – to Spain, the east – the Indies – to Portugal. European ships and cannon gave these new traders an unchallenged military superiority to the Oriental powers. Large numbers of merchants and adventurers began to settle in enclosures and trading stations, and to travel across India. After the establishment of the English East India Company in 1600 the bloody struggle for Indian and Southeast Asian trade between the European powers entered a new phase.

Merchants and missionaries. It is no part of the purpose of this book to describe the history of this era. It is, however, of interest that some of the early merchants and missionaries were among the first dimly to discern something of the actual quality of ancient Indian culture. The Italian Nicolo dei Conti early in the 15th century left an account of the splendor of the Hindu kingdom of Vijaynagar. And the English Jesuit Thomas Stevens, who reached Goa in 1579, was one of the first to study Indian languages seriously – for his own missionary purposes of course, though he much admired the qualities of the Marathi language. More interesting still was the Florentine merchant, Filippo Sasetti, who lived for five years in Goa (1583–88) and recorded his experiences in letters sent home. He was an educated man who had studied at the University of Pisa, and pursued a special interest in science, medicine and folklore. He studied Sanskrit texts on these subjects, and seems to have been the first person to have observed a relationship between Sanskrit and European languages. This was unusual; for the trading enclaves tended to be in the south, where south Indian languages were the most likely to be learned by Europeans for their immediate practical purposes. Many other travelers of all kinds visited India during the 17th and 18th centuries, mostly in pursuit of wealth by trade or of missionary converts. Many of them wrote impressionistic accounts of what they saw; and Europe tended to accept their exotic but inaccurate descriptions. But then under the influence of the Abbé Dubois' grossly distorted account of *Hindu Manners, Customs and Ceremonies* (1817) Hinduism

Portuguese and Indians, portrayed in a 17th-century Portuguese album of the customs and costumes of the people of Africa and Asia.

View of the great modern temple of the Reclining Buddha in Bangkok, with a Buddhist monk in the foreground. It was in such temples that Europeans first encountered Buddhism as a living religion, and met monks of non-Christian faith.

ultimately came to be regarded as especially noisome and gloomy.

There were, however, several travelers who did write accurate accounts. J. B. Tavernier, a jewel merchant, probably saw more of India than any other man during his five visits between 1641 and 1688. His account is not, however, nearly so valuable as that of François Bernier (1670–71), a French physician who lived for 12 years at the Mughal court. He is still a prime source of information about the India of his time, and of hearsay about parts of Southeast Asia. He returned to France and, through his acquaintance with the fable writer La Fontaine and the philosopher Pascal, passed on a far more accurate knowledge of India into French society than was current in other countries. He brought back a manuscript of the *Upanishads* in Persian – the Mughal court language. This manuscript came into the hands of Anquetil Duperron, who had already translated in 1771 the ancient Persian

religious classic, the *Avesta*, after 12 years' work. Duperron published his strange mixed-language translation of the *Upanishads* in 1801; and this was the book which deeply impressed the German philosopher Schopenhauer. A French Jesuit, Father Bouvet, wrote in 1687 the first clear description of the painted and gilt Buddhist architecture of Thailand, mentioning that its "pyramids" – stupas – were ornamented with an architectural order like the western, but "more charged with sculpture," and so less attractive to western eyes.

In fact, scholarly and relatively accurate accounts of Indian literature were not lacking, though they were not widely distributed. The German priest H. Roth (1610–88) produced the first Sanskrit–Latin grammar; but it remained in manuscript. The first European mention of the Vedas was in a book by a Dutch preacher called Abraham Roger who had lived both in south India near Madras and in Indonesia. He included translations of some of the famous songs of Bhartrihari. It was in his book, translated into German in 1663, that the great German Romantic writer Herder (1744–1813), of whom more will be heard later, first encountered Indian literature. But the first solid and definitive work of Sanskrit scholarship was carried through by two Jesuits. The German Hanxledon, in Malabar from 1699 to 1732, composed a manuscript Sanskrit dictionary. This was then used by "Fra Paolino de St Bartholomeo" (his real name was Wessdin) who also lived in Malabar, learning much about Indian culture, and later retired to Rome to write a definitive Sanskrit grammar and other texts, which *were* published. A Saxon missionary Ziegenbalg published the first Tamil grammar in 1716. A French missionary called Coeurdoux, who worked with a south Indian pandit, Maridas Pillai, in the 18th century at Pondicherry, suggested once more the relationship between Sanskrit and European languages. As scholarship progressed, the first serious attempt to grasp Sanskrit learning as a whole was made by Alexander Dow in the preface to his *History of India* (1768). He pointed out that Hindu history extended further back than that of any other nation – an epoch-making recognition, which heralded the search for ancient India.

The first scholars. The subsequent history of Europe's direct knowledge of India has run along two parallel channels. One is the Romantic, literary and philosophical interest in the content of Indian culture; the second, the scholarly interest in the facts of history. The two, of course, were mutually influential; for scholarship benefited from the Romantic impulse to explore an admired exotic culture; while the interest in content relied on scholarship for its material and benefited from its results. Both trends survive today in modern forms. In practice both took their rise from the same sources, the work of Sir William Jones (1746–94) and of two of his colleagues who labored with him in India, Charles Wilkins (1749–1836) the first Englishman to become a Sanskrit scholar, and

Henry Colebrook (1765–1837). All three were given direct encouragement by the greatest British administrator ever to work in India, Warren Hastings. Jones succeeded in gaining an appointment in India as a judge of the high court at Calcutta in 1783, and lived there for ten years till his early death. He already knew Arabic and Persian, and, as soon as he reached India, he began to study

Portrait of Sir William Jones, the great English scholar who first brought Indian literature to the notice of Europe, and founded the Asiatic Society of Bengal.

Sanskrit with Wilkins' help. In England his reputation was already quite extraordinary. The impetus behind his scholarship was no mere dispassionate desire for knowledge, but a profound admiration for Indian culture.

In 1784 Jones founded the Asiatic Society of Bengal, in whose journal and series of *Asiatick Researches* the first systematic attempts to discover the ancient roots of Indian culture were published. In 1786 he even published an amazingly accurate account of the system of Indian music. His most influential work, however, was his translation from Sanskrit of the play *Shakuntala* by the great Gupta poet and playwright Kalidasa (4th century AD?). It was published in 1789, and within the space of five years was taking Europe by storm. Jones and his colleagues continued to bring out further translations of Sanskrit classics, which all added to the impact on Europe of Sanskrit literature.

J. G. Herder (1744–1803) was the writer chiefly responsible for initiating the wave of enthusiasm for Indian literature in Germany. Even before he read a German translation of Jones's *Shakuntala* in 1791, he had already proclaimed his conviction that India was the source of humanity, and of a truth and wisdom which contrasted sharply with the coldness of European intellect. He spent the remainder of his life propagating his enthusiasm for Indian literature and wisdom, and ardently studying all the Indian literature he could find. Goethe (1749–1832), Germany's greatest poet-dramatist, shared his enthusiasm for Kalidasa, several times describing the impression it made on him, and how the Indian writer had influenced his own writing. He too sought out other translations of Sanskrit works as they appeared. What charmed these authors was certainly, in the first place, the radiant atmosphere of sweetness and eroticism with which *Shakuntala* is imbued; but they also perceived the depths both of artistic skill and philosophical implication it contained. Schiller, Novalis, Schelling and Heine were other German writers who were also deeply affected – a list that could be greatly extended. Beethoven's papers are full of quotations from Indian religious writings. But the most important diffusers of knowledge about Sanskrit literature in Germany were the brothers Schlegel. Friedrich (1772–1829) learned Sanskrit from Alexander Hamilton, whom he met returning from India in 1802; he became the first man to translate Sanskrit texts directly into German. His brother August Wilhelm (1767–1845), the famous translator of Shakespeare, also studied Sanskrit and translated many major Sanskrit classics.

Indian influence on western cultures. Two of Germany's greatest philosophers were deeply influenced by the content of Sanskrit literature. The first was Immanuel Kant (1712–1804). The scholars Jacobi and Stcherbatsky have pointed out several of his principal ideas whose form and expression owe a debt to Buddhist philosophy and the theory of Hindu poetics. The second is

Arthur Schopenhauer (1788–1860) whose entire philosophy, which he himself regarded as a direct continuation of Kant's, culminates in a version of Indian monist thought. In later life he was deeply impressed by Buddhism, and kept a statue of the Buddha in his study, referring to himself and his followers as "we Buddhists." One of the most important of those followers, both as philosopher and as Sanskritist, was Paul Deussen (1845–1919), translator and commentator on the *Upanishads*. Another was the composer Richard Wagner (1813–83), who used Indian motives in his early plays. And the philosopher Friedrich Nietzsche (1844–1900), despite his hostility to Wagner, esteemed the moral code expressed in the ancient Sanskrit legal code, the *Manusmriti*, so highly that he asserted all other codes to be merely its imitations and caricatures.

Although the Germans were, perhaps, the most enthusiastic in their assimilation of Indian ideas, there were many writers in other countries who also found inspiration in the Indian classics. Among them were Victor Hugo (1802–85), who wrote one poem in direct imitation of an *Upanishad*, and Mihai Eminescu, Romania's greatest poet, who was also a Sanskritist and follower of Schopenhauer. The thought and writings of the American R. W. Emerson (1803–82) were devoted to expressing his intuitions of the unity of all life and the transcendent principle of reality; repeatedly he described his debt to India. H. D. Thoreau (1817–62) was another important American who read Indian literature extensively. His major work *Walden* is full of references to Sanskrit scriptures. In 1850 he wrote that the inspiration of the Vedas had fallen on him like light "from a higher and purer luminary"; and the "natural" life he attempted to live imitated that of the vegetarian and abstemious upper-caste Hindu.

This stream of inspiration flowing from the content of Indian literature and thought has run on into modern times. Sir Edwin Arnold's book on the Buddha, *The Light of Asia* (1879), went through many editions. Poets such as W. B. Yeats integrated Indian philosophy into their own world views. The German Hermann Hesse (1877–1962) has impressed a whole modern generation with his novels dealing with Indian themes. The last two were indebted especially to the work of the early Russian theosophist H. P. Blavatsky, who vigorously propagated her own interpretation of Indian spirituality. Despite the low point at which her reputation now stands, the movement she initiated played an important role in both Indian politics and European cultural life. P. D. Ouspensky (1878–1947) was another Russian whose extremely significant speculations on the nature of time were stimulated by Indian ideas.

European scholarship. The stream of scientific scholarship dealing with India took its rise in the 18th century. The French had begun collecting Sanskrit and Tamil texts, including the Veda, as early as 1718, although they were unable to read them until later in the century, when, with the help of the Tamil pandit Maridas Pillai, certain scholars who visited Pondicherry learned Indian scripts and languages. It is likely that the 18th-century French historian Desvignes, working from manuscripts collected by the traveling astronomer Le Gentil, was the first to fix the chronological correspondence which put the study of Indian history on a sound footing. This was the identity of the king "Sandrakottos," recorded by Megasthenes, with Chandragupta Maurya. Jones publicized this correspondence as the essential basis for Indian history. Once again it was, in practice, the members of the Asiatic Society of Bengal who first published and translated the corpus of Indian literature by which the scientific interest was nourished. Jones, Wilkins, Colebrooke and H. H. Wilson all worked with helpful Indian collaborators. Colebrooke was particularly interested in scientific material; Wilson composed a dictionary, translated the *Vishnupurana*, and only in 1832 became the first Boden Professor of Sanskrit at Oxford University, 18 years after de Chèzy had been appointed to a chair of Sanskrit in Paris. And this fact is the first indication of the degeneration of interest in Indian culture in Britain, as distinct from the continent, despite the British occupation of India.

To this day Britain has very few chairs of Sanskrit, and those are held primarily by philologists, in contrast with

The philosopher Schopenhauer, who was deeply impressed by Indian philosophy and assimilated it to his own. Portrait by F. von Lenbach.

Palm leaf of Buddhist Wisdom manuscript, the illumination
representing the Buddha; 10th century AD, Nepal. British Museum.

Germany, where, since the first chair was established at
Bonn in 1818, almost every university has had flourishing
departments covering a wide field of Indian studies. The
great exception was F. Max Müller (1823–1900), the vastly
productive German Sanskrit scholar, who held the chair of
comparative philology at Oxford for many years. He was
both a scientist and a committed advocate of Indian ideas.

In practice, however, dispassionate and objective study
of Indian affairs advanced among the British living in
India, at first those working for the East India Company
which administered vast tracts of the subcontinent,
especially Bengal; and then after 1860 for the crown.

Only during the 20th century did most British
administrators, lawyers and military men again become
able to commit themselves more than superficially to
Indian religion, literature and life. Chief among them is
perhaps Sir John Woodroffe, a judge of the High Court in
Calcutta, who under the pseudonym Arthur Avalon
devoted his life to expounding and advocating Tantrik
religion.

In continental Europe a long series of distinguished
scholars took up the study of Sanskrit literature and Indian
history. In France the Société Asiatique, the first such
society, was founded in 1822. J. L. Burnouf made much
progress with the comparative study of Sanskrit and
European languages. His son Eugène read widely in
Indian literature, and discovered the nature of the Pali
language used for Theravada texts; in 1840 he translated
from Sanskrit the vast *Bhagavata Purana*. But one of the
characteristics of French Oriental scholarship was its
breadth, embracing within its purview China and
Southeast Asia. When the French took over as colonies
first Saigon (1859), then Cochin China (1867), Vietnam
(1883) and Cambodia, and then Laos (by 1893) the specific
French interest in Southeast Asia was formulated. Émile
Guimet founded, first at Lyons, then in Paris, the museum
which now bears his name, and contains collections
reflecting that broad French scholarly and aesthetic
interest. A whole series of French scholars worked in India
and Southeast Asia. Dutreuil de Rhins explored Khotan,
bringing back early birchbark manuscripts; he also
worked on Buddhist inscriptions. Émile Sénart, Sylvain
Lévi, Edouard Chavannes, Louis Finot and Alfred
Foucher all worked on Indian material, both in the east
and in France; Foucher in particular studied what he called

the Greco-Buddhist art of Gandhara. He it was also who founded three other important institutions in the east: the École Française d'Extrême Orient in Indochina, which sustained a long series of the most important publications on Oriental art; the French archaeological mission in Afghanistan; and the Franco–Japanese at Tokyo. A whole series of distinguished scholars worked in these institutions, outstanding among them Joseph Hackin (died 1941), the excavator of Begram.

Germany had no colonial stake in eastern countries. Her scholarship therefore remained academic, aesthetic and linguistic, with some interest in numismatics. Its achievements were nevertheless considerable. Th. Benfey published in 1859 his edition of the great collection of Indian stories, the *Panchatantra*, which caused a furore. He was able to illustrate in detail how the stories in that collection had gradually penetrated through Persian, Arabic, Hebrew and Latin into European languages, many to be introduced by La Fontaine. In 1852 A. Weber published the first consistent history of Indian literature. In Holland, Italy, Czechoslovakia and Hungary Indian studies also flourished. The Hungarian Csoma de Körös (1784–1842) visited and worked in India, studying especially language and literature on the fringes of Tibet, where he died. The interest in Indian Asia was thus virtually continent–wide.

First encounters with Indian art. It is fascinating to read the early accounts by British officials of their first sight of what are now recognized monuments of Indian art. Examples may give the flavor of the time. In the first volume of *Asiatick Researches* (1784) the architect William Chambers describes the visit he made in 1772 to the Pallava remains at Mahabalipuram. "The rock or rather hill of stone on which a great part of the works are executed, is one of the principal marks for mariners as they approach the coast ... and is known by the name of Seven Pagodas ... Some such number formerly stood there, and in time have been buried by the waves ... [the hill] is that which first engrosses the attention on approaching the place; for, as it arises abruptly out of a level plain of great extent, consists chiefly of one single stone and is situated very near to the sea-beach, it is such a kind of object as an inquisitive traveller would naturally turn aside to examine. Its shape is also singular and romantic, and, from a distant view, has an appearance like some antique and lofty edifice. On coming near to the foot of the rock from the north, imagery and sculpture crowd thick upon the eye, as might seem to favour the idea of a petrified town, like those which have been fabled in different parts of the world by too credulous travellers."

A footnote explains that "Among these, one object, though a mean one, attracts the attention, on account of the grotesque and ridiculous nature of the design; it consists of two monkeys cut out of one stone, one of them in a stooping posture, while the other is taking the insects

Above: three of the *rathas*, small monolithic shrines of the 7th century, at Mahabalipuram, near Madras, a site often visited in the 18th century by Europeans.

Opposite above: the sculpture of "two monkeys" picking fleas, at Mahabalipuram, scorned by William Chambers.

Opposite below: the Mauryan pillar, now at Delhi, which bears an incised inscription of the Emperor Ashoka, 3rd century BC, in the Brahmi script deciphered by James Prinsep in 1837.

out of his head." Further on, Chambers records the mythological account given him by Indians of the founding, history and abandonment of the great site, in which gods and kings of legend figure. "Such," he writes, "is the mode in which the Brahmins chose to account for the signal overthrow of a place devoted to their wretched superstitions." The 18th-century cultural assumptions with which this account is permeated are fascinating in their own right, and go a long way to explaining the manner in which the early study of Indian art developed.

Further articles in the Asiatic Society's publications give accounts, for example, of Buddhism in Ceylon, of the cave temples at Elephanta (vol. 6) and of temples in other parts of India. Francis Buchanan described the language and religion and literature of the "Burmas" (vols. 5 and 6); he wrote of Burmese pagodas: "... Godama commanded his images and relics to be worshipped. The largest and most celebrated temples are generally in the form of a pyramid, and are supposed to contain some of these relics; such as a tooth, a bone, a hair or a garment. To these temples, as containing the sacred relic, the prayers of the devout are addressed, and their offerings presented. The pyramids are often of great size, constructed of solid brick-work plastered over, and generally placed on a prodigiously elevated terrace. The base of the pyramid is frequently surrounded by a double row of small ones; and the summits of the whole are always crowned with umbrellas, made of a combination of iron bars into a kind of fillagree

work, and adorned with bells. Many of these pyramids are from three to five hundred feet high. In the larger temples the umbrella and at least the upper part of the pyramid, and often the whole, is entirely gilded over: and the title of shwe or golden, is bestowed on the edifice."

Attempts at chronology. The variety of topics tackled in the early publications of the Asiatic Society of Bengal is truly impressive. The tradition these writers followed was that developed in late 17th-century England, when scholars like Wharton were evolving an accurate history of Britain. One of the most important themes was the question of the chronology of Indian culture. In *Asiatick Researches*, vol. 2, an attempt was made to embrace the whole within a single scheme and correlate it with the Biblical; but without success. Captain Wilford's study of the chronology of kings in Magadha and Andhra was another more detailed, erroneous, but important preliminary study. Elphinstone, in his important *History of India* (1839), had to write that for Indian history "no date of a public event can be fixed before the invasion of Alexander and no connected relation of the national transactions can be attempted until after the Mahometan conquest." It needed the devoted research of generations of scholars, reporting, sifting and collating inscriptions and coins throughout the 19th century, to establish finally a valid sequence for Indian history. Even this sequence, however, is only very broadly brushed in, and lacks detail compared with western notions of proper history. And crucial details – for example era base-dates or any dates for the great Kushan king Kanishka – are still not yet decided Study of Indian source materials has been structured by epigraphy and numismatics. These are the essential tools of history; and the Society's publications, from the earliest *Asiatick Researches* on, were filled with accounts of ancient inscriptions, accompanied by copies of the originals for later scholars to use. Perhaps the most important breakthrough in the field of inscriptions was when James Prinsep, secretary of the Society, published in 1837 the key to the Brahmi alphabet used by the great early emperor Ashoka (272–232 BC) for his proclamations cut on stones and pillars.

The chief reason why the creation of a coordinated Indian history was so difficult was that, although there are bodies of historical tradition in India, they tend to be combined with myth and somewhat confused or extravagant. Native Indian scholarship had not synthesized dated historical records as had been done in China and the west. This was partly the result, first, of the repeated fragmentation of India's empires, with the consequent absence of many continuous records of events; second, in earlier times especially, of the use of an assortment of different base-dates for the eras giving the years recorded in inscriptions; and third, of the fact that history does not seem ever to have been the major cultural effort in India it was in the west and China. For European

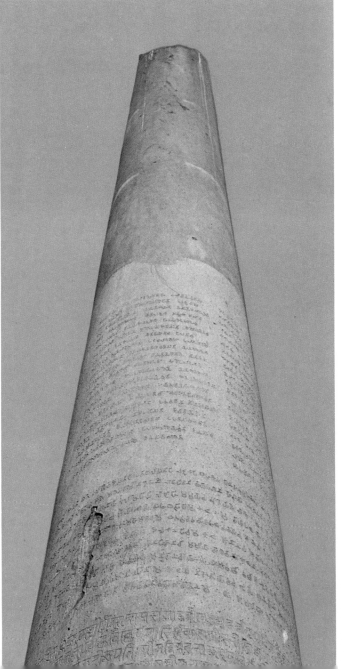

scholars, therefore, building up a chronological framework for Indian civilization was chiefly a matter of combining synchronisms and sequences. Synchronisms are those events which can be related in date, by documentary evidence, first to the established time scales of non-Indian cultures, and second to each other. Many such synchronisms will be noted in this book. Sequences are the lists of successive events in India which can be compounded from such records as king lists in the *Puranas* or inscriptions and coins; most often they are simply the names of members of families of kings. Some of these names may then be identified with figures appearing in otherwise undated literature to give new synchronisms. An example is the identification of a king "Milinda," who appears as interlocutor in a Buddhist text, with King Menander, a Greek ruler of Gandhara and the Punjab, whose coinage and place in history are relatively well known. Such work may be amplified by the study, for example, of ancient place names and geography. Needless to say, the prose in which such scholarship is conducted can be very dry.

The chief Indian traditions which do survive, and were of fundamental value, as comparative material, include the annals contained in two Pali Buddhist texts of Ceylon, called the *Dipavamsa* (4th century AD?) and the *Mahavamsa*, both of which include versions of Indian history – especially of the Maurya dynasty – which do not tally. Then there are five of the 18 *Puranas* which contain king lists, the most reliable being the *Vishnupurana*. A poem on the "Deeds of King Harsha" was written by Bana c. 620 AD; and in the 12th century a poet Bilhana wrote a comparable "Deeds of Vikramanka," his own royal master. The *Rajatarangini* is a 12th-century chronicle of early and medieval kings of Kashmir; and there are numerous Jain sacred chronicles in manuscript, some now studied, many not yet. There are, as well, a few other texts available to specialists. But it is interesting how archaeological research is now vindicating the accuracy of descriptions of cities, of daily life and events as they are recorded in early undated literature, so as to give general dates to what had previously been historically rootless, even suspect. The sequences established by archaeology can also throw light on history from the material point of view, though it has concentrated on certain periods to the almost complete exclusion of others. Activity in the field of Indian history, however, is intense and has been increasing for almost two centuries.

Epigraphy. Epigraphy, or the study of inscriptions, applies itself to the records inscribed on stone, seals, reliquaries or copper plates, which those who commissioned them wished to be preserved. Along with numismatics, finding, collecting and studying inscriptions constituted the chief activity of archaeologists right up to the beginning of the 20th century. Inscriptions usually commemorate dead kings or royal conquests of territory, record the pious dedication of buildings and sculpture, or testify to the virtuous deeds of people in all walks of life, including pilgrims. They also often document the transfer of lands and income to religious foundations. They may be very long, and amount to panegyrics on the virtues of the patron – which may rather reduce their accuracy. Some record that they were written by an "overseer of records" – which suggests that much must have been compiled which now has been irretrievably lost, like so much else in India.

It is impossible to give here any account of the course of Indian epigraphic studies, as the material is so vast and the progress of argument and assessment has been virtually unbroken. Along with Prinsep the chief pioneers between about 1783 and 1821 were Colin Mackenzie, who was a considerable topographical draughtsman, and later (1815) Surveyor General of India, who collected numerous written records from the old Madras Presidency; and Walter Elliot, who published papers on "Hindu inscriptions" in numbers of the *Journal of the (London) Royal Asiatic Society*. Later, Theodore Hope collected and photographed many ancient records in Madras and Mysore, which were edited by J. F. Fleet. Three long series of publications contain much of the fundamental material: the *Indian Antiquary*, started by James Burgess in 1872; *Epigraphia Indica*, also edited by Burgess (1888–92), continued by E. Hultsch, who later became professor at

Silver roll impressed with an inscription in Kharoshthi script, from Taxila. An example of epigraphy's raw material, dated to 78 AD.

The most recent major publications have been the continuing series of *Epigraphia Indica*, and since 1945, the Annual Report on Indian Epigraphy of the government epigraphic department. A most distinguished recent government epigraphist for India has been Professor D. C. Sircar, who retired from that post in 1961.

Numismatics. Numismatics, the study and classification of coins, especially to establish sequences, proceeded hand-in-hand with epigraphy, of which in a sense it is a branch. The inscriptions on coins, however, are usually brief; but the sites and levels at which coins are found supply important additional evidence.

The first publications of Indian "Greek" coins were by Mionnet in 1811 and Visconti in 1814. Then in 1824 Colonel Tod published, in the first volume of the *Transactions* of the Royal Asiatic Society, a full memoir on Greek, Parthian and Indian "medals," with engravings. Charles Masson traveled in Afghanistan, and published three memoirs (1834–36) on the coins he discovered there. They supplied the immediate condition for Prinsep's deciphering of ancient scripts. Many other officers and explorers collected and published, notably General Ventura, an officer in the service of Ranjit Singh, the Sikh ruler of the Punjab, in the 1820s. Tod's plates were used by A. W. von Schlegel in the *Journal Asiatique* of 1828 for the first valid attempt to construct an Indian chronology from coins. His work was followed ten years later by Lassen's history of the Greek and Indo-Scythian kings, based on coinage, first in German, then two years later in English. In 1841 H. H. Wilson published the first summary of numismatic research in relation to other archaeological work.

Through the middle of the 19th century the most important work was probably done by E. Thomas, who brought out a full catalog of Bactrian coins in 1857, and edited Prinsep's essays. It is significant how much emphasis was laid, and still is laid, on the northwest and Afghanistan. For it was here that west and east met, and that synchronisms might best be set up. But vital lists of museum collections, made by Rodgers at Lahore, Delhi and Calcutta, provided the basis for broader numismatic study across northern India. For the south, Bhagawanlal Indraji surveyed Shaka-Shatavahava coins; and Walter Elliot published *Coins of Southern India* (1886).

The major work of codification took place in the later 19th century. Von Sallet's series of essays on the coins of Alexander's followers in Bactria and India (1879) was the first. Then followed Vincent Smith's studies of Gupta coinage (1884, 1889, 1894) and Percy Gardner's British Museum catalog of the coins of the Greek and Scythic kings of Bactria and India (1886). E. J. Rapson's general book *Indian Coins* (1898) first synthesized the work of generations of scholars into a comprehensive survey, and is still of value. In 1908 he completed his British Museum catalog of the coins of early western India. J. Allan's

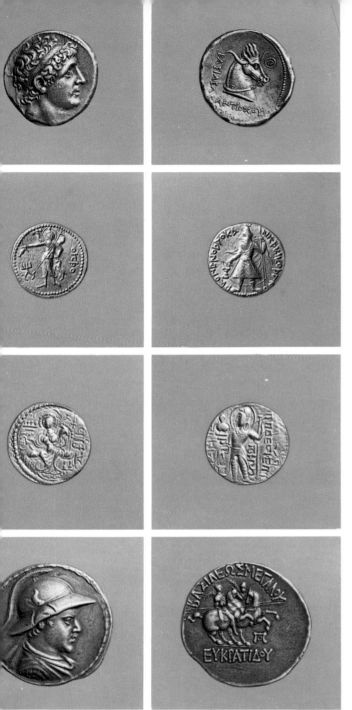

Obverse and reverse of coins of (from the top) the Seleucid ruler Antiochus II, the Kushan Emperor Kanishka, the Gupta Emperor Samudragupta and the Bactrian King Eucratides. British Museum.

Halle University in Germany; and *South Indian Inscriptions* first published by Hultsch in 1890. These are supplemented by numerous additional works, many by Indian scholars. The most important, perhaps, was Fleet's study of *Gupta Inscriptions*, following his crucial discovery in 1887 of synchronisms that established the opening date of the Gupta era, about which opinion had fluctuated wildly. But as an illustration of how prolonged epigraphical research may be, it is interesting that only with the discovery of a broken clay seal at Nalanda in 1943 was one of the greatest Gupta kings, Buddhagupta, finally given his true place in Fleet's sequence. Another important work was F. Kielhorn's *Inscriptions of Northern India* (1898–99).

British Museum catalog of *Coins of the Gupta Dynasties etc.* (1914) was another landmark. Work continues, now in close association with archaeological excavation.

In 1904 the Numismatic Supplement to the *Journal of the Asiatic Society of Bengal* was started, and scholarly interest in medieval and later coinage developed – a field in which a whole series of Indian scholars have published major research. Notable among them were R. D. Banerji, Professor Altekar and Dr Agrawala. Another Indian scholar, who has worked especially on the early punch-marked coins of the city-states is D. D. Koshambi. An important auxiliary text is Dr B. Sahani's *Technique of Casting Coins in Ancient India* (1945). During this century work on refining numismatic scholarship has continued in every field, and has been published especially in the *Journal of the Numismatic Society of India*. For continuing archaeological excavation often brings fresh numismatic material to light. Particularly important are foreign coins, such as the Roman hoards found at many early sites, which can be used to provide solid synchronisms.

The Archaeological Survey of India. Another important writer on Indian coins was Alexander Cunningham. His *Coins of Ancient India* (1891) and *Coins of Medieval India* (1894) were the product of decades of study – and of excavation; for he had been India's first Director-General of Archaeology. In 1848, as an engineer officer, he had proposed the survey and preservation of India's monuments. In practice, a number of officers who were also competent draughtsmen (as many were in those days) had already begun making records of ruins and remains in India; and tentative steps had been taken to gain official recognition of what was needed. Only in 1860 was Cunningham's idea given some substance, when the government of India was taken over by the British Crown. Cunningham was then (temporarily) appointed as the first Archaeological Surveyor of India, working in Uttar Pradesh and Bihar. There were financial difficulties; but aided by pressure from, among others, the architectural scholar James Fergusson, a full Directorate of Archaeology was eventually set up, with Cunningham as director, to work in northern India. In 1874 its activities were extended to the west and south, where James Burgess was appointed Surveyor.

The three scholars named here produced an extraordinary series of reports and publications on discovery, epigraphy, architecture and conservation, to which the study of ancient India is still greatly indebted. The Survey also initiated a large number of site museums. But Cunningham retired in 1885, Burgess in 1889 and the Survey fell on bad days. The provincial administrations made only token contributions to the conservation of remains, though they were beginning to set up museums, some of which became extremely important. There are now over 80 museums in India. Some of the chief are the Madras Museum (begun 1857); Lucknow State Museum

(1883); the Indian Museum, Calcutta (1878), which was based on the collections of the Asiatic Society of Bengal; the Prince of Wales Museum, Bombay, originally the defunct Poona Museum (1870s); and the Curzon Museum at Mathura.

In 1899 Lord Curzon was appointed Viceroy of India – a landmark in the history of archaeology in India, as well as in politics. In that year an attempt had been made to organize the Survey into five regional circles. Curzon, however, was personally determined that India's past should be recovered and recorded, and he accepted the government's responsibility to do so. In 1902 Sir John Marshall was therefore appointed Director-General of the revived Archaeological Survey, at a very young age. He remained at work in India till 1931. Despite financial shortages and Marshall's inexperience, substantial work was done on excavating, photographing and conserving sites. Between 1906 and 1909 the explorer Sir Aurel Stein excavated the first sites around the fringes of the desert Tarim basin in Central Asia – work in which he was followed by the German von le Coq and the Frenchman P. Pelliot – thus for the first time beginning to clarify the archaeology of Buddhist Central Asia, and the geography and chronology of the ancient trans-Asiatic trade routes.

As the department grew, archaeological interest shifted somewhat away from its old primary concern with epigraphy and numismatics in favor of prehistoric excavation. Some bitterness was caused by the radical shift of resources, which left the epigraphic scholars in a backwater. The shift is, however, understandable in view of the great discoveries that were being made during Marshall's tenure, notably the Indus valley civilization

with its two capital cities of Harappa and Mohenjo-Daro. The excavation techniques used were relatively rough and ready. To remedy this state of affairs, first Sir Leonard Woolley, excavator of Ur, was asked in 1938 to advise on methods and training – though with little effect. Then Mortimer Wheeler, an experienced British excavator and museum curator, was engaged as Director-General of the Survey, from 1944 to 1948. The task he accomplished in his four years was to bring methods of excavation and the organization itself up to date. The Survey as it exists today, and the Indian archaeologists whom he trained, owe a great deal to his administration. During the life of the British Survey the picture of the material culture of ancient India gradually began to catch up and become correlated with the work of historians and literary scholars. In this latter activity Indian authors were naturally of particular importance, especially Rajendralal Mitra, Sir R. G. Bhandarkar and Bhagavanlal Indraji. Since Indian independence perhaps the most significant work of the Survey has been that done by Indian archaeologists – many of them Wheeler's pupils – in excavating the early historical city-sites, such as Hasti-napura and Kaushambi, whose reports in the journal *Ancient India* have not yet been integrated into a unified overall picture.

As sites have been discovered, surveyed, excavated, photographed, and some restored, a series of publications have attempted to draw together the results of detailed research into coherent unity. Particularly important were the works of Vincent Smith in his *Histories of India* (1904–19) and *Fine Art in India and Ceylon* (1911); of J. Ph. Vogel on the sculpture of Mathura (1910 and 1930) and

Indian Serpent Lore (1928); of H. Cousens on Deccan architecture (1926 and 1931); and of H. Jouveau-Dubreuil on southern archaeology and architecture (1916 and 1926). Notable scholarly work has also been published by French scholars in the series *Arts asiatiques*, and by Americans and Germans in *Artibus Asiae*. Stella Kramrisch, founder of the Indian Society of Oriental Art and its journal, has pioneered the study especially of theoretical texts on art.

Exploration of Tibet and Burma. In volume 1 of *Asiatick Researches* (1784) the Hon. John MacPherson gave a general account of his perilous visit to the "Teshoo Loomboo" (Tashi Lunpo monastery) in Tibet. Tibet was a country only rarely visited in the 19th century by a few eccentric Europeans, some of whom met their death in that difficult and dangerous terrain. In the *Journal of the Asiatic Society of Bengal* of 1881, the Indian Savat Chandra Das published the first well-informed "contribution" on the history and religion of Tibet. It was, however, only with the publication of L. A. Waddell's *Lamaism* in 1895 that the first clear and wide-ranging account of Tibetan religion and art was given. The Younghusband mission to Lhasa in 1904 brought back many objects and much information, as well as opening up contacts with India. Since then many scholars have learned Tibetan, and the culture has been studied from its voluminous printed literature. Only the Italian G. Tucci has made any serious and sustained attempt, under great difficulties, to make archaeological sense of the numerous monuments. That effort is, for the time being, in abeyance.

It is perhaps strange, but, despite the initial impulse of early members of the Asiatic Society of Bengal, the

Opposite: timber baulks used in the 3rd-century BC foundations of the Mauryan capital city Pataliputra, modern Patna, during excavation in the early years of this century.

Right: collection of medieval sculptures at Tewar, central India, as they were photographed in the late 19th century immediately after excavation by the Archaeological Survey of India.

Below: the Maniyar Math, a circular shrine excavated at old Rajgir, near Patna. The fine Gupta stucco sculptures have now been washed away by heavy monsoon rains.

Above: view of the "Great Dagon Pagoda of Rangoon and scenery to the westward of the Great Road"; drawn by J. Moore, engraved by H. Payli, published in 1825.

Below: a treasure-trove collection of fine medieval temple bronzes photographed in the early years of this century at Bagalkot in the Bombay Presidency, by the Archaeological Survey of India.

archaeologists of British India made little effort to synthesize their work with that of archaeologists working in other parts of south Asia. The Indian scholar R. C. Majumdar was a notable exception. The British, however, after they conquered Burma, did begin to take a serious interest in the country in 1858, when Sir Henry Yule's account of his mission to the Burmese court at Ava was published. A group of missionaries led by A. Judson had arrived in 1813 and begun work on the language, and Dr Burney had begun searching out sources for history in 1825. Crawford, returning from a mission to the court at Ava in 1827, wrote a cynically accurate assessment of the exhibitionistic motives for temple building in that country. Then in 1860 Harwell began to study the Mon language, and in 1892 the Burmese and Pali texts were published by Forschammer. Phayre published a history in 1883. An archaeological survey was established in 1899 and Charles Duroiselle, professor of Pali at Rangoon, became superintendent. It started its own series of publications: Duroiselle acted as adviser to the Burmese royal scholar Taw Sein Ko, and initiated excavations first at Prome (1905) then at Pagan (1907). The work of the survey continued throughout the 1920s and 1930s, much of it conservation; and two scholars in particular, G. H. Luce and U Pe Maung Tin, synthesized source material as it accumulated to build up a history of the country. Unfortunately, no consistent picture has yet been achieved of the evolution of Burmese art styles after the medieval Pagan period; and much archaeology remains to be done.

Investigation of Indonesia and Indochina. The study of art and archaeology in Indonesia was initiated by an Englishman, T. Stamford Raffles, who founded Singapore as a British colonial trading post in 1819. The Dutch East India Company had ceded its interests in 1799 to the Batavian Republic, which could not hold the terrain. The British then occupied Java for five years (1811–16), during which time Raffles conducted energetic research, discovering Borobudur, the greatest Buddhist monument, and writing a *History of Java*. Indonesia was then returned to the Dutch, who ruled it until 1949, at first without pursuing Raffles' initiative. There were grave troubles and unrest.

Although some exploration and photography had been done 40 years earlier by individual administrators, only in 1901 was a Dutch Archaeological Commission set up, becoming an archaeological service in 1913. Our knowledge of ancient Indonesian culture owes an immense debt in particular to one man, Th. van Erp (died 1958). An architect, archaeologist and scholar, he was principally responsible for recovering the major monuments of Javanese art from decay and publishing them. Among many others, two notable Dutch scholars N. J. Krom and W. F. Stutterheim poured out books and monographs which filled in the picture of Indonesian archaeology.

In Indochina, especially Cambodia and South Vietnam, French scholars were active only after 1860, when the naturalist H. Mouhot reached Angkor. His colorful newspaper publication focused the attention of the learned world on these colossal ruins lost in the jungle. In 1866 the Scot John Thomson photographed them, and read their symbolism from Hindu parallels. Work then began on describing and deciphering the inscriptions. In 1873 casts were taken of sculptures at Angkor, and carried to the Trocadéro in Paris, where they aroused amazement and admiration. The monuments of the Cham kingdom in South Vietnam were first discovered by the French in 1885. Discoveries and scholarship followed as the French administration consolidated its position in the region.

In 1865 the Société des Études Indochinoises was founded, after the pattern of British institutions in India. In 1898 Alfred Foucher set up the École Française de l'Extrême Orient, which was responsible for publishing the major part of research in that region. When France compelled Thailand to return Angkor to Cambodia in 1907, a conservancy was begun; and in 20 years more than 800 sites were found. George Groslier, one of the leading French scholars, founded the great museum at Phnom Penh to house the vast hoard of finds from Indochinese sites. Over decades of scholarship and controversy G. Çoedes, Ph. Stern, P. Dupont, P. Mus and the Grosliers, father and son, have inspired intensive development of the archaeology and history of the region. H. Parmentier and L. Finot contributed especially to work in Champa and Laos. An immense amount of conservation was also undertaken. Aerial surveys have helped to reveal the vast extent of what remains to be discovered; for the present, however, work is inevitably at a standstill. Only in Thailand has research continued, but as yet a modest amount of excavation has been done at the great city sites, though conservation is going forward and works of scholarship are in hand.

European attitudes to Indian art. The artistic aspect of the remains of Indian and Southeast Asian civilization was not readily appreciated by the Europeans who exhumed and studied it. There was a battle to fight. During the last decades of the 19th century the prevalent and influential opinion in Britain on the quality of Indian art – which was, of course, generally known only through photographs – was represented by John Ruskin. In his second series of lectures as Professor of Art at Oxford University (published in 1871 as *Aratra Penteleci*) he used a photograph of a south Indian Nandi-bull sculpture "as a sufficient type of the bad art of all the earth. False in form, dead in heart, and loaded with wealth, externally. It may rest in the eternal obscurity of evil art, everywhere and forever. Now," he continued, "beside this colossal bull here is a bit of Daedalus work, enlarged from a coin no bigger than a shilling" – in fact, the obverse of a Greek coin of the 5th century BC bearing an indubitably splendid bull. "Look at the two together," he says, "and you ought to know, henceforward, what Greek art means, to the end of your

Drawing "NNE view of the Great Pyramidal Temple of Bara Budur in the Cadu District, Java," made in 1815 during the British occupation of Java in Raffles' time.

days." He certainly had in mind some kind of ideal of truth or morality which he found in the beauty of the Greek image.

Nine years later Sir George Birdwood printed a famous opinion along similar lines, which he repeated in a paper read in London to the Royal Society of Arts in 1910. He said of a Javanese Buddha that its "senseless similitude, by its immemorial fixed pose, is nothing more than an uninspired brazen image, vacuously squinting down its nose to its thumbs, knees and toes. A boiled suet pudding would serve equally well as a symbol of passionate purity and serenity of soul." This severe judgment notwithstanding, Sir George was, in fact, a great friend to contemporary Indian craftsmanship, especially that of Muslim descent. He had organized a number of exhibitions designed to stimulate the Indian craft economy, and written what is still a classic book on the *Industrial Arts of India* (1880). But even the official handbook to the Indian collections of the South Kensington (afterwards Victorian and Albert) Museum had stated "The monstrous shapes of Puranic deities are unsuitable for the higher forms of artistic representation: and this is possibly why sculpture and painting are unknown, as fine arts, in India."

These quotations, typical of many, amply illustrate the European attitude to the artistic heritage of India current in the later decades of the 19th century. "Monstrosity," "ugliness," "brutish," "debased" were a few of the words applied to it. There existed only a slender thread of appreciation parallel to that accorded to Indian literature; and even among the officials who worked in India itself there was little enthusiasm for the content of the art they studied. Their interest was in history and its physical documents. The task of breaking down such deeply entrenched prejudice was by no means easy. James Fergusson, in his *History of Indian Architecture* (1876), had referred to Europe's natural affinity for its own Greek and medieval traditions, but had then continued: "How different is the state of feeling when from this familiar home we turn to such a country as India. Its geography is hardly taught in schools, and seldom mastered perfectly; its history is a puzzle; its literature a mythic dream; its arts a quaint perplexity. But, above all, the names of its heroes and great men are so unfamiliar and so unpronounceable, that, except a few of those who go to India, scarcely any ever become so acquainted with them, that they call up any memories which are either pleasing or worth dwelling upon." He writes of his own admiration: "Were it not for this, there is probably no country – out of Europe at least – that would so well repay attention as India. None, where all the problems of natural science or of art are presented in so distinct or so pleasing a form. Nowhere does nature show herself in such grand and such luxurious features, and nowhere does humanity exist in more varied and more pleasing conditions."

Nowadays most people would heartily agree with the sentiments, though India's problems may have slightly diminished the charm. But the change in attitude has taken virtually a century to consummate. It happened in three principal phases. First came the recognition that some Indian art at least had Greek affinities. Second a strong revivalist movement developed among certain teachers in Indian art schools and scholars captivated by the atmosphere of Indian art. Third was the enthusiasm of western artists.

The awakening of enthusiasm. The first phase began in 1870, when Dr Leitner presented in England a large number of what he revealingly called "specimens" of sculpture which he named "Greco-Buddhist" – a name which made it acceptable. The earliest discovery of this Gandharan art, which is in fact both Buddhist and influenced by a late Greek phase of art, had been in 1833, when the first relief, a Buddha, had been dug up from a stupa near Kabul by Dr Gerard. Hoenigberger (1833–34) and Masson had explored further, and in 1848 Cunningham had excavated more Buddhist works at the site of Jamalgarhi; these had been published in the *Journal of the*

Sculpture of a Bodhisattva from Shahbazgarhi in Gandhara, 2nd century AD, in the style labeled Greco-Buddhist, which first attracted aesthetic interest in Europe. Musée Guimet, Paris.

One of the copies of the ancient Buddhist wall paintings at Ajanta (Cave 15), executed c. 1880 under the supervision of James Griffiths, sent to London and published in 1896. Victoria and Albert Museum, London.

Asiatic Society of Bengal in 1853 with wretched pictures, and brought to England. Unfortunately they perished in the 1866 fire at the Crystal Palace, where they were on exhibition, though they had made something of an impression. They had prepared the ground for Dr Leitner's "specimens"; and the name Greco-Buddhist was adopted by Alfred Foucher for his fundamental study *L'Art Gréco-Bouddhique du Gandhara* (1905).

The second phase in the awakening of genuine enthusiasm for Indian art was partly connected with the setting up in the 1870s of a series of art schools on the British pattern in the chief cities. After an initial period, when an attempt was made to transplant British academic methods, the British and Indian staff of these schools came to exercise a powerful influence on the general Indian attitude to the arts. Some helped the revival of Indian consciousness of their own artistic heritage which took place towards the end of the 19th century, from both the aesthetic and the practical points of view. The awakening was focused to begin with by events connected with the wall paintings in the great Buddhist cave monastery of Ajanta (executed between about 100 BC and 600 AD). They were first visited by a group of British officers of the Madras army in 1819. Their description, then published, aroused little interest. In 1843, however, James Fergusson, the architectural historian, published a fuller description.

His discerning eye led him to persuade the East India Company to have copies made at public expense. An engineer officer, Major Gill, who was also a distinguished artist, was commissioned to execute these with the help of a *camera-lucida* machine, supplied by the East India Company. He made over 30 large oil copies, which were sent to England in batches. They were exhibited in the Crystal Palace, where all except five were also burned in 1866, but not before they too had made some impact on the public. Then between 1872 and 1885 James Griffiths, head of the Bombay School of Art, supervised the execution by some of his pupils of fresh sets of copies. These were sent back to South Kensington and published in 1896 in two huge volumes. They revealed to the western world for the first time something of the extraordinary quality of Indian art. Unhappily many of these copies also perished in another fire at South Kensington. And the fame they brought to Ajanta also had a disastrous effect on the originals. For the walls were pillaged for decades without any official protection, and unfortunate attempts at conservation did not help matters. Now Ajanta's wonderful murals are far fewer than they were in 1819.

The copies, however, did have a significant effect on public attitudes. There had long been heated discussion as to whether India had contributed anything or nothing to world culture. But, by 1910, it had become possible for a group of 13 artists and critics to write an indignant letter to *The Times* declaring their deep admiration for Indian art and culture. The letter was prompted by Sir George Birdwood's paper to the Royal Society of Arts, in which he repeated the opinion described earlier. In 1904 Laurence Binyon, of the British Museum, had written with great insight of the genuine artistic relationship between the Ajanta paintings and the 8th-century AD wall paintings in the great hall of Horyuji temple at Nara in Japan. In Paris Rodin, the great sculptor of the early decades of this century, had expressed his deep admiration for the Southeast Asian art which he knew through casts in the Trocadéro, and had purchased actual pieces of Indian and Cambodian sculpture. In his admiration he was following in the footsteps of Gauguin and Degas.

This awakening of aesthetic interest was consummated in India by the work of E. B. Havell, who had gone to Calcutta as Principal of the School of Art. His book *Indian Sculpture and Painting*, published in 1908, electrified Indian society, and played a major role in restoring to modern India that pride in her ancient past which submission to Muslim and European domination had almost entirely obliterated. Artists who had worked with Griffiths on the Ajanta copies also worked with Havell alongside other artists: among them were members of the Tagore family who, for decades, helped to sustain the artistic movement known as the Bengal Revivalist School. This played a major part in establishing a truly national 20th-century art in India.

Publication of ancient texts and modern scholarship. In practice, neither artistic enthusiasm nor archaeology could, on its own, open up for western consciousness the meaning of the Indian artistic achievement. A new and vitally important element was introduced into understanding of the Oriental past by the publication of ancient texts, many of which had been among the manuscripts carefully listed by traveling scholars during the 19th century. One or two, such as the medieval *Sadhanamala*, which bore directly upon the interpretation of Indian artistic imagery, were readily accepted. But the implications of the contents of others only began to make their way slowly into the consciousness of scholars, western and eastern; though it should be said that in this respect the French and Dutch were far in advance of their British counterparts. Among the most important published series were the Trivandrum Sanskrit Series (1905–), the Gaekwad's Oriental Series published in Baroda (1916–), the Kashmir Series of Texts and Studies (1911–), and Tantrik Texts, edited from Calcutta by A. Avalon (Sir John Woodroffe) (1913–). In the United States Lanman edited a very important set of Sanskrit texts in the Harvard Oriental Series (1891–). All these, as well as others published by the Theosophical Society, by universities and wealthy patrons, brought a new element into the understanding of Indianized art, which made possible an interpretation of the meaning which monuments, sculpture and painting had had for the people who commissioned them. This was the study of iconology and symbolism, which paralleled, where it did not precede, similar study applied to European medieval and Renaissance art. Its insights were able to breathe life into the bare bones of knowledge, illuminating the significance of material objects.

This work was partly based on comparative study of the symbolisms appearing in different eastern cultures, and was inspired by the same interest as that which led Sir James Frazer to publish his massive study of "primitive" religion, *The Golden Bough*. Its early monument in India was James Fergusson's *Tree and Serpent Worship* (1868). Another contribution was by W. Crooke, a district officer, called *Popular Religion and Folklore of Northern India* (1893). A huge collection of Indian material was also made in Hastings' *Encyclopaedia of Religion and Ethics* (1908–), which remains a wonderful source of information. Major works of synthesis, without which no study of this field is possible, were Edgar Thurston's *Castes and Tribes of Southern India*, in seven volumes; and T. A. Gopinath Rao's *Elements of Hindu Iconography* (1914–16). The most important scholar of the early 20th century was perhaps A. K. Coomaraswamy (1877–1947), half-British, half-Ceylonese by birth, who began his career in 1903–08 as a geologist in Ceylon before he turned to art in 1910. He lived in England from 1908 to 1917, with short spells in India. He then went, in 1917, to the Boston Museum, U.S.A., where he remained till his death. His *Medieval*

Sinhalese Art (1908) and *History of Indian and Indonesian Art* (1927) remain standard texts; but it was in his long series of essays on symbolism and figuration that he demonstrated a new awareness of meanings which is now an indispensable part of the interpretation of cultural facts. It should be mentioned that his arguments, insofar as they apply to art rather than theology, were filled with a zeal to reform current artistic practices, complete with censorship, after the pattern of an imagined ideal state of affairs in ancient India.

Serious work was also done on the content and meaning of Indian art – made possible by the publication of texts – by the German scholar Heinrich Zimmer. His amazingly far-sighted book *Kunstform und Yoga* (*Art Form and Yoga*, 1928) explained much Indianized art from a new point of view, as the architectonics of meditation. In later life he emigrated to the United States, and there produced other important work, especially *Myths and Symbols in Indian Art and Civilization* (1946). He knew the psychologist C. G. Jung and his work on symbolism and archetypes, which encouraged Zimmer to develop his personal lines of thought. In fact, during the 1920s in Germany there was a public aware of the arts of the east, and interested in them in a specifically aesthetic way. Their interest was met by publications such as Karl With's *Java* (1920) – still an important book – and a series edited by William Cohn which included the first widely distributed photographs of the erotic sculptures of Konarak (1921). This aesthetic concern probably had a great deal to do with the expressionist movement in German art, which had explored exotic arts for their own sake, and drawn inspiration from them.

During the first decades of this century, however, French and Dutch scholarship was far more prepared to assimilate symbolic interpretations of art and anthropological knowledge than was British. Most archaeologists in Cambodia and Indonesia regarded it as part of their responsibility to interpret what they studied. One of the greatest works to emerge, both in bulk and achievement, was by the Frenchman, Paul Mus. His study of *Borobudur* (1935), published in Hanoi, established a new plateau for the interpretation of art; and the text was prefaced by an immensely long and detailed survey of virtually all older opinion as to the significance of the elements synthesized in that great Javanese compendium of Buddhist architecture and sculpture. A similarly indispensable work of scholarship appeared in F. D. K. Bosch's *The Golden Germ* (1948), which elucidates the widespread Oriental artistic symbolism of the lotus and its vegetation. A considerable amount of work along similar lines has been done by many other western and Indian scholars. Such study combines at once a profound interest in the content of Oriental culture, a high appreciation of its aesthetic value, and the most detailed scientific information. In this respect, Indology is probably unique, and sets a valuable pattern for scholarship in other fields.

The Excavation of Taxila

Taxila was one of the great cities of northern India, founded probably about 600 BC. It lies in the Kabul river valley, in modern Pakistan. It was the city entered by Alexander the Great in 326 BC when he first reached India from Bactria. The site was excavated, along with adjacent religious monuments, between 1912 and 1934, notably by Sir John Marshall, with later work being done on nearby sites by others. The city was occupied by a whole series of peoples after Alexander, including Bactrian Greeks, Scythian-Parthians, and Kushans. In the 3rd century BC it was the western capital of the Mauryan empire of Bihar, and the great Mauryan emperor Ashoka served as governor there during his youth. Its most productive period artistically came under the Kushans in the early 2nd century AD.

The first Buddhist stupa at Taxila was probably the Dharmarajika, built perhaps in the 3rd or 2nd century BC. But under the Kushans, who became wealthy by trade, a large number were built around the city, lavishly decorated in the Gandhara style, with monasteries for monks. Here (*below*) is the base of a smallish stupa of the Kushan period.

Above: Sir John Marshall, the excavator of Taxila, standing in the excavated walls of the Bhir mound. He was Director General of the Archaeological Survey of India from 1902 to 1931, during which time much exploration was done of the Central Asian trade routes on one of which Taxila lay.

Left: plinth of the temple of the double-headed eagle, Sirkap. Between Corinthian-type pilasters are Indian gateway forms, and two of Greek pattern. On four of these are "eagles," one double-headed, a motive perhaps introduced from western Asia by the Scythians or Shakas.

Below: panoramic view of the site of Sirkap during the excavations.

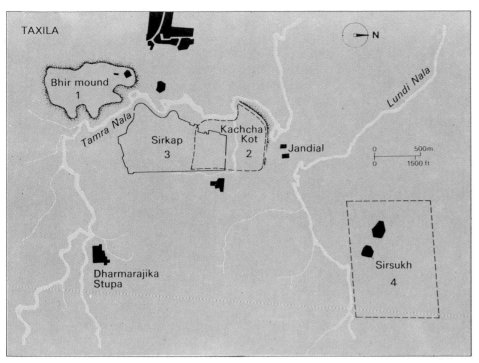

Above: a map of Taxila, showing the shifts in occupation of the site. The Bhir mound to the southwest contains the oldest city, built of rather rough, rubble stonework. The street plan was not regular, and the houses varied much in size. Among them was a large mansion with courts and a hall with three pillars. A public building had an apsidal end and bases for wooden pillars. Kaccha Kot was a fortification of mud brick, built before the Hellenic city of Sirkap was laid out, on a regular plan, in the 2nd century BC. It contains a large palace complex to the south, a probable Buddhist temple, and a possible Zoroastrian fire temple with a portico having Ionic capitals to its pillars. In the 2nd century AD Sirkap was succeeded by the Kushan town Sirsukh.

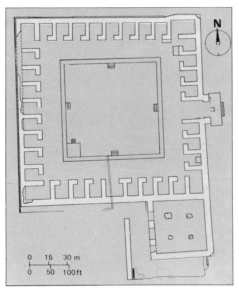

Above: small–scale stupa at the monastery of Mohra Moradu, which lies nearly 1 mile southeast of Sirsukh, and belongs to the Kushan period, executed in Gandharan style. Before excavation its buildings were mostly covered by detritus from the hillside above. Buddhas look out from the base of the structure.

Left: plan of the living quarters of the "monastery of Kunala," beside a stupa said to have been erected by Ashoka to commemorate the blinding of one of his sons called Kunala. The plan is of typical "sarai" pattern, a court surrounded by cells, 3rd century AD.

Below: excavating pottery *in situ* in the Bhir mound.

Left: the Bhallar stupa, which crowns a spur about 5 miles from Taxila, is a medieval construction, a fine example of the later, taller type made up originally of six or seven tiers. It is said to occupy the site where Ashoka built a stupa of his own to mark the spot where, in a previous incarnation, the Buddha sacrificed his head.

Right: meditating Buddha from one of the chapels of the Jaulian monastery on a hill above Sirsukh. This was a Kushan foundation, 2nd century AD, and was probably destroyed in the late 5th century. The art-style is pure Gandhara. Jaulian contained many important inscriptions in Kharoshthi script. Taxila Museum.

Above: stucco head of the Buddha in course of excavation, late Gandhara type of the 5th century. Such heads, and their bodies, were often repaired by being given fresh layers of stucco modeling.

Left: this stupa base, now in Taxila Museum, would once have supported the dome, crowned by tiered umbrellas. The Buddhas which face out at each level represent the multiplicity of the Buddha nature; and, although they wear Roman-like garments typical of Gandhara art of the 2nd century AD, they certainly do not illustrate merely human Buddhas. For the terraces are borne up on the backs of mythical animals, thus suggesting that the whole structure is a "celestial apparition," like stupas described in Mahayana texts.

Above right: stucco image of the Buddha lying to die and pass into Nirvana, in course of excavation at the Bhamala monastery. An icon of this type, some 1000 feet long, is reported to be lying somewhere in the Gandhara region, buried under detritus no doubt. This one is probably c. 300 AD.

Right: diaper stone walling of the Dharmarajika stupa. The stages of evolution in the stonework at Taxila may be used for the general dating of buildings. The earliest stonework consisted of large, irregular stones, set in a rubble of small stones, under the Scythians or Shakas in the 1st century BC. True diaper, with the large stones more regular and the small trimmed carefully and laid, was introduced in the 1st century AD. This was refined under the early Kushans, as here; then in the 4th century AD both larger and smaller stones were carefully trimmed to each other, and bands of even ashlar separated each course of large stones.

Right: the base of a stupa being excavated, of a similar type to that opposite, from Jaulian monastery.

Right and far right: a group of Buddhist figures during excavation, and after conservation and display in the museum. These are a set of stucco over clay sculptures from Jaulian monastery, cell 29, dating to c. 300. They show many Romano-Hellenic characteristics, including the draped, toga-like garments and the bare torso. Among them are clearly recognizable the Buddha, celestials, a monk and a foreign king. This may refer to a specific episode in Buddhist legend or to a donation.

Left: stucco polychrome head from a shrine at Taxila. This illustrates the extraordinary finesse of which the stucco workers in Gandhara were capable. It is sometimes suggested that masters may have come along the overland route from Roman-Hellenic cities of the eastern Mediterranean, perhaps Alexandria, to take advantage of the wealth being spent on Buddhist art in Gandhara. The expression of ecstasy on this head of a celestial has never been surpassed. Museo Nazionale d'Arte Orientale, Rome.

Below: silver disk of Romano-Hellenic workmanship, representing a bearded philosopher type, excavated in Sirkap at Taxila. This may have been meant as a mirror back or the center of a bowl; it must have been imported. Such heads lie behind those on the terracotta panel from Harwan in Chapter 2. Many other Classical bronzes have been excavated at Taxila, and a whole collection of Alexandrian (?) plaster models for such work was excavated at Begram.

Right: pot-shaped reliquary in turned steatite, from the Dharmarajika stupa. Such reliquaries were used to contain relics of the Buddha and Buddhist saints deposited in stupas.

Below: gold bracelet found at Sirkap, one of a pair. Actual examples of ancient Indian jewelry are naturally rare. The discovery of many fine pieces at Taxila suggests that they were hidden, perhaps under threat of invasion, and never recovered.

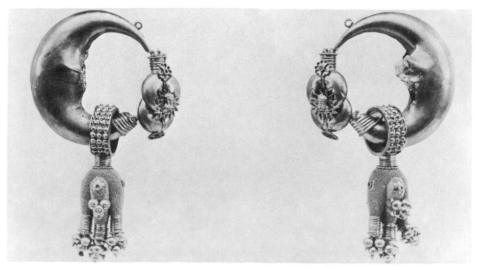

Superb gold jewelry, like these earrings found in Sirkap city at Taxila, suggests that the city itself must have been splendidly adorned, if its citizens were able to ornament themselves with gold so beautifully and inventively shaped. It testifies to the wealth which trade with both west and east must have brought to the inhabitants of this great metropolis.

3. The Growth of Indian Civilization

The arrival of the Aryans. The beginning of historical India is usually connected with the arrival of the Aryans in the northwest, sometime not long after 2000 BC. The earlier Indus valley civilization had existed from soon after 3000 BC in what was then a fertile and forested river plain. Its large principal cities, notably Harappa to the north and Mohenjo-daro to the south, had survived, with their streetplans virtually unchanged, for over 1,500 years. The encounter between its population and the Aryans is undocumented. Certainly elements of the Indus valley culture and its arts survived into later times. These include pastoral techniques of cattle and buffalo raising and technological inventions such as carts, the weaving of cotton cloth, implements still in use today, as well as motifs of religious art, such as the ithyphallic deity "lord of the beasts," a bull cult and images of ritual bullfighting – a custom which certain Adivasi groups still practice. So it is likely that the population remains as an ingredient in modern India's. Harappa may perhaps have fallen to invading Aryans; Mohenjo-daro is more likely to have been abandoned; both cities were anyway in some sort of decline during the later centuries of the second millennium BC.

The Aryans seem to have sprung from a large population group that expanded in the steppes of southern Russia and Central Asia. They spread west and east, appearing as invaders on the territory of several ancient civilizations. They spoke a number of languages which are the ancestors of most modern European and north Indian tongues. The whole Indo–Aryan group thus has strong affinities of grammar, vocabulary and especially of conceptual structure. The name "Arya" is that by which this people called themselves in India. The name of "Iran" comes from the same root. It is clear that they established themselves in a dominant position in India, at the top of the social hierarchy, which they organized according to their own ideas. The term "Arya" is still a complimentary form of polite address. They brought with them into India the horse – not usually ridden, at first, but harnessed in pairs to war-chariots – and a leaf-bladed bronze sword. Perhaps they brought iron at a slightly later date. Most important of all, they brought their sacred literature standardized in the Veda, which has provided the nucleus of Indian culture for almost four millennia, and still does.

The basic Veda consists of four groups of hymns, each finally arranged about 900 BC according to its own system, each for a different use. Originally composed by inspired sages called *rishis*, the hymns were chanted at sacrifices, to invoke named gods (*devas* = "shining ones") who would receive the burned offerings and respond favorably to the requests of those for whom the sacrifices were being offered. Varuna, Indra, Agni, Surya and Soma are a few of the chief deities. The priestly officiants at the sacrifice, whose business it was to know and chant the hymns, as well as carry through the rituals in which they formed the chief element, were called Brahmans. They were a hereditary caste; they learned by rote their hymns and rituals, never writing them down until quite lately, preserving their texts unchanged for some 3,000 years. The texts were in an archaic and complex form of Sanskrit. As time went on, and this language became more and more remote from spoken tongues as they developed, the Brahmans composed first a mass of explanatory material, and then easily remembered summaries of this, all of which they committed to memory. They were thus compelled to become philologists, grammarians and semanticists of their own sacred language at an early date. The great linguist Panini is said to have written his grammar of Sanskrit about 450 BC.

In addition to the hymns, the chief Vedic texts are the *Brahmanas*, and the main group of *Upanishads*; they were all complete perhaps by 400 BC. The *Brahmanas* are huge compilations of myth and legend which "explain" the significances of ancient ceremonies. They preserve the largest and probably the oldest known systematic exploration of myth and folklore. The major *Upanishads* are summaries of metaphysical thought and imagery derived from the rest of the Veda. To this day they are regarded by those who know them as one of the most profound religious texts of mankind; and they have been read as inspiration by many western philosophers. Virtually the whole of later Indian thought takes its rise in one or other Vedic tradition. Even the unorthodox religions, Buddhism and Jainism, are couched in language and conceptual forms which are only intelligible in terms of the *Upanishads*.

Aryan society and art. Early Aryan society was broadly divided into four hereditary social strata, called *varna*, "colors." The Brahmans were one. The next were the Kshatriyas, the warriors, whose duty it was continually to be active in warfare and government, and who formed an aristocracy supporting closely the Brahmans. Third were the Vish, the "everybody else" who mattered. They later tended to become merchants, artisans and farmers. Fourth were the Shudras, the nonentities, who had no social standing. And then there were the rest, conquered non-Aryan populations, alien slaves, the "noseless ones." For Aryans prided themselves on their high-bridged long noses and on their light skin color, still important today in marriage advertisements. Within the set of *varnas*, which is, after all, a fairly broad and non-confining classification, there evolved a set of occupational categories, also governed by birth, which were arranged on a scale of

Previous page: pillar from the railing of the now-vanished Barhut stupa, 2nd century BC, carved with a king or deity on horseback who carries a pillar crowned with a winged being. Indian Museum, Calcutta.

Opposite: terracotta figures of dancing girls, with swirling skirts, excavated at the Mauryan capital city of Pataliputra. Dance, and other pleasures, interested the inhabitants of the great early Indian cities, influencing later aesthetic traditions. Patna Museum.

relative "cleanness" or "uncleanness." This developed by the early centuries AD into the caste system, which is now outlawed. At first it was designed as a means of ordering society. Later it certainly became oppressive.

The Aryans were settled in the region of the five tributaries of the Indus (*panch-ap* = five-waters = Punjab) by about 1300 BC. But as they did not build their villages in brick or stone they have left little for archaeology to dig up. They moved gradually down into the Ganga valley, and probably towards the Narmada region, clearing and beginning to cultivate. By about 500 BC they had established large cities, and begun what we call the normal processes of civilization, including trade, for which the earliest "punch-marked" coins were struck, and the consolidation of kingdoms within what earlier had been a tribally structured society.

During this epoch some of the cardinal formative events of Indian history took place. Probably about 800 BC lived a sage called Kapila to whom is attributed the original conception of the profoundly important Sankhya system, a seminal element in the whole of Indian philosophy, and the philosophical counterpart to Yoga: which suggests that Yoga too was then in existence. Then during the 6th century BC lived the two teachers who founded the great unorthodox non-Hindu religions of India, which flourish to this day: Mahavira (c. 599–527), the founder of Jainism, and Gautama Shakyamuni, the Buddha (c. 563–489?), founder of the world religion Buddhism. In 483 BC the first great council of Buddhists was called to fix and authenticate the Buddha's original verbal teaching. It took place at one of the cities where he had lived and taught, old Rajgir, near modern Patna. For centuries this

was a sacred pilgrimage site for Buddhists. The hill nearby called the Vulture Peak, once looking over a huge ancient reservoir, is where the Buddha is said to have uttered many of the teaching texts attributed to him. The city lay in a valley shielded by a ring of Cyclopean walls running along the hilltops around. It was one of the early cities about which Buddhist literature tells us; and archaeology is now confirming the physical reality of the literary descriptions. The ruler of Magadha during a large part of the Buddha's lifetime was Bimbisara (544–493 BC) who also appears in Buddhist literature.

About 450 BC King Ajatashatru, son of Bimbisara, founded the city of Pataliputra, in the suburbs of modern Patna on the Ganga river. Here a large timber palace-hall has been excavated, and many beautiful small terracottas found. These miniature sculptures seem to have been a feature of art in the Ganga basin during the centuries before the birth of Christ. They represent such secular subjects as animals, dancing girls and scenes of pleasure in a simple graphic style. No doubt there were major arts of wooden sculpture, and probably painting, that have vanished. So these modest, fired-clay objects set for us the tone of later Indian art by their sweetness, their emphasis upon the mode of delight and their imagery both of desirable beauty and of the wealth represented by lavish jewelry and elaborate coiffure. At Chandraketugarh on the lower Ganga there has been discovered a factory of such terracottas, and many have been excavated elsewhere. They were clearly produced in response to the demands of city populations, at least a proportion of whom were able to devote themselves to enjoyment. For so far as our information goes, the great early cities of the

३री सदी ई॰ प॰
मौर्य काल पटना
G. 417

३री सदी ई॰ पू॰
बुलन्दिबाग पटना

Map of India, showing the major sites where excavations have been done or remains survive.

Ganga plain were very well governed, and their rulers accepted it as part of their responsibility to provide pleasure gardens outside the walls for the enjoyment of the populace. Buddhist texts describe the cheerful noise resounding through such gardens in the cool evening. The Buddha himself was born in one, the Lumbini in Nepal. And Panini records that full-fledged drama, as well as dramatic criticism, existed already in his day.

The first cities. A large number of major cities seem to have come into existence about 600 BC. They were the capitals of ancient states whose names and memory have been canonized in the two ancient Sanskrit epic poems, the *Mahabharata*, and the *Ramayana* by Valmiki; both were probably composed initially about this time, though they may have been rewritten later. Cities referred to in literature, some partly but none fully excavated, include Ujjayini (modern Ujjain) and Vidisha in central India; Mahishmati, on the Narmada river and Nasikya on the Godavari. Rupar on the Sutlej river (Ambala district) has given archaeology a linked series of pottery types reaching back to the Indus valley period. In the Ganga valley region down into northern Orissa excavation has revealed a whole series of major city sites, many of them occupied continuously from c. 600 BC to 1100 AD. Ahicchatra

(Bareilly district) and Hastinapura (Meerut district), once the capital of the *Mahabharata* heroes, are now both deserted. Kaushambi (Allahabad), perhaps the earliest foundation, going back to c. 850 BC, had a splendid palace in the southwestern corner partly roofed by the only true stone vaults known in pre-Muslim India. Rajghat was old Banaras; at Rajgir was found a shrine inscribed with the name of the local snake deity, who is mentioned in the *Mahabharata*, Maninaga. Vaishali (Muzaffarpur district) was a city associated with the Buddha, where the second Buddhist council was also held about 100 years after the Buddha's death. In the northwest, Taxila and Charsada have been excavated. They were the chief cities of the region called Gandhara from which one of the Achaemenid emperors of Iran, Darius, claimed to receive tribute in c. 590 BC.

Tamluk was a port in eastern India, known to the 2nd-century AD Greek writer Ptolemy. Here was found rouletted ware and pottery of Roman type. In Orissa, at Shishupalgarh, substantial remains of huge earth fortifications have been found. Many other discoveries have been recorded, and many will yet be made. These cities can be linked chronologically by a complex pottery sequence, which runs through a painted gray ware, and a coarse gray ware c. 600 BC, to a finely polished black ware, called Northern Black Polished (NBP), from about 300 BC to 150 BC, which was probably made in one or more centers on the Ganga. Overlapping with it are red wares, among which a later, finely polished red is said to have been inspired by Roman Samian imports. From all the available evidence, literary and archaeological, we are able to reconstruct the image of a lively cosmopolitan civilization, in some ways broadly comparable with the Greek, based upon city kingdoms which fought each other – as Kshatriya rulers were in duty bound to do – but otherwise maintaining close relations. They conducted a lively trade among themselves, which was carried along the roads and rivers. Its chief goods were gold, ivory, fabrics, slaves and artisan work. Most important, perhaps, was the growth within the cities of the class of educated merchants and craftsmen, who had become wealthy by that trade, and to whom the new religions of the Buddha and Mahavira especially appealed. Early Buddhist texts refer to convoys of 400 or 500 laden ox-carts traveling the roads; and they describe gifts made to the Buddha and the Buddhist order by wealthy patrons who were members of that class of society.

The growth of Buddhism. The centuries between 500 and 300 BC saw the growth especially of Buddhism. It seems that the cosmopolitan populations of the cities became interested in religions which involved them as individuals. No doubt the sacrificial ceremonies the Brahmans performed for the aristocracy had begun to seem conventional, perhaps complacent, exclusive and remote. There had grown up orders of ascetics and wandering teachers of many different sects and persuasions, who offered instruction and inspiration to apprentice ascetics, usually of the upper classes. Initially the Buddha himself, after being born a petty prince, became such a one, and the stories of his life describe him trying out a succession of different teachers and their doctrines, but finding satisfaction in none. He therefore took a vow to obtain true enlightenment. He achieved it at Bodhgaya, after prolonged meditation and spiritual struggle under a pipal tree. This became known as the Bodhi tree. He spent the rest of his life as a wandering teacher, building up his order of monks and nuns, which still embodies his teaching to the present day. On his death he passed into Nirvana. The essence of his doctrine was its direct appeal to the individual, whoever he might be. No one, whatever his class, was left without hope for his or her own salvation. All had at least a prospect of attaining enlightenment similar to the Buddha's own.

Over the centuries a great body of Buddhist teaching and rules for monastic and lay discipline was built up in the memories of members of the Buddhist order, on the basis of what those who knew the Buddha himself had heard him say. Buddhist councils were held at intervals to check over and authenticate those remembered teachings. After a few centuries, however, the teachings developed regional and sectarian variations which the councils could not contain. They were finally written down at some uncertain date in two languages. The best opinion suggests that this was not until late in the 1st century BC. The tradition recorded in Pali, a language derived from Sanskrit, is usually called Theravada, "the way of the elders," or Hinayana, "the lesser vehicle." It tends to be strict, slightly archaic, and to emphasize the individual's personal pursuit of his own enlightenment. The tradition recorded in Sanskrit at about the same time is called the Mahayana, or "great vehicle." It developed elaborate visionary philosophies, and emphasizes the Bodhisattva ideal of total unselfishness. The Bodhisattva is a being who, reaching the status virtually of Buddha, and becoming entitled to Nirvana, dedicates the results of his own spiritual effort to the salvation of all other living creatures. He vows not to depart into his own Nirvana until he has led all other suffering beings to attain theirs.

Buddhism is based upon a doctrine of detachment. The Buddha taught that everyone's craving for objects, possessions, pleasures and personal status, even for identity, was the source of strife, of human suffering and individual despair. The Buddhist should learn to stop his cravings; and then he may reach the peace of true wisdom. But, of course, this is no easy matter. The Buddhist orders, with their discipline and meditation, exist specifically to make it possible. But the very existence of the orders, who can own nothing and must beg to live, depends on a faithful body of laity. Partly to meet their religious needs, there grew up in Buddhism a strand of personal devotion both to the Buddha and his memory, and, in Mahayana, to infinitely compassionate Bodhisattvas, which prompted the development both of the stupa and of the personal icon, a phenomenon studied in detail later on. There can be little doubt that it was the challenge and example of Buddhism in this respect that awoke the Brahmans to parallel efforts of their own, inducing them to cultivate popular devotion to deities and saintly teachers within their own system.

The Maurya dynasty and Ashoka. A new historical epoch began with the Maurya dynasty, founded by Chandragupta, who began rule from the city of Pataliputra in 321 BC, two years after the death of Alexander the Great. In 326 Alexander had passed through the Khyber pass and entered the Indus valley with his army to investigate the fabled land of India. Chandragupta is said to have spent some months in Alexander's camp. His army then returned to Iran, part by sea, part by land along the coast. Alexander himself returned to Babylon to die in 323. He left behind officers of his garrisons as petty princes in Bactria and the Upper Indus valley. The dynasty of Seleucus became dominant in the area, the first of several Greek and Parthian families to maintain courts at which Greek plays were performed, and which left as artistic traces of their presence some important sub-

The Mauryan dynastic site of Sarnath during excavation. The famous pillar and capital are shown.

Classical architecture at Taxila, many Indo-Greek coins, and Hellenistic gems inscribed in Greek, Brahmi and Kharoshthi. The temple of the double-headed eagle in the Jandial mound at Taxila will be discussed later. The impact of the Greek incursion on the art of mainland India, however, was otherwise minimal. Seleucus himself is important to Indian history partly because a Greek ambassador he sent to the court of Chandragupta, Megasthenes, wrote a vivid description of life in the Maurya capital, much quoted by other Greek writers, though the original is lost. He describes in particular detail the huge and splendid wooden palace of which fragments have been excavated.

Chandragupta laid the foundations of an empire that was vastly extended and consolidated by his grandson, the legendary Ashoka (272–232 BC), one of the greatest emperors known to history. After prolonged and bloody battles, including a genocidal campaign in the south, Ashoka underwent a conversion, and adopted pacific teachings, probably based on Buddhism. He is said to have constructed vast numbers of stupas. The colossal army he had used was partly disbanded. But the great administrative and economic system which had underpinned the conquest was adapted to running a unified state almost 2,000 miles from east to west, and something like 1,000 miles from north to south. We know about Ashoka's ambitions and something of his achievements, partly from Buddhist legend, but also from an extensive body of inscriptions he ordered to be cut on pillars and rocks over the extent of his empire; most are in a script called Brahmi; two are in Kharoshthi. They were deciphered by James Prinsep in 1837, though it was not until one inscription identifying the king specifically as Ashoka was found in 1915 that his identity was confirmed. The inscriptions urge the people, whom the king calls "my children," to obey their governors, who are like an "experienced nurse" appointed for the children's welfare and happiness; to avoid bloodshed; and to respect "Brahmanas and Shramanas" (the latter word probably referring to non-Brahman religious orders).

Ashoka was responsible for the conversion of the kings of Ceylon to Theravada Buddhism, sending to their capital Anuradhapura a cutting of the Bodhi tree. Around that city the kings built palaces, monasteries and many stupas. The Theravada Buddhism of Ceylon became important in the later history of Southeast Asia, because it preserved what was believed by fundamentalist Buddhists to be the pristine form of Buddhist teaching. As such its monks and texts were in great demand, notably in Burma and Thailand.

Post–Mauryan society and literature. The Mauryan empire had dissolved by about 185 BC. It was succeeded in the heartland of Magadha by a series of lesser dynasties: the Shunga (c. 187–75 BC), the Kanva (75–30 BC) and a series of even less significant families, until the

Above: ancient stupa at Sarnath, the site where the Buddha preached his first sermon, visited by many people today, although Buddhism was eclipsed in India in the late 12th century AD.

Below: female head, cut in stone, from a lost monument of the Shunga period, 2nd century BC, with elaborate coiffure and turban illustrating ideal wealth and chic. Delhi Museum.

rise of the Gupta in the 4th century AD. The history of these kingdoms illustrates very clearly the usual Indian dynastic system which survived right through the Middle Ages. It was semi-feudal, in the sense that each area was under the control of a dominant family. Among these families might be one more powerful than the rest, whose head ruled the others as their king, compelling their allegiance, taking princesses of their families into his harem, and counting their accumulated terrain as his kingdom. The countryside supported the dynasty's capital, usually one of the old cities, though sometimes a new capital was founded. Kings would build reservoirs (called tanks) and shrines, granting land and villages to support them. For all rulers claimed the sanction of religion for their dominion. Hinduism and Buddhism both offered metaphysical authentifications of royal power, as we shall see. Kings claiming the ultimate imperial title might perform the horse sacrifice, which is prescribed in the Veda. A white horse would be turned loose to wander for a year and a day. If no one dared molest it in all its peregrinations, it would be sacrificed with elaborate ceremonial; the king would then claim a uniquely sublime status, blessed by the gods. Empires and large kingdoms could wither back to their constituent petty kingdoms if the central authority lost its grip. Fringe areas might fall under the control of some other neighboring dynasty whose power was waxing. Thus the fortunes of cities might rise and fall along with those of their royal families. Many of India's modern cities go back to 600 BC. Others are far younger. Yet others have either vanished completely or fallen to the status of a village of peasants who stable their cattle in ancient dynastic shrines, and use the finely cut stones to build their houses and wall their fields.

There are two important texts which illustrate very different aspects of city life during the immediate post-Maurya period. Both are summaries of ideas and knowledge accumulated over a fairly long period and both became classics to later ages. The first is the *Arthashastra*, the second the *Kamasutra*. The *Arthashastra* is attributed to a minister of Chandragupta Maurya, but is probably not by him. It is a text on the science of government, including civil administration, taxation, law, inheritance, the army and secret service, the planning and layout of cities and towns, on loans and interest, on slavery and gambling. It also deals with what we call prostitution, which in ancient India was an honorable profession, protected by the state which drew income from its individual courtesans. Kings and wealthy men maintained groups of salaried prostitutes, who attended their personal courts, even in battle, and could expect to make good marriages.

The *Kamasutra* (c. 200 BC) is a famous manual on the techniques of love, now a world classic. As well as describing the mechanisms of sex and the physical endowments of women from different parts of India, it also describes the life of pleasure normally lived by the man-about-town in those north Indian cities, where pleasure was regarded without guilt as a normal part of life. It mentions in passing that one of the accomplishments expected of a young man is that he be able to paint a likeness of any of his mistresses; it is not surprising, therefore, that many of the Ganga valley terracottas mentioned above are explicitly sexual. They are the material vestiges from this Ganga culture which best illustrate the formulation of what became the cardinal Indian mode of aesthetic expression – the erotic. As we shall see, the idea that a being of divine status would naturally be surrounded by beautiful people engaged in supernatural pleasures lay behind the schemes of decoration developed for Indian religious buildings.

Art and architecture. A series of Mauryan works in stone mark the earliest stages of the development of historical Indian art. Many will be discussed in more detail later on. The earliest caves were excavated at Barabar, on Nagarjuni hill, initially, it seems from an inscription, to shelter an order of monks during the monsoon rains. The interiors were polished, as much other Mauryan stone-work was, perhaps in imitation of imperial stonework at Persepolis, the capital of Achaemenid Iran. The series of inscribed pillars mentioned above were also polished monoliths, crowned with figures of symbolic animals. Polished railings and fragments of dedicatory sculpture have been found at Sarnath (Banaras), the site which seems to have been adopted as the Mauryan Buddhist dynastic shrine. Its main stupa was either constructed or enlarged under the Mauryas, as was Stupa I at Sanchi (Bhopal district). In the same period the excavation of the Buddhist cave shrines at Ajanta was begun, with the polished cave number 8. So too was a series of colossal free-standing stone sculptures, representing opulent males and females holding fly whisks, usually called *Yakshas* and *Yakshis*. Most are damaged, and were found with no context. But it is likely that they were statues set up at sacred shrines on behalf of royalty as dedications of themselves, carved by an imperial Mauryan guild of craftsmen.

After the Mauryan eclipse, during the reign of the Shungas, the great, highly ornate stupa of Barhut was built; so too was the railing of Stupa II at Sanchi. From elsewhere in India fragments of work in related styles are known, no doubt of similar date. For example, at the important city of Mathura (modern Muttra) stupas, both Buddhist and Jain, must have been ornamented in a very similar way to Barhut; and, in the southeast, around Amaravati on the Krishna delta, somewhat similar work was done, probably at the first major dynastic sites of the Shatavahana dynasty, whose rule began in the area c. 150 BC. Altogether it seems that Buddhism played by far the most important role in the patronizing of Indian art in these centuries. There is very little to suggest that Hinduism made much use of art at all. But at a sanctuary in

Carved ivory from India excavated at Pompeii in Italy, which was overwhelmed by Vesuvius in 79 AD; this was probably a mirror handle. Museo Nazionale, Naples.

Vidisha (central India) a pillar was dedicated to a deity called Vasudeva by one "Heliodoros," perhaps a Greek, about 113 BC. Interestingly, the first sea voyage direct from Egypt to India was said to have been made by Eudoxos in 120 BC. "Yavanas" – people of Hellenic descent – become familiar as traders and soldiers. One of the guardian figures on the railing of Barhut is a man

wearing un-Indian tailored garments, an unusual sheathed sword and a Greek diadem headband. Under the Kanvas (75–30 BC) Buddhism continued to be patronized, and a railing was built at Bodhgaya, the scene of his enlightenment, around the Buddha's "walking place."

Overseas trade and colonies. In the west of India it is certain that trade contacts with the western world were well established by the later part of the 1st century BC. The ports, chief of them Bharukaccha (modern Broach) and Kalyan, north of Bombay, were actively importing and exporting goods, with the balance of trade pretty much in favor of India. The rulers of this area were probably at first the Shakas, though the Shatavahanas competed strongly for control of the area and its trade. In the 1st century BC, under Shatavahana rule and in a Shatavahana style, the Great Stupa at Sanchi finally received its four gateways. Between 26 and 20 BC the dynasty sent embassies to the Roman emperor Augustus, probably with a view to developing their trade routes around the southern part of the peninsula, up to the area of the Krishna delta, of which they were taking control. In about 45 AD a Greek sailor called Hippalos is said to have learned the trick of sailing on the monsoon winds across the Indian Ocean, to make landfall on the Malabar coast of the southwestern Deccan. The port of Arikamedu, already mentioned, was active about that date, with Roman pottery and wine in jars passing through. The Roman writer Pliny (1st century AD) lamented the extravagance of the Romans in buying immense quantities of luxury goods from India at great cost. These included spices, perfumes, fine textiles, dyes, slaves, jewels, sugar, iron, and ivory both uncut and worked. In Italy an Indian ivory carving has been found at Herculaneum, overwhelmed by Vesuvius in 79 AD. Fine jewelry has been found at Pompeii which, from its style and opulence, may well be identified as Indian. Elephants, lions, tigers and buffaloes, parrots, peacocks and monkeys were transported live for the Roman circuses and private zoos. These imports were paid for in gold, constituting a tremendous drain on the resources of the Roman Empire, and a vast gain to the Indian traders. Many hoards of Roman gold coins have been found in India, especially in the Deccan and Ceylon.

The Buddhist Shatavahanas were also developing trade into Southeast Asia. One of their kings struck coins with the device of a two-masted ship. The first evidences of Indian presence during the 1st century AD in Malaya, Sumatra and the coasts of Thailand and Indochina are probably due to the efforts of their merchants searching for gold (especially in Sumatra), precious stones and the spices which those regions were already cultivating. These the Indians passed profitably westwards into the Roman world. The trading posts then set up in Southeast Asia became the nuclei of Indianized kingdoms, and Buddhism traveled with the trade. It is conceivable that the early committal of the Hinayana scriptures into Pali, which

some scholars believe took place in this epoch (c. 70 BC?), may have been partly a response to the need to record authentic versions of the texts for the benefit of remote overseas monastic communities. There are many passages in the scriptures themselves referring to long voyages across the ocean.

The role of the so-called Shaka dynasties in western India is still not sufficiently recognized by many western scholars. About 140 BC Shakas were ruling the Taxila area; and about 70 AD the Greek author Arrian called the lower Indus region, then ruled by Shakas, "Scythia." But it is more than likely that even during the 2nd century BC Shakas were already ruling, from their capital city of Ujjain, the still fertile regions of the Indus valley and Punjab including Mathura, stretches of the west coast, the adjacent Ghats and even areas of the Deccan. Some Indian scholars believe that it was in this region under the Shakas that pure Sanskrit was preserved, and that Patanjali, the second great grammarian of India, who is also said to have written the Yoga sutras in which the fundamental doctrine of Yoga is defined, lived in their kingdom, along with some of the greatest writers of Sanskrit poetry usually dated far later by western scholars. It is also possible that the Sanskrit texts in which Mahayana Buddhist doctrine is condensed, the "Wisdom Literature," were composed in the Shaka domains. Certainly the earliest pure Sanskrit inscriptions in India were cut by the Kshatrapas, a Shaka dynasty of the west (e.g. the Rudradaman I inscription at Girnar). And Sanskrit was the official language of the western region, while even kings in the rest of northern India went on cutting inscriptions in Prakrit until the 4th century AD when they too adopted Sanskrit. The first of the great series of Buddhist caves in the Western Ghats was cut in the 2nd century BC, probably under the Shata-vahanas, who were then finally forced from the area by the Kshatrapas during the 2nd century AD, when the latter began to cut and inscribe their own caves. The first colonization of Java was by a prince "Aji Shaka," from western India about 75 AD, and the 1st-century founder of Funan probably came from the same region. So it is probable that the Shakas played a substantial role in the Indianization of Southeast Asia.

The Kushans. The 1st century AD was, in fact, one of the most crucial in the history of India's colonial expansion. The first Hindu colonies were founded in Kambuja (Cambodia) by Kaundinya, in Malaya by Lankesha and his son Bhagadatta, in Champa by Shri Mara, and in western Java by Devavarman. Expansion in another direction was made possible by the arrival in northwest and west central India of the Kushan dynasty, founded by the Yüeh-chi people from Central Asia. In 126 BC the

Yakshi, or aristocratic attendant, from Didarganj, Bihar, 1st century BC. The colossal figure is cut in sandstone and its surface is highly polished; it probably stood at a now vanished shrine. Patna Museum.

Chinese had sent an embassy to them, while they were living in the Oxus river valley. Already in 2 BC they had presented Buddhist scriptures to the Chinese court; and about 65 AD the first Buddhist monastery, the "White Horse," was built at Chang-an, the Chinese capital. The Yüeh-chi must in practice have commanded the roads of Central Asia throughout this period. By the 1st century AD they had taken command of ancient Gandhara, the region of the Kabul valley and Upper Indus, with its capital Taxila (Sirkap sector), and driven the Shakas from Mathura, which they made their second capital. They sent embassies to Rome, and, in collusion with the Romans, broke the Parthian control of the land trade routes to the Mediterranean through Iran, Mesopotamia and Syria.

By about 120 AD they had opened direct roads to the eastern shores of the Mediterranean, and trade – especially in silk – began to flow overland under their auspices from China and India to Rome. In 129 the Chinese first reached Bactria, which then to them was "India." The Kushan merchants became immensely rich, and much of their wealth was spent on art to adorn Buddhist shrines and monasteries. There is little doubt that Mathura, known to the Greeks as *Modoura ton theon*, "Mathura of the Gods," already supported flourishing schools of art, especially

Right: standing dedicatory figure of a Bodhisattva, from Mathura, of the Kushan period, early 2nd century AD. Mathura Museum.

Below: figure of a celestial girl carrying a bird cage, carved on a railing pillar of a vanished stupa at Mathura, 2nd century AD. Mathura Museum.

sculpture in a pink sandstone; from the characteristics of some of the reliefs of the Shaka period at Mathura it also appears certain that painting must have existed. There are many motives derived from Mediterranean or Egyptian prototypes. Under the Kushans sculpture at Mathura continued to develop, and its works were exported to other parts of the Kushan empire, including Sanchi. At Mathura were laid the foundations for the unified traditions of both Buddhist and Hindu iconic art in later India.

The greatest Kushan king was Kanishka, whose dates are uncertain; his accession is variously held to be 78, 124 or 144 AD. He ruled a huge empire which extended deep into Central Asia, across Afghanistan and down to Banaras on the Ganga. Mahayana Buddhism remembers him as a great patron; for under his rule that faith flourished, in Gandhara especially. Huge shrines and monastic com-

Ivory panels, from the hoard excavated at Begram, which would have been parts of a box. They are incised with pleasing ornament and figures in a style like that of Amaravati in the 2nd century A.D. Kabul Museum.

plexes were built there near every major town, paid for by princes, chiefs, merchants and even peasants. They were encrusted with sculpture in a style strongly influenced by the art of Rome's eastern Mediterranean Hellenistic provinces; the early work was in schist, the later in stucco. Figures stand in Classical poses wearing toga-like garments; there are Hellenistic torsos, putti supporting swagged garlands; and Greek legends appear among the ornament. Two known names of artists suggest Classical connections: one Tita (Titus) painted the shrine at Miran in Central Asia, and Agishala (Agesilaus) smithed the golden reliquary casket found in Kanishka's own colossal stupa at Shah-ji-ki-dheri, in Gandhara. Many Classical jewels, small bronzes and terracottas have also been excavated in the northwest. Kushan coins tended to follow Greco-Roman types and weight standards.

It was Kushan Gandharan art that provided the basis for the Buddhist art of Central Asia, of China, Korea (528) and Japan (538). It lasted into the 6th century at Hadda, Akhnur, Ushkur. A related Buddhist style appeared in other parts of western India in the Kushan dominions, where it endured into the 7th century. A most important hoard of art was discovered by Hackin at Begram in Afghanistan, a summer resort of the Kushans. Crowded into one room, whose roof had fallen in and so protected the hoard, were quantities of Syrian painted glass, eastern Greek silver patterns and stucco reliefs, Indian ivories, possibly from the Shatavahana kingdom, and some Chinese Han lacquer fragments. This gives a unique insight into the international character of commerce during the epoch when the Kushans controlled the roads. Their power somewhat decreased after the 3rd century, and the Kushan kings of Kabul became vassals of the Persian Sasanians. The empire gradually dissolved into a multiplicity of lesser Kushan states, many of which continued to produce major religious art.

2nd-century developments. The 2nd century AD saw developments in other parts of Indian Asia. In the southeast the Shatavahanas continued to build in carved white limestone a major series of Buddhist shrines on the banks of the Krishna river, superbly decorated in their indigenous style. But most important was the growth that then took place of the trading colonies in Southeast Asia. In Malaya and west Java true kingdoms were set up. In 192, near Hue in Vietnam, the first royal temple foundation (no longer extant) was laid in the kingdom of Champa. The kingdom of Funan on the lower Mekong river in Cambodia, the basis of the later great Khmer empire, was first described by the Chinese in this century as having many splendid buildings, carved, painted and gilt. The founder was probably a Brahman trader, again from western India, whom local legend describes as marrying the daughter of a serpent deity. Many sites of canal towns and of forts with great earthen ramparts belonging to this kingdom have been identified around Oc-eo, now in South Vietnam. The houses seem to have been built on piles. Only one site has so far been excavated, but it yielded, among other finds, Indian seals, jewels and rings, Roman coins, Hellenistic engraved gems, Sasanian jewels, and Chinese bronzes of the Han and Wei dynasties. From the 2nd century to the 5th Funan repeatedly sent ambassadors to China, no doubt to help maintain the flow of seaborne trade. And although we know that by about 500 the kings of Funan were Hindu, Buddhist monks were being called to China from Funan only a little later to teach Buddhism there.

Alongside the significant developments of material culture, and no doubt inspiring some of them, a number of the most important developments in Buddhist thought took place in the late 1st and 2nd centuries AD. Ashvaghosha wrote his great Sanskrit poems on the life of the Buddha, the *Buddhacharita* and *Saundarananda*, partly perhaps with the aim of giving Buddhists epics of their own to rival the Hindu *Ramayana* and *Mahabharata*. He is also known to have written plays, none of which survives intact. A definitive collection of stories about the previous lives of the Buddha, called the *Jatakamala*, was made by a poet called Aryasura. Two of the greatest Sanskrit Buddhist doctrinal texts were composed probably in the Kushan dominions: the *Saddharmapundarika* (the "Lotus" sutra), which was one of the fundamental sutras for Mahayana Buddhism in China and Japan; and the *Lalitavistara*, scarcely less important. In the southeast, the Buddhist philosopher Nagarjuna, for whom a stupa was set up and decorated under the Shatavahanas, developed his *Madhyamika*, a cardinal theoretical work of Buddhist philosophy. This philosopher is also said to have written hymns, as well as an epistle to a Shatavahana king to whom one of the classic collections of Prakrit lyric poetry is attributed, the *Saptashataka*, which deals with village life and love. Also living in the 2nd century AD was India's greatest known early dramatist, Bhasa. His works give us our first comprehensive view of the flourishing classical drama. His masterpiece is the *Dream Vasavadatta*, a full-fledged historical realization. Other Sanskrit plays survive from the same epoch, only a few of the many composed.

The 3rd and 4th centuries also saw important developments in the spread of Buddhism across Central Asia. In the 3rd century the Lotus sutra and the *Divyavadana* were translated into Chinese; and near Bamiyan, in Afghanistan, huge rock-cut Buddhas were carved at a monastery cave-site which became the pattern for the earliest Chinese cave complexes at Yun-kang and Lung-men, cut during the 4th to 6th centuries. We know that the Chinese monk Chu Shih-hsing came to Khotan to study Buddhism, the first of many to make pilgrimages which penetrated gradually ever closer towards the Buddhist heartland of India. Between 344 and 412 the great Indian teacher Kumarajiva lived in the Chinese capital Chang-an, supervising the translation into Chinese of 106 Mahayana texts – a colossal task, for which he was highly honored. All over India during these centuries Buddhist monasteries flourished in the regions – in the western Deccan, where Ajanta continued to expand; in the southeast, where the Shatavahana style had reached its apogee by about 300 at Amaravati, Nagarjunakonda and

Jaggayapeta, before that dynasty gave ground to the Pallavas; in the west, under late Kushan patronage, for example in Sind; while at Mathura a whole series of Buddha and Jaina icons was cut which fixed the patterns for major icons which were to be made elsewhere. Colonies with Buddhist monasteries were also founded in Borneo and perhaps in the Philippines. In Champa the first inscriptions in Sanskrit, and a little later in Cham, record that the founder of what became the northern Cham capital, Mi Son, was a devotee of Shiva.

The Gupta empire. During the 4th century a new empire, that of the Guptas, emerged in India, based in Magadha, and supplanting the Kushan power in central India. It endured till the 6th century, though it suffered temporary eclipse at the end of the 5th when it lost most of its western terrain to invaders called Hunas; but it was brought back to something like its former size and glory by King Harsha of Kanauj (606–47). This dynasty founded one of the most glorious legendary courts of ancient times. It fostered a whole galaxy of Sanskrit literary talent, most of whose productions have been lost and are known to us only through the discussions of later critics. Their very existence indicates an appreciative and highly literate public. There were poems, epic, satiric and lyric, many novels, and especially plays. One of the greatest of the Gupta poet-playwrights was Kalidasa (c. 440) whose play, *Shakuntala*, was translated into English by William Jones in 1789 and whose poem, *Meghasandesha* ("Cloud-messenger"), was familiar in translation to Goethe, among others. Gupta theater was outstanding. Its illustrious names include Vishakhadatta, Bharavi, Bana, Bhavabhuti, Dandin and the Emperor Harsha himself. The cardinal text of Indian aesthetics, the *Natyashastra*, was probably compiled during the Gupta period (4th to 5th century), although it certainly contains much older material. It gives the most complete description of ancient techniques of acting, mime and dance with full details of bodily postures, gestures of arms and legs, glances of eyes, surviving anywhere in the world, and is still far too little known. India's great mathematician Aryabhatta (c. 476–99) also flourished at this time.

Buddhism remained doctrinally creative; for Sanskrit Mahayana texts seem to have been composed in the 4th century which were translated into Chinese during the 5th: for example, the immense *Avatamsaka* by Buddhabhadra in Nanking (429) and the *Lankavatara* by Gunabhadra (435–43). Many Indian monks and nuns were then reaching China, and a group of 61 Chinese pilgrims visited India (399–414), among them Fa-hsien, who left a valuable written account of what he saw. About 420 King Kumaragupta founded what was to become the greatest Buddhist university city, at Nalanda in Bihar. At Sarnath, as well as a few other Buddhist centers in Magadha, highly refined stone icons of the Buddha and Bodhisattvas were executed during the 5th to 8th centuries, based initially

Colossal rock-cut standing Buddha, 175 feet high, at the Buddhist cave site of Bamiyan on the trade road through Afghanistan, probably 3rd century AD; much damaged by Muslim vandalism.

upon developments at Mathura, as well as many smaller bronze images. In the Deccan a dynasty called the Vakatakas, allied to the Guptas by marriage, at whose court lived the great writer Vishnushaiman, author of the *Panchatantra*, continued to patronize the Buddhist caves of Ajanta; work went on there till about 600; at Ellora (Caves 5–9), at Bagh and Aurangabad other Buddhist caves were cut during the 6th and 7th centuries.

The major artistic departure under the Guptas was, however, Hindu. The earliest Hindu temples belong to the early 5th century. By the 6th century their sculpture both introduced a whole new iconography, and developed a superb and polished style of execution. In the Udayagiri caves (Bhilsa, Malwa) a whole series of Hindu mythical figures appears for the first time. Courtly conceptions of body movement and gesture, certainly connected with the flowering of the dance-drama, make their way into legendary narrative reliefs on many shrines. Extraordinarily elaborate ornaments appear, as do hairstyles that are mops of curls or fantastic coils. We must suppose that in the sophisticated courts and cities of the time a secular art no less developed than the religious must have flourished, and that it contributed something of its sweetness and chic to religious imagery. All that remains to us is the sculpture on a series of Hindu temples that

Above: Bodhisattva preaching, a sculpture of the 9th century in stucco on a building at the great Buddhist university at Nalanda, Bihar, photographed during excavation.

Above left: figure of the Hindu god Vishnu, in the sweet Gupta style of the 5th century AD, from Mathura. Delhi Museum.

Below: view of excavations in progress at Nalanda, the old Buddhist university city in Bihar. It is now possible to visit the site and walk through its streets and courtyards.

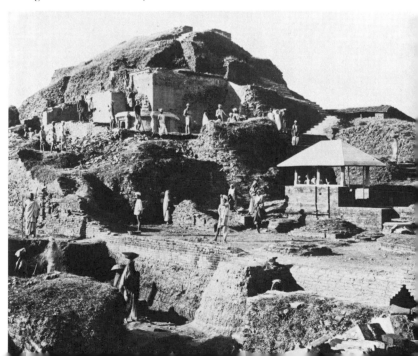

continued throughout the Gupta period well into the 7th century. Few are at all well preserved. The architectural and sculptural conceptions they embody, however, made their way into other regions of India, and into Southeast Asia, there to fertilize the local art styles.

During the 6th and 7th centuries in the Deccan, major groups of Hindu temples were made by the Chalukya dynasty at their successive capitals, at first Aivalli, then later at Badami. Here Hindu sculpture seems to have developed as a function of the compilation of those huge Sanskrit encyclopedias of Hindu legend called *Puranas*. Sculptors were called on to invent images not of human but of cosmic events; so that between 700 and 800 in rock-cut temples made first for the Chalukyas, and then for the Rashtrakutas after c. 758 in the Western Ghats, the art of sculpture reached an extraordinary scale of accomplishment. Echoes of its massive and energetic forms appear in many of the carvings executed in Southeast Asia. For these were centuries of major developments in Hindu stone sculpture overseas. It is not surprising that the 8th century was also rich in secular literature, allegorical novels in

Bodhisattva figure from Sarnath, sandstone carving in the gently rounded Gupta style of the 5th century; the garment hangs in a characteristic fish-tail shape. Similar images influenced Chinese Buddhist art in the 6th century. Delhi Museum.

particular. In the 9th century Jainism made great headway in the Deccan, and many of the Rashtrakuta kings abdicated to die as Jain monks. There is a major series of Jain caves at Ellora.

Links with Southeast Asia. It seems that during the 6th century the Roman Empire had ceased to trade with the east by sea. But India's maritime trade area had begun regularly to include south China. For the Chinese knew of the great Pyu city Shrikshetra (Hmawza, Prome) in Burma, which had been founded about 470. Inscribed Pali Buddhist texts have been found there, and excavation has revealed many early remains. The Chinese also reported the existence of flourishing, recently discovered kingdoms in lower Burma and Malaya. By 560 they knew of the existence of the Mon kingdom of Dvaravati, which endured until the 8th century; it was centered on Thaton in Burma and Nakhon Pathom in Thailand, its Buddhism was based on Pali Theravada, and some of its art was influenced by Pala India. During the 7th century Chinese art began to show the effects of regular direct contact with the Indian Buddhist art of Magadha, and its original Gandharan types began to lose ground. By the 5th century the Chinese also recorded that the original kingdom of Funan on the middle Mekong, in modern Cambodia and Laos, had been replaced by a kingdom they called Chen-la. None of Chen-la's many sites has yet been excavated, though many fine iconic sculptures have been collected.

In 616 Chen-la itself was superseded by the Khmer kingdom of Cambodia, whose empire was destined to become probably the greatest in Southeast Asia. It was founded by Isanavarman I (616–35), who built his capital at Sambor Prei Kuk, basing its planning and ornament on Indian models, though the full-round iconic sculptures – the glory of the Funan–Chen-la art tradition – far transcend any Indian prototypes. The early phases of this kingdom had to endure great difficulties and setbacks throughout the 8th century – not least from the Hindu Cham. The people of this kingdom enriched themselves by piracy, preying on ships sailing the monsoon routes. Their tribal society had a matrilineal element, at the center of which the Hindu temple, served by priestesses, acted as focus for social ceremonial, maintaining itself from the economic byproducts of pilgrimage. There was a vigorous culture, partly based on corrupt versions of Sanskrit literature, astrology and magic, including native folktales and extravagant legends of marvels. The irregularity of the surviving manuscripts, with their mixed papers and writing styles, suggests that Cham literacy was not of the highest. They were continuously under pressure from the Chinese, who took their capital in 605, but retired. Then in the 8th century the kingdoms of Indonesia took a hand in the maritime power struggle; first of all the dynasty of Shrivijaya, which was visited by the Chinese monk pilgrim I-Ching (671–95), and whose kings ruled parts of Malaya, Sumatra and western Java; then, later, the

Balconies of Jain caves at the great religious center of Ellora in the Western Ghats, probably 9th century AD. The glorified pillars and fine carving transform the cave into an image of heavenly palaces.

Shailendra of central Java, who built so many great Mahayana Buddhist monuments, including Borobudur (c. 800). Out of this period of conflict first the Shailendra, then the Khmer emerged as predominant powers, their dynasties linked by marriage alliances.

It seems probable that the Pallava dynasty, who had ruled the southeastern Tamil coastal plains of India since about 360 AD, participated substantially in the politics of Southeast Asia during the later 7th and the 8th centuries. They certainly maintained close trade connections all over Southeast Asia. It is possible they were of Shaka descent; they inscribed in Prakrit, although ruling a Tamil people. Worshipers of Shiva, they built many temples (e.g. at Mamallapuram, Kanchipuram) to Vishnu as well as to Shiva through the 7th and 8th centuries. During their rule the literature of the Tamil south attained its greatest flowering. From the early anthologies of bardic songs (2nd and 3rd centuries AD) through the Kural – called the Tamil Veda (6th century) – to the 9th-century epics *Manimegalai* and *Silappadigaram*, a continuous stream of secular inspiration flowed. But from the 6th century a parallel stream of religious devotionalism also gathered force, to culminate in an ecstatic poetry of adoration for Shiva and Vishnu composed by generations of saints through the 8th and 9th centuries. This knowledge can greatly add to our insight into the visual art that survives. The Pallavas continued to dominate their terrain, in conflict with the

Chalukyas of the Deccan, until they were ousted in the 10th century by the Cholas.

The Hindu dynasties. The Pallavas were probably responsible for the virtually total eclipse of Buddhism in the area. A Chinese pilgrim who visited India during the time of Harsha of Kanauj (606–47), Hsüan Chang, wrote the longest and most interesting Chinese account of India. Like I-Ching (672–96) he was saddened by the evident decline of Buddhism. He found Kapilavastu deserted, Kaushambi and Vaishali falling to ruin. Everywhere were signs that, despite the number of Buddhist sites, the "Deva temples of the unbelievers" were gaining popular support everywhere. Certainly for the next few centuries in central and western India Hinduism was completely in the ascendant, fortified by the teachings first of Guadapada (late 7th century), a great monist philosopher, and then in the 9th century by the greatest philosopher of all, Shankaracharya, a Brahman from Kerala, prime teacher of the Vedanta, who is looked on by many Hindus as an incarnation of Shiva himself.

The Hindu dynasties of north and western India are interesting to us chiefly for the Hindu temples they have left, which will be surveyed in a later chapter. Most were built between about 750 and the arrival of the Turkish Muslims in the 11th and 12th centuries, who conducted one of the most devastating campaigns of total destruction known to history. They looted cities and temples, burning libraries expressly to exterminate non-Muslim culture, and spending immense effort on smashing, stone by stone, many hundreds of shrines. It is therefore not surprising that we know relatively little of the material culture of the Hindu dynasties of medieval India, whose tangled and fluctuating fortunes are of interest chiefly to the pure historian, and must be deciphered from coinage and dedicatory copper plates. The languages, however, could not be destroyed, and in both Sanskrit and northern vernaculars (Hindi, Braj, Rajasthani, Maithili, etc.) an extensive classical literature was composed, much of which survives in manuscript. In the light of the fact that the only visual art we know from this whole epoch happens to be religious work cut in stone, it is as well to remember that, although some literature was religious, a very great deal was secular; and we must again suppose that there was a secular visual art in impermanent materials.

Some western and central Indian dynasties were themselves descendants of earlier invaders who had been assimilated to the 36 Rajput clans recognized in later medieval times. Among the dynasties we know, chiefly for their patronage of temples which have survived the Muslim devastation, are the Chandellas of Bandelkhand (mid-9th to 11th century), whose capital was Khajuraho; the Gurjara-Pratiharas of Kanauj (725–1036); the Paramaras of Dhara (c. 950–12th century) in the west; and the Chalukyas of the Western Deccan (8th–13th centuries);

Pallava dynasty temple at Kanchipuram on the coast of Madras, 7th century AD.

even the Hoyshalas (c. 1100–1386) of far southern Mysore, whose kingdom was also destroyed by Muslims. Only two major Hindu regions survived the first Muslim onslaught culturally intact: Orissa, and the Chola-Pandya kingdom of the Tamil plains. Both produced magnificent architecture as well as vernacular literature. A testimony to the great importance of the strictly Shaiva Chola Hindu influence in Southeast Asia is the fact that about 1005 AD the king of Shrivijaya dedicated a temple at Negapatam in the Tamil plains. In Kanchi, a Chola city, one of the most important texts of medieval Hinduism was compiled, the *Shrimad Devibhagavatam*, a Sanskrit Purana in honor of the goddess, which became the focus of a vast devotional movement over the whole subcontinent.

The fortunes of Hindu culture overseas were bound up primarily with those of the dynasties of the Khmer, the Cham, and of eastern Java. The Khmer empire arose on the old terrain of Chen-la. In 802 a Khmer king, Jayavarman II, established his capital by Phnom-Kulen, building many shrines. Indravarman I (877–89) expanded the empire, and moved its capital to Angkor, some 20 miles away. Here the kingdom flourished, maintaining a broadly based Indian culture, including a Tantrik form of Hinduism introduced probably from south India in 802. The very great importance of the Khmer empire and its connection with the south Indian Cholas is borne out by a sudden increase in maritime trade reported by Chinese Sung dynasty sources. The Chinese, between 960 and 1200, seem to have become aware of the value of seafaring trade in an unprecedented way. Eleven of their seaports – the largest number until the 19th century – were actively trading with Southeast Asia. Thirty-six Chinese treatises are known to have been written dealing with the geography and culture of Southeast Asia; and new Chinese mercantile initiatives took place. Angkor was sacked by the Cham in 1177. During the brief revival of Angkor's splendor under Jayavarman VII (1181–c. 1215) Buddhism became the state religion. Such it has since

remained. The temporarily victorious Hindu Cham were themselves gradually forced out of existence by the pressure of the racially Vietnamese people from the north, who adhered to Theravada Buddhism, like their ethnic kin, the racial Burmese and Thai. The Hindu dynasty was finally eclipsed in the 15th century. Yet another Hindu kingdom, that of eastern Java (927–16th century), lasted until gradually eliminated by the forces of Islam; a much-modified form of Hinduism survives to the present day in the small but famous and beautiful island of Bali.

Buddhist revival under the Palas. Buddhism and Buddhist culture received a great, renewed impetus under the Pala kings, whose fortunes rose during the second half of the 8th century. They ended by ruling Bengal, Bihar and part of Orissa. Their peaceful reign lasted right through the 9th and 10th centuries and into the 11th. Then it was disturbed, first when the Cholas seized part of the Bengal coast, and then when the Senas, a Hindu dynasty, repulsing the Cholas, took over all of the more southerly part of their dominion, including northern Orissa, sometime before 1040. But Pala rule persisted in most of Bihar and Bengal until 1196. Their kingdom was so peaceful that in that year it was possible for a small party of Muslim horsemen to ride direct to the Pala palace and slaughter the dynasty's last king. The Muslims went on to destroy the great Buddhist university of Nalanda, which had been founded nearly 700 years earlier. Although

Tibetan Thang-Ka representing the Indian magician-saint Padmasambhava enthroned on his miraculous island surrounded by saints and demi-gods; early 19th century, Gulbenkian Museum, Durham.

Hinduism had been by no means eliminated, it did not enjoy royal patronage as Buddhism did; for the Palas had founded many other Buddhist centers of learning, including the great complexes at Vikramapura and on the hill Ratnagiri in Orissa. They too were destroyed by the Muslims. Some of their monks who escaped the massacre took refuge in Burma, Nepal and Tibet.

Throughout the relatively peaceful centuries of the Pala dynasty's rule the major events were religious and literary. The form of Buddhism was Vajrayana, in which a mass of various earlier teachings was combined. It is sometimes called Tantrik. For it was the Buddhist counterpart to Hindu Tantra, emphasizing a yoga based on the assimilation of the generative energy of the phenomenal universe to the individual's own bodily energy. Its special learning and associated magical practices were therefore of interest not only to the individual monk, but also to the public and the state; for experienced practitioners were supposed to be able to control the forces not only of the inner but also of the outer world, and so affect the course of phenomenal events. Although the earliest surviving written Tantrik texts are Buddhist – the *Hevajra* and *Guhyasamaja*, both pre-600 AD – in fact Tantra had long been an element of cult in southern India, central India, and especially in Bengal. The earliest surviving text in what became the Bengali language is a collection of 10th-century Tantrik hymns called the *Dohas*, ascribed to a Buddhist master called Sarahapada. One of the greatest encyclopedic philosophers and aestheticians of medieval India, Abhinavagupta (fl. 1000 AD), traveled from his home in Kashmir to Bengal, there to absorb Tantrik learning, which enabled him to achieve his great work of synthesis. He thus became one of the masters of the important school of Kashmiri Shaiva philosophy.

The influence of Tantrik Buddhism, Vajrayana, spread widely during the Pala epoch, especially into Tibet. As early as 640 the Tibetan king Srong-tsen-gampo had been persuaded by his Indian wife to import Vajrayana Buddhism, along with a version of the Indian script in which to write the previously unwritten Tibetan language. Buddhism was recognized as the state religion in 779. Thereafter, in spite of a persecution in 838–42, Vajrayana Buddhism gradually entrenched itself in Tibet, expanding greatly in the later 9th and 10th centuries – as well as in Sikkim and Bhutan. A series of great Indian teachers made their way from the Pala universities to strengthen Tantrik traditions in Tibet, where they remained alive into modern times. The first of these was Padmasambhava (c. 747), a colorful and powerful magician and miracle worker as well as a practitioner of sexual yoga, who founded the Red Hat sect. His life has become the focus of a great deal of symbolic legend. During the 11th century other great masters left Pala India for Tibet, notably Marpa the translator (d. 1098), who was the teacher of Tibet's most famous native Buddhist poet-saint, Milarpa; and Atisa (d. 1042), who came from Bengal.

We also know that, through western Tibet, connections were maintained with the so far little-studied Buddhist monasteries of Kashmir, centered on Hasaraja, whence many works of art were imported. Rinchensangpo (958–1055) is stated to have gone to Kashmir, and then returned to found a temple in western Tibet. It may have been through such contacts that the late Gandhara Fondukistan-Ushkur techniques of painted stucco sculpture made their way into Tibet. At the same time we know from native records that the very first traditions of Tibetan art go back to artists called Diman and Bhitpala, who lived in the 8th and 9th centuries in the Pala epoch, and may have worked at Nalanda. Other works of art and artists came from Nepal, central India, and even from southern India. One artist from Khotan is known to have been especially admired by a 10th-century Tibetan king. Other artists migrated from China. All this helps to account for the variety of stylistic characteristics which can still be recognized in Tibetan art. One most important event was the meeting between Tibetan leaders and Genghis Khan, Great Khan of the Mongols (1206), whose invasion of China led to the founding of the Yüan dynasty. This ensured that the head of the Sakya monastery became the official hereditary teacher of the dynasty – an event which helped to introduce a powerful Vajrayana movement into China. Only in the 14th century was the primacy transferred from Sakya to the Dalai Lama at Lhasa.

Buddhist Burma and Thailand. We have, unfortunately, no comparable documentation of the way Pala Vajrayana, with its art, also penetrated into Java, Sumatra, and especially upper Burma under the Pyu, where it flourished among their Ari priesthood. The Pyu spoke a Tibeto-Burmese language, and may themselves have originated in Central Asia. The magnificence of their cities was recorded in the Chinese T'ang history. In the 8th century one city was reported as being some 50 miles in circumference. Their capital, Hmawza, has been partly excavated, and the finds are discussed in a later chapter. After the Pyu were conquered (c. 900) by unidentified neighbors, their terrain was gradually infiltrated from the northeast by the racially Burmese people, kin of the Thai and Vietnamese, who were also pressing south at this time. They were converted to Buddhism by the Pyu, and as they moved on into the Mon kingdom of lower Burma they finally adopted the Theravada Buddhism of the Mon. In 1056 their king Anawrahta decreed that this should be the state religion of all Burma – and so it has remained into this century. The Ari were proscribed, though some of their magical skills were acquired by the state Buddhists; and the traditional animist religion of the Burmese with its 36 Nats, named spiritual beings, was skillfully combined into the Buddhist system. Mon monks and craftsmen were carried off from the conquered Mon capital (probably Thaton). The monks were given the task of organizing the

Wall painting from the Buddhist shrine of Pagan in Burma, in style close to that of northeast India.

new kingdom; the craftsmen were employed on building the huge new Burmese capital on the old site of Pagan, much of which still stands today – the only ancient city to do so. It represents the culminating achievement of Mon art. Work continued there until it was sacked and garrisoned by the Mongols in 1287.

In neighboring Thailand the racial Thai also moved into an already Buddhist country. In the south of this region, however, the eastern Mon kingdom of Dvaravati had already been annexed by the Khmer. Khmer Hindu shrines were built as foci of the dynastic cult, the most important being at Phimai. There a cult statue of Jayavarman II (c. 802) has been found. So too have bronze figures of Vajrayana deities, indicating that Pala influence was also at work. Only when the Khmer power was finally broken in the 13th century did the Thai succeed in

Vista of surviving buildings at Pagan. Those painted white are still in use; the Ananda is at center left.

occupying most of their modern country which was not united into a single kingdom. Partly because of this phase of its history Thailand, which is extremely fertile, has remained divided into northern and southern regions. The capital of the north was Chiengmai, of the south Ayutthaya. Between the two stands the city of Sukhodaya, held either by the northern or the southern Thai kingdom at different times, being independent at others. Sukhodaya, which lies on a major land trade road running east to west, seems to have been a center of Theravada Buddhist culture, remaining in direct touch with Ceylon long after the Muslims had destroyed Buddhism in Pala India.

The Thai also had an animist religion combined with trance Shamanism. They had and still have a splendid tradition of high-gabled wooden architecture; and they adopted Theravada Buddhism, but far more slowly and less completely than the Burmese. As they had moved into the north of Thailand the Thai maintained some relationship with a primitive mountain kingdom called Nan-chao, in present Chinese Yunnan. The rulers of this kingdom seem to have adopted a Bodhisattva patron, and produced modest bronze images of him based upon an unknown but seemingly Pallava prototype (c. 9th century). As they moved south, the Thai kings also adopted Buddhism as their dynastic cult, entrusting the spiritual organization of their kingdom to monks, but treating the great bronze images of the Buddha they made from the 15th century on as repositories of an unequivocally magical power. Again and again the kings attempted to "purify" and strengthen the religion of the people by importing monks and images from Ceylon. But to this day the Buddhist culture of Thailand remains idiosyncratic. The Indian influence has been profound, but has adapted itself, as it did elsewhere in Southeast Asia, to the customs and life-style of non-Indian people to produce a civilization which has endured for well over 1,000 years.

4. The Buddhist Stupa

The spread of Buddhism. Buddhism seems to have spread as widely and as swiftly as it did in India, and later in Central and Southeast Asia, largely because it was adopted by traveling merchants and by workers in gold and ivory, whose goods were continuously exported. India's very oldest Buddhist sites are at dynastic capitals, but the spread of later establishments followed the chief trade roads. Across Central Asia the spread followed the great caravan routes to China; and into the archipelagoes of Southeast Asia it penetrated with the seagoing merchants. Indeed monasteries seem, during the early centuries of the Christian era, either to have served as caravansarays, or at least to have stood close by the markets or bazaars. This association is reflected in a number of artistic phenomena.

First is the constant presence on Buddhist monuments of a symbolism of wealth, with appropriate deities: a jeweled Sri on the earliest sites, and a quite elaborate iconography of the pot-bellied god Kuvera, with his open sacks of money, on later ones. The late 2nd-century BC railing from Barhut is even sculpted with a continuous

Stupa I at Sanchi, Bhopal, restored to something like its early 1st-century BC shape; it contained relics of the Buddha himself. The pillars on the left are from a later preaching hall.

coping-band representing the "wish-granting tree," an element from Indian legend, which virtually identifies the structure with the source of all material benefits the heart can desire. The Indian fertility goddess Sri had even traveled to Japan by the 8th century AD. And on the main approach to Borobudur in Java, about 800 AD, was built a special shrine called Chandi Pawon, whose external iconography is mainly devoted to the cult of Kuvera, as god of wealth. To this day in Buddhist countries the stupa is looked on as the supernatural source of fertility and fortune. The inscriptions on some of the carved stones of which the earliest Indian stupas were built, give the names of donors who came from quite distant parts of the subcontinent. And, in a society such as India's at that date, this too suggests that they were involved in some way in the flourishing trade that flowed along the trunk roads.

Though in early Buddhism only the higher castes were admitted to the order, the merchants may well have resented the fact that their experience, wealth and education counted for so little in the orthodox Brahmin scheme of things. Anyway frequent long-distance travel caused problems over food taboo and ritual purity to the very highest castes. So it is not surprising that the merchants embraced the personally relevant religion of Buddhism with its somewhat "commercial" outlook on the accumulation of merit as a kind of metaphysical bank account, which was increased by means of carefully graded good deeds, and which thus could in theory lead to ultimate salvation.

A natural consequence of this association between Buddhism and the roads was that pilgrimage became an entrenched custom. Not only in India, but from every other country of Buddhist Asia, the pilgrims had begun by the 3rd century AD to stream vast distances along the trade routes to the central sites of Buddhism, where the great events of the Buddha's life occurred. This continuous migration of devotees was a most important medium for the dissemination of Buddhist artistic patterns no less than

Terracotta plaque representing the goddess of abundance, Sri, heavily jeweled, 2nd century BC from the Ganga valley. Probably a domestic image. Ashmolean Museum, Oxford.

doctrinal ideas. The evidence suggests that Buddhist pilgrimage over immense distances long antedates the later Hindu custom of pilgrimage, and may well have stimulated it.

It is, however, true that Buddhism was also adopted in India as a state cult by many kings. Ashoka (272–232 BC) was certainly not the first of these, though he may well have been the most important, both as greatest emperor and as pattern for later rulers. One view holds that he built the main stupa at Sanchi. He was almost certainly responsible for the development of the great site called Sarnath near Banaras, the "deer-park" where the Buddha's first preaching took place, as a dynastic cult center. Fragments of Ashokan polished sandstone railings have been found there. At Bodhgaya has been found an early railing which once enclosed the space where the Buddha practiced his walking meditation, as well as sculpture and a stone throne-slab which probably marked the spot where the enlightenment took place. It may be that dynastic interest in Buddhism was the chief reason for the architecture of Buddhist buildings being based directly upon that of secular palaces, even to their luxurious and often sensual ornament and figure sculpture. It is also possible that the pillars crowned with symbolic animals, which occur at a number of the earlier sites, signified that they were under royal patronage. For we know that it was normal from Maurya times for kings to erect "pillars of victory" in conquered terrain; and that in more recent times, in Hinayana countries, kings set up pillars of wood or even bronze as testimony to their devotion at a major monastery. Of course, Buddhism seems to us, with our direct scholarly knowledge of its texts, a religion requiring of the monks total renunciation of worldly things, and has no real place for a king, with his pride of status and self-indulgent life of royal luxury. But it appears that Buddhists pragmatically accepted that, if their religion was to flourish, royal patronage was necessary.

The Buddha himself was of a petty "royal" family; and the early texts refer to him before his enlightenment as "the Bodhisattva" ("enlightenment-being"), qualified for future Buddhahood, a term that later came to have deep metaphysical interpretations. The earliest surviving stone statues of Bodhisattvas, from Mathura and Gandhara (late 1st and early 2nd century AD), have an affinity with the series of older colossal, polished dedicatory statues called *Yakshas* (male) and *Yakshis* (female), who hold fly whisks like the early attendant Bodhisattvas on Buddha icons (e.g. the early Katra Buddha). For this reason, and because they are dressed in sumptuous clothes, gems and diadems, it seems likely that they testify to the devotion of some kind of royalty. Certainly by 600 AD the status of Bodhisattva had been formally accorded to kings, no doubt because their generosity to the monastic order was taken as a demonstration that they, like the Bodhisattva Sakyamuni, were on the way to becoming Buddhas themselves. This conception both justified and stimulated during the early centuries AD a most important and fruitful doctrine: that the Buddha nature, one and indivisible, was also capable of manifesting itself as a vast infinity of individual Buddhas. We know from the account of the Chinese pilgrim Hsüan Chang that in 644 King Harsha had a monastery built with a Buddha image equal to the king in stature, and himself participated in state rituals dressed as and impersonating the god Indra holding an umbrella over another image of the Buddha. It is proposed (by Paul Mus) that such royal rites were the reason for one type of Buddha image appearing about that time – the Buddha adorned with crown and royal jewels. Once it had appeared, the image was developed in northeastern India under the Pala kings, as the carrier of a special doctrinal function in the type of Buddhism known as Vajrayana.

Since the Middle Ages the royalty of Buddhist countries have ceased to claim extravagant Buddhist titles. Probably the last king to do so, at least by implication, was Jayavarman VII of Angkor (c. 1181). In more recent centuries the royal families of Buddhist countries have been content with rituals recognizing them as protectors of the Buddhist faith, perhaps as titular heads of the secular side of the organization. They have often spent, in their youth, token periods enrolled into the monastic order, and have frequently abdicated and retired into the order in later life.

The doctrines of Buddhism. One of the doctrinal developments most significant for art history is the concept of the three bodies of the Buddha. It seems probable that it evolved during the 1st century AD. Buddhism teaches that all men may expect to attain by merit the state of enlightenment, at which point their nature as transmigrating beings is transformed into the Buddha nature. This Buddha nature, exemplified by the Buddha himself, has three forms. The first and highest is the Body of Truth (*Dharmakaya*), attained at total enlightenment (*Buddhi*). This is indescribable and unrepresentable. To attempt to describe or represent it would be grossly offensive. The earliest surviving Indian sculptures of scenes illustrating episodes in the Buddha's life, at Sanchi and in the southeast of India, before about 20–50 AD, never represent him in the body at all. His presence is simply indicated by a lotus flower, a cushion on a seat, a pair of footprints or an emblem. After all, he was the paragon of those who were no more to return to the limited world. The third and lowest body – not represented in India, though in later Buddhism it becomes a focus of profound teaching – is the actual human frame in which the Buddha appears with all the attributes of individuality. It is called the "Body of Limitation" (*Nirmanakaya*) and is only really represented in Chinese and Japanese art.

The second, intermediate body is called the "Body of Glory" (*Sambhogakaya*). This is a golden symbolic body, which refers by its emblematic attributes to inner spiritual status – a typical Indian invention. It is the tranquil figure represented in practically all the Buddha icons of the world. Among its most obvious emblematic attributes are: a twist of hair between the eyebrows; a protuberance on the top of the head; webbed fingers and toes; arms so long that the fingers reach to the knees; sexual organ covered by a membrane; lotus or wheel marks on the palms of the hands and the soles of the feet. The characteristics of this body are probably derived from an ancient pre-Buddhist code of fortune telling. But the theory of the three bodies made a full-fledged Buddhist art possible, and conditioned every Buddhist's visual conception of his ideal. The Sambhoga is the bodily form in which the Buddha may legitimately be represented in all Buddhist narrative sculpture and painting.

By about 400 AD it seems that the doctrinal concept of the Bodhisattva had been extended far beyond its early limits, and ideas developed in philosophical literature had penetrated into art. The earliest Bodhisattva images which represent the new concept fully developed are probably those of the 5th century painted by the door of a cave at Ajanta. A number of major Mahayana texts, and a special

Relief in limestone from Amaravati, 2nd century AD, illustrating the attack of Mara, god of death, on the Buddha, who is symbolized only by a cushion under the Bodhi tree. Musée Guimet, Paris.

section added to the Lotus sutra, suggest that the philosophical concept was evolving during the 3rd and 4th centuries AD. The earliest icons of the Buddha from the late 1st and early 2nd centuries AD show him in his "body of glory" flanked by the two royally adorned attendants with fly whisks, one on each side. These are susceptible of a variety of interpretations, but most likely they illustrate the generic idea of devotion and dedication to the Buddha. In Gandhara, however, we find icons of the next two centuries which set the Buddha into the frame of a palatial structure inhabited by listening, royally clad figures. Some have one knee cocked up; and this type was not long after, in the 4th century, adopted in China as a pattern for large sculptures of major Bodhisattvas. These icons reflect descriptions of great metaphysical congresses of Buddhas, Bodhisattvas and celestial beings in mysterious regions beyond normal space and time, the apparitions of worlds and vanishing aeons, which are ecstatically recorded in those great Mahayana texts.

The Bodhisattva, according to this newly evolved concept, is a being who is entitled by his vast store of accumulated merit to attain full Nirvana; but he takes the "Bodhisattva vow" and refuses to "depart" into Nirvana out of compassion for all the suffering creatures who remain unliberated in the worlds of the cosmos. Instead he dedicates to all creatures his own merit. His spiritual status gives him the freedom of time and space, so that he is able to work miracles of compassion in many different guises. He hastens to help those who suffer and address him with true faith. Although his nature is identical with the Buddha nature, and the Buddha's doctrine is the wellspring of his being, he seems to the Buddhist peoples of Asia especially approachable. He, when they pray, would be the one to listen to their prayers and do something in response. Hence his icons show him as gentle, compassionate, offering protection and blessings. In his headdress sits a Buddha, emblem of his own enlightened status. He wears the crown and jewels of the king, to suggest his power, which in some regions during the Middle Ages was interpreted as cosmic, on the pattern of Hindu gods.

Early Buddhist architecture and imagery. The architecture of Buddhism is focused on a structure called the stupa, also known as dagoba in Ceylon, pagoda in Burma. The earliest stupas resembled tumuli, being simple circular mounds of earth, perhaps with inner reinforcing walls. The latest still preserve the fundamental idea of the circular dome under accretions of spires and often some auxiliary structures. It is most probable that the very first stupas were erected on the terrain of those kings who fought for and divided the bodily relics of the Buddha immediately after his cremation.

In fact Buddhism was committed to the cult of relics, despite the Buddha's own opposition to such cults. They formed one of the foci of the custom of pilgrimage. The relics most treasured were of the Buddha himself; but they were naturally few. The remains of enlightened Buddhist saints, however, were scarcely less revered. The stupa was intended to accommodate relics, though by the 2nd century BC it had come to be used purely as an emblem of Nirvana. All the earliest ones contain relic chambers in a shaft let into the summit of the mound, thus elevating the sacred fragments above the earth. (A recent excavation has revealed one relic casket resting on the virgin soil, beneath a false upper chamber.) In this they differ from the more familiar western Bronze and Iron Age tumuli. The stupa's development consisted essentially in an increase of the height and elaboration of the fundamental architectural units of the early stupa. And it seems that relics in the Buddhist world were looked on as a supernatural source of benefits of all kinds to the land where they stood – increasing its fertility, as well as the people's wealth, piety and social morality. This last factor is stressed in the inscriptions cut to the order of the Emperor Ashoka on rocks and victory pillars over the extent of his empire. These include the earliest intact monuments of Buddhist art.

The common rite performed at Buddhist stupas, which always governed their architectural form, was *pradakshina*. This consists of walking around a sacred person or object, keeping it on one's right hand, imitating the direction of the sun's path, as it is seen by someone who looks towards it in the northern hemisphere. The rite expressed reverence, as well as setting up a special kind of supernatural connection between the visitor and the object of his reverence. All stupas thus have at least one processional path for *pradakshina*. The great stupa of Sanchi, in Bhopal state, completed c. 20 BC–20 AD and now restored, has a raised processional terrace around its foot, as well as a path at ground level. And early representational art in the southeast of India illustrates stupas with two, or even three, such terraces. These were the root of later developments in north India and Southeast Asia.

A most important feature of the early stupas in India was their enclosing stone railing. All sacred sites are marked in India by being enclosed. The Buddha himself is said to have visited older sacred places, called in the texts *cetiyas*. The earliest surviving section of stupa railing, that from Barhut, erected probably by Shunga kings (187–75 BC), is elaborately carved with figures of godlings, emblems of supernatural power and abbreviated narrative scenes. The relief is shallow, on two stages; the designs are angular; and the outstanding impression the ornament conveys is of opulence, the figures accentuating this by their jeweled belts, armlets, anklets and hairdressing. Elaborate ornament became a constant feature in all Indian figurative sculpture, reflecting the status symbolism of Indian society.

At Sanchi the history of relief sculpture can be traced through an earlier as well as a later evolutionary phase than at Barhut. On the railings of Stupa II and the stairways of

Stupas I and III an extremely crude version of what emerged at Barhut as the Shunga style appears. But on the four superb gateways of Stupa I, with their posts and three slightly arched lintels (c. 10 AD), appears a magnificent style of high-relief sculpture which is the direct antecedent of the developed Kshatrapa-Shatavahana styles of the western Deccan and of the Amaravati region (1st to 3rd centuries AD). It is also related to the style of similar fragments of railings and gates which have been excavated around the site of the great ancient city of Mathura some 280 miles away – where there may be important discoveries still to be made. The panels of relief sculpture on the Sanchi gateways are one of the chief sources for our knowledge of early Indian civil architecture, costume, customs and life; for they illustrate narrative scenes taken from the life of the Buddha, possibly incidents from Buddhist history, and episodes from the *Jatakas*.

These are especially important, for they provide the imagery for a huge quantity of Buddhist painting and sculpture at sites throughout the Buddhist world, right down into modern times. Such imagery conveys at the same time the basic morality and metaphysical doctrine. The *Jatakas* are stories, long recited but first collected by Aryasura in the 2nd century AD, which recount the previous incarnations of the being who became the Buddha, as he was reborn in animal and human forms. In each incarnation he performs some supreme act of self-sacrifice for the good of others, and thus vastly increases his store of merit, advancing him along the road to ultimate Nirvana.

In practice, apart from the images of godlings, all the representational art in early Buddhist monuments was couched in very human terms. Its events are seen on the scale of actuality; although the figures are somewhat idealized, they take place in our ordinary world. Even when the Buddha-to-be appears in a *Jataka* episode as a mythical animal such as a six-tusked elephant, or the scene is set in the palace-like heaven of the 33 gods, the art preserves its sense of human scale. As the centuries passed,

Buddhist art, based on these literary sources, developed hieratic and narrative aspects, to appear on different parts of buildings in different ways. In addition, the story of the Buddha's ascent to heaven was used to justify the interpretation of the Buddhist monastery as a heavenly palace, the resort of attendant gods, who would be represented in their beautiful persons on various parts of the structure.

During the period between about 250 BC and 400 AD a large number of domed stupas were built or enlarged throughout the north of India. Many have been excavated, but none has been so thoroughly restored as Sanchi. Each must have played its own role in history, but as yet the state of our knowledge does not permit us to trace the sequence exactly. Most were located at major city sites, usually the capitals of kingdoms or along trade routes. Among the earliest is Piprawa, perhaps the only pre-Ashokan brick structure known. Other early stupas are known at Vaishali, the birthplace of the Jain founder Mahavira, and a favorite resort of the Buddha's; at Bairat (Jaipur district), where it was enclosed in a circular shrine like sacred sites represented in early reliefs; at Kasia (Deoria district), the original site of the Buddha's demise, when he passed into Nirvana, one of the holiest spots in India until the 12th century; at Saheth-Maheth (Uttar Pradesh) where the Buddha's own garden refuge, the Jetavana, was located; and at Kaushambi (Allahabad district), where the Buddha's Ghositarama refuge was marked by a large complex of buildings. Only the plans of these structures are now at all clear. The main buildings have gone. In Ceylon the remains of stupas of Ashoka's time have been preserved, including that at the place of the surviving Bodhi tree, grown from a sprig sent by Ashoka. All are at the old capital city Anuradhapura (e.g. Tissa maharama, Yatthala, Thuparama, Runvanveli seya).

Below left: rear view of the north gate of Sanchi Stupa I, showing the wide range of symbols associated with early Buddhism.

Below: early Thuparama Dagoba, 3rd century BC restored, at Anuradhapura, Ceylon.

Ancillary buildings and monasteries. At all Buddhist sites in India which were occupied and revered for some 15 centuries, in addition to the stupa, there are usually many other religious structures of different sizes and ages. The most important was the preaching hall aligned in some way, sometimes even combined, with the main stupa – a relationship preserved at virtually all later sites. The reason for the existence of this hall – often called a *chaitya* – is not far to seek. The earliest stupas were founded well before any of the Buddhist texts were written down, and they were still preserved in the memory of individual members of the order. The only way, therefore, in which either junior monks or lay supporters could be instructed in Buddhist legend and doctrine was by recitation. This probably took place within the hall. In later times we know it was also used for communal meditation by members of the order, and by the laity on ceremonial occasions; and it may well have been so used in early times. For one of the earliest excavated religious caves, a Mauryan one at Udayagiri in Bihar, is expressly described by inscription as a shelter for an order during the monsoon rains – no doubt to ensure that their contemplative life could continue as normally as possible throughout the deluge.

The existence of the hall implies the presence of a number of monks at least temporarily, but by about 100 AD probably permanently, resident at the site. Theoretically, Buddhist monks were not supposed to live anywhere specific, so as to avoid becoming attached to any "home." They were to be "homeless ones," living in the open, meditating in remote places, only visiting villages or towns to beg their food. But in practice monasteries developed, probably with written versions of the scriptures and doctrinal and philosophical literature. For these had become by 100 AD very bulky; so libraries became an important feature of Buddhist monasteries. In one sense Buddhism only exists in the persons of the yellow-robed members of the order, originally aristocrats both spiritually and temporally; for only members of the higher castes, who had demonstrated by their being reborn into a "good family" their merit during previous incarnations, were admitted to the order. Monasteries became the natural strongholds of the Buddhist order and their existence at first presupposes a body of faithful laity large and rich enough to support the monks they accommodated.

Structurally the earliest monasteries, whose foundations have been excavated, appear to have been enclosures of wood and brick, on an ageless Oriental pattern: small courtyards surrounded by little living rooms or cells for the monks. Later monasteries however, especially outside India, adopted the dormitory principle. But in India, as the monasteries grew in size, they became virtually villages of multistoried courts with their own streets, focused around the primary and secondary stupas. A count of the available bed-shelves in the rock-cut monastery at Ajanta suggests

Above: facade of the rock-cut Buddhist preaching hall at Karli, 2nd century BC; the *mithuna* couple at left are original, the Buddha preaching at right is 6th-century AD palimpsest work.

Below: interior of the rock-cut Buddhist preaching hall at Bhaja, 2nd century BC, its vault imitating the roof of wooden buildings.

that at the peak of its development in the 6th century it was probably capable of accommodating about 600 Buddhists – perhaps not all full monks; and this assumes that the earliest excavations were still available for use, which they may not have been. Outside India, in Southeast Asia, monasteries were always capable of expanding by the addition of extra buildings. We know, for example, that in the 12th and 13th centuries at Pagan in Burma many of the fine monastic buildings were originally palaces given by royalty and wealthy donors to accommodate monks who may have previously lived in less substantial structures. The same happened during the Middle Ages in Suk-hodaya, Ayutthaya and other cities of Thailand. And more recently in Burma additional new courts and pavilions have been built for monasteries by wealthy people as acts of merit, even when they were not strictly necessary. In practice, a large amount of Buddhist artistic activity was inspired by the hope of acquiring merit as the essential aid to ultimate Nirvana.

The same motive seems to have lain behind the building of most of the auxiliary structures added to major sites. The commonest are smaller stupas. The chief of these may enshrine the relics of Buddhist saints. But there may be many, far smaller ones, made of brick and stucco or of stone, containing no relics, ranging in size from some 40 feet in height to a mere 2 feet or so. These were set up as emblems of the ultimate Buddhist goal wherever space was available within the monastic complex, simply as a merit-gaining exercise. In Thailand we also know that when a sacred old stupa was enclosed in a new structure, a small version of the old was set up beside the new. The merit-building custom survives into modern times in the Buddhist countries of Southeast Asia and Ceylon. More modest merit-earning dedications are the small images of the Buddha, which are stocked in magazines, or the sticking of wafers of gold leaf onto stupas or major Buddha images.

Cave sanctuaries. The Buddhist cave sanctuaries of the Western Ghats, in the kingdom of the Shatavahana dynasty in peninsular India, have a history of their own. They form a unique continuous sequence within the otherwise fragmented history of early Indian art; and their forms must reflect those of vanished wooden architecture. One important custom has previously somewhat confused the issue of the dating of these caves: palimpsest working. Later sculpture has frequently been added, especially to the facades on older caves. Earlier scholarship assumed that the architecture of the caves progressed smoothly from those having most wooden additions – roof ribs, porches, inset window-grills – such as Bhaja, c. 200 BC, to those in which these elements are carved in the original stone, such as Karli c. 200 AD. It is now generally agreed that fundamentally Bhaja and Karli, as well as Pitalkhora, where recently there has been careful excavation, belong to the 2nd century BC; and that none of the others, save Kanheri (2nd

century AD), is more than 100 or so years later.

The main cave at each of these sites is a long preaching hall, its axis running in at right angles to the rock face. Its inmost end has a semicircular apse; a pair of aisles and continuous ambulatory run around a rock-cut and purely emblematic stupa standing at the inner end of the nave. It would thus be possible to perform *pradakshina* along the aisles and ambulatory. The interior, and the external facade are carved in strict imitation of a piece of wooden architecture, down to balconies, trellises and projecting joist-ends. At Bhaja there are even relief female figures on the facade, and couples carved in the balconies. Such a *chaitya* cave represents an early amalgam of stupa and preaching hall into a single architectural unit.

Carved into the rock on one or both sides of the *chaitya* may be living caves, called *viharas*, small at Bhaja, larger at Nasik. These constitute at least part of the monastery; for it is impossible yet to estimate how much wooden temporary building there may have been as well. They are often decorated with sculpture, the earliest probably being the low-relief mythical scenes – including the legend of the wish-granting tree – at Bhaja. From Pitalkhora a stone pot-bellied *yaksha*, of the same type as those on the gateposts at Sanchi, but with a hairdo and clothed in a *dhoti* like those on the earliest stairway reliefs at Sanchi (hence early 1st century BC), bears the name of a goldsmith Kanhadasa ("slave of Krishna") – more likely donor than carver. This figure probably comes from some additional structure now destroyed. On the facade of Karli a superb colossal pair of embracing couples was carved in palimpsest in the 1st century AD. Kanheri's similar but later ones were carved probably with the rest of the cave.

The epitome of the cave series is at Ajanta. This huge site, cut into the outer face of a curved gorge above a river, contains 27 caves. Four are *chaityas*, the oldest being numbers 10 and 9, 2nd century BC. The rest are *viharas*, some two-storied, the latest outermost caves being probably of the 7th century AD. Their architecture and sculpture register a history of Buddhist art in the region. There is much palimpsest work, many additional carved Buddha images of the 5th and 6th centuries having been commissioned as acts of merit by individual donors. The massive rock-cut icons of Buddhas and deities in cells at the rear of a number of the caves are the closest parallels we know to some of the great icons in Java. It should be mentioned that related sculpture of similar date appears in the Buddhist caves at Ellora (numbers 8, 9, 10) and some striking, almost full-round compositions of a most unusual character in *viharas* at Aurangabad.

Ajanta, however, is especially famous and important for the wall paintings that remain in a number of caves. The oldest, in Cave 10, are contemporary with the Sanchi gates. The latest are probably some of the last work done at the site. In places there are several layers of painted plaster of different dates. A few comparable fragments survive at other places, notably in the Buddhist caves at Bagh and in a Hindu cave at Badami. But in principle the Ajanta paintings are almost our only evidence for what literature tells us must have been a widespread and flourishing pictorial art, executed in thousands of public buildings and private houses. If we assume that the paintings were done by professionals engaged only for a time on each Buddhist panel or series, this may explain why the figures, who represent the usual Buddhist subject matter, are executed in such a lush and sensually stimulating style. Most of the 3rd- and 4th-century work is, in fact, a pictorial parallel to the style of sensuous and elaborate decorative sculpture used on the great structural stupas of the southeast, around Amaravati, at the other side of the Shatavahana kingdom; which fact suggests that this sculpture, too, was a religious version of a secular art.

Here, at a group of major sites (Amaravati, Ghantasali, Bhattiprolu, Jaggayapeta, Nagarjunakonda), we can trace the evolution of a sculptural style from a stage similar to the oldest at Sanchi, to its full development by the 3rd

Right: vista of the rock-cut Buddhist monastery at Ajanta, where paintings (1st century BC–c. 600 AD) survive.

Below: plan of the Ajanta cave monastery. The oldest caves are nos. 9–10 at center, the latest on the outer ends.

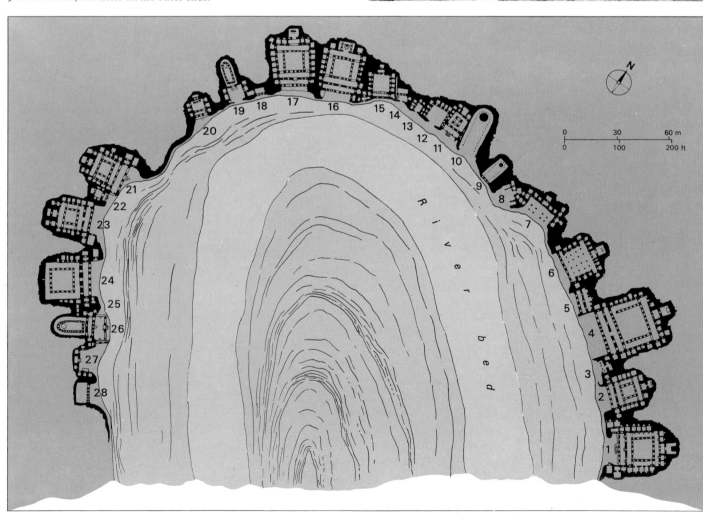

Above: the veranda of the late cave no. 1 at Ajanta, 6th century; it contains the dance painting illustrated on page 26.

Left: wall painting in Ajanta cave no. 16, representing an aristocrat with moustache and tailored jacket, perhaps a Shaka, with his ladies, 5th century AD.

century AD. These stupas were mounted on *pradakshina* terraces, some heightened by a circular drum, and surrounded by railings. Their gates were not always adorned with linteled gates, but were fronted by five standing pillars (perhaps symbolic of the "five Buddhas," four past, one to come). Their truly special feature, however, was the relief sculpture which effloresced all over the white limestone railings and the drums of the stupas. Such lavishness applied to the monuments of an ascetic religion dedicated to poverty can only have been justified as a function of the intention to offer praise and testify to the glory of the Buddha. An analogy would be the ancient custom of hanging garlands upon sacred trees and other hallowed sites.

One important type of sculpture, developed around Amaravati, is the life-size standing draped Buddha figure, which seems to have been erected at the base of each stupa, facing out of the gateways, during the later 3rd century AD. This type seems to have provided the pattern for the earliest Buddha icons to be exported to Southeast Asia. The people of the region seem to have been much involved in trade enterprises, having received influence as well as objects from the Eastern Roman Empire, and dispatching colonists overseas. In fact one of the finest and the earliest bronze Buddhas from Southeast Asia, excavated on the river Kamara in Celebes, follows the Amaravati pattern, perhaps mediated through Ceylon. For the early Buddhist art of Ceylon seems to have derived much from this lively school of Shatavahana art. And the superb ivories excavated from Pompeii (pre-79 AD) and Begram (2nd century AD) in Afghanistan testify to the

creative productivity of the kingdom. The fragmentary rock paintings at Sihagiri in Ceylon, representing heavenly girls among clouds bearing offerings, dated either to the late 5th or early 6th century AD, are close in style to Shatavahana work. Also based on such work is much art at Anuradhapura in Ceylon (e.g. Jetavana Dagoba). The stupa in Ceylon was often enlarged to colossal size, however (Ruanveli being 300 feet, Abhayagiri 350 feet and Jetavana 400 feet high), while preserving the Shatavahana pattern. Sculptural ornament based on the mainland style developed on semilunate door sills and snake-god stelae, even after the end of the Shatavahana tradition. Some sculpture even shows Pallava affinities.

Gandharan stupas. In the northwestern region of the Indian subcontinent, called in antiquity Gandhara (now shared between Pakistan and Afghanistan), one of the most important developments of stupa art took place. This was a critical region. Its main towns and cities lie along the valley of the Kabul river and the Khyber pass; and that became during the 2nd century AD the main artery through which flowed India's trade with the eastern Mediterranean and China. A Central Asian dynasty, the Kushans, had by then taken control of the region, and, probably in collusion with the Romans, had broken the power of the Parthians to the west. By trade the area became wealthy; and much of that wealth was spent on Buddhist monuments. Splendid stupas were built; one, at Shah-ji-ki-dheri which contained a relic casket dedicated by the great Kushan king Kanishka, was said by the

Chinese pilgrim Sun yün to be 700 feet high. They, and their many associated buildings, were encrusted with relief sculpture in the style called Gandharan, strongly influenced by the art of the Helleno-Roman eastern Mediterranean. There are Classical togas and torsos, Roman putti with swags, and scenes from Greek legend. Even the risers of steps were carved. This art supplied the patterns for the original Buddhist art of Central Asia, China, Korea and Japan. Its earliest work was carried out in a gray schist stone; its later work, some of it extremely lively and vivid, in stucco. The other chief sites are Manikyala and Taxila, Takht-i-Bahai, Sahr-i-Bahlol, Jamalgarhi, Charsada; and at a Bamiyan cave site there are standing rock-cut Buddhas 120 feet and 175 feet high. Work at these sites seems to have ceased in the 6th and 7th centuries. On the plains of Sind, during the 3rd to 6th centuries, several brick stupas with stucco and molded brick ornament were constructed in a style related to that of Gandhara. The most famous is at Mirpur Khas, and it was decorated with terracotta panels in a manner, if not a style, similar to other significant stupa buildings further east, as will appear. A somewhat similar massive stupa at Devnimori (Gujerat) was raised on two square platforms also faced with superb terracotta relief sculptures. An inscription on a reliquary found in its main chamber dates it to c. 327 AD. At many sites on the fringes of Gandhara an elaborate style of painted stucco sculpture, increasingly sweet and sinuous, continued until well into the 9th century, notably in Fondukistan, Ushkur, and also probably in Kashmir, where a fine art of bronze image casting also flourished.

The central architectural development of the Gandharan epoch was the stupa itself. It became tall in proportion to its breadth, raised on two or more high square plinths, its drum greatly deepened and amplified, often in diminishing tiers, and its crowning umbrellas multiplied so as to resemble a tapered pinnacle. Around its base appeared a courtyard lined with shrine-cells containing icons. These provided for the cult of the increasingly numerous hierarchy of Buddhist deities. The plinths of the stupa also bore Buddha figures and groups facing outward in arcaded niches. The Shah-ji-ki-dheri stupa showed features which became architectural constants on the stupas of Burma and Thailand— additional towers on the corners of the main plinth, which was of cruciform plan.

There can be little doubt that much of this vanished architecture, with its accompanying sculpture and painting (to which Central Asian survivals must be an index) was intended to produce a distinctive atmosphere of mystery and transcendent opulence. Certainly the Nara and Heian monuments preserved in Japan, of later date but partly comparable in style, achieve such an atmosphere. For one of the outstanding features of the great Mahayana sutras (for example, the Lotus) is that they describe teaching-assemblies as taking place in a realm of time and space far beyond the scope of normal human experience. They present cosmic visions of multitudes of Buddhas, Bodhisattvas and Arhats, imbued with unearthly radiance, surrounded by ranked orders of flying gods and celestial beings, meeting in a kind of time out of time; supernatural showers of blossoms rain down; phantom pavilions float in the sky. The Buddha shows himself in the guise of Cosmic Man, brilliant as 100,000 suns, with tens of thousands of universes glimmering in each of his hair pores. Confronted with the sad ruins of so many once-magnificent shrines we are obliged to use our imaginations if we are to envisage what they must once have been like.

Buddhist icons. In fact Roman influence of a kind can be found in the sculpture of what was probably the greatest Indian city at that time, Mathura, which was also ruled by the Kushans. So far, little excavation has been carried out here but what has been discovered enables us to say that it produced probably the most inventive and crucially important school of art to appear in India. There are fragments of gates and pillars which cover the period of Sanchi; but most important are magnificent, bulky and

Mahabodhi temple, Bodhgaya: marking the site where the Buddha gained enlightenment, it was a pattern imitated in southeast Asia. The tower was restored in the 12th century by the Burmese.

sensuous figures cut in the characteristic pink sandstone during the later 1st and earlier 2nd centuries AD, many of which were exported to other sites. Some were godlings for stupa decoration; but the most important were the icons. For our present knowledge suggests that the Indian icon as such was invented and developed here. Mathura probably produced the earliest Buddha figure; it certainly produced the earliest Hindu icons. But it also developed themes – some derived from Helleno-Egyptian terracottas – which became standard ingredients in Buddhist and Hindu ornament. These include a standing Bodhisattva figure, which is the prototype of certain pre-Khmer images in Cambodia; and drinking celestial beings. Buddhist icons were certainly made for now vanished stupas. A few reliefs show that the history of sculptural art here had at least paralleled, if not preceded, similar developments at Barhut and Sanchi. But the gradual evolution of what became the canonical type of suave and sweet Buddha icon distributed all over the Buddhist world can also be traced in detail at Mathura from (probably) the later 1st century AD to the 5th.

The site where this type of icon reached its perfection under the Guptas was Sarnath, where the great ruined Dharmarajika stupa is probably originally Ashokan in date. Many examples in different sandstones are known, both standing and seated. Many have haloes carved with beautiful foliate ornament in low relief. They must come from vanished shrines and stupas at the site. There is, however, one stupa which illustrates a later Indian development of the fundamental concept which is only occasionally known elsewhere, notably in Indonesia. It is the Dhamekh stupa, 143 feet high, 93 feet in diameter. This has become essentially a cylindrical, round-shouldered tower somewhat resembling a Hindu temple spire. Its lower part is adorned with finely rhythmical shallow moldings, and foliate ornament like that on the Buddha haloes, with eight faces on its base to accommodate now vanished sculpture. Like the great sites of north India which were associated with the life of the Buddha, Sarnath was continuously added to and reworked by succeeding generations of Buddhist rulers. This was partly connected with the growing custom of pilgrimage. Buddhists, especially monks, had been traveling along the great trade routes to the sacred sites of Buddhism since the 2nd century AD. Among them were the three Chinese pilgrims who have left valuable accounts of their journeys to India, Fa-hsien (399–414), Hsüan Chang (629–45) and I-Ching (673–95). The sites the pilgrims visited were in early centuries great monasteries, centers of learning, at places which the Buddha himself never visited (though legends were invented) such as Khotan in Turkestan and Hadda in Gandhara. But by the later 3rd century AD pilgrimage was confined to the flourishing and crowded centers of the faith, the places actually associated with the Buddha's life – particularly Sarnath where he preached the First Sermon, Rajgir where he lived and often taught; but especially Bodhgaya, where he achieved his enlightenment.

The site of Bodhgaya is one of the most ancient and continuously developed. There are the fragments of Ashokan sculpture already mentioned, and work was also done during the Gupta epoch. Its outstanding feature, however, is the Mahabodhi temple, whose broad shrine chamber is surmounted by a huge pyramidal tower some 180 feet high with four smaller towers at the corners. The date and exact character of this tower are controversial, as it was restored by a mission sent by King Kyanzittha of Burma in the 11th century. It seems to date essentially from the 2nd century AD at the latest. Architecturally it must have inspired a series of imitations in the great Buddhist city in Burma, Pagan (e.g. the Mahabodhi and the Wet-kyi-in, Ku Byauk-ki), and in Thailand (e.g. the Mon Wat-Kukut and Wat-Mahathat at Lamphun, overworked later, and Wat-Si-Liem and Wat-Chet-Yot at Chiengmai). Another important feature of the Mahabodhi shrine was its great Buddha icon, now vanished. Its replica was duplicated thousands of times in fired-clay votive tablets and small bronzes and distributed all over Buddhist Asia. The oldest image was probably lost when the Hindu King Shashanka cut down the Bodhi tree itself about 600 AD (its offshoot, sent to Ceylon, has now been propagated anew at Bodhgaya). The image shown on these clay tablets and bronzes seems to be of early Pala date; and the Buddha type thus distributed into medieval Burma and Thailand follows this later pattern.

Buddhism under the Palas. This historical possibility illuminates an important transition in the fortunes of Buddhism which took place in the 8th century when the Pala dynasty took control of northeastern India. There can be little doubt that elsewhere Buddhism had declined by about 600 AD, as popular and dynastic Hinduism developed. Only in Ceylon did a fundamentalist version adhering to old stupa types retain its hold almost unchallenged. But the Vajrayana school ardently supported by the Pala kings was very different, and conceived its monuments in a new way. Thus was a polarity within Buddhism and its art set up. This polarity seems to be both historically and doctrinally more genuine than what has often been called the Mahayana-Hinayana polarity.

Pala patronage seems to have been focused initially at the great site of Nalanda, where an Ashokan foundation is said to have existed earlier. By 600 AD, however, the building complex had grown piecemeal into an immense center of Buddhist learning, sometimes called a "university," which has been thoroughly excavated. The heart of the complex was a row of shrines raised on a double plinth, confronting a row of monasteries. Many buildings had been frequently rebuilt and redecorated. For example, one shrine, Temple 3, was overworked at least seven times between 600 and 1200. The shrines were lavishly ornamented with stucco sculpture in Gupta tradition; and from the whole area has come a rich collection of iconic bronzes. The Palas founded another great Buddhist university at Vikramapura, not as yet properly excavated. From here the great teacher Atisa left for Tibet. Another major center of late Buddhist learning was on the hill called Ratnagiri and two nearby hills, in Orissa. We know that these universities were not narrowly sectarian. Lay students were admitted, and there were also at Nalanda courses on the Veda, Sankya philosophy, logic, medicine, linguistics and practical magic. Students came from as far afield as Korea and Japan. Large quantities of small-scale sculpture were produced at all these places, some even signed with the names of the artists. And the earliest finely illuminated palm-leaf manuscripts of Buddhist texts that we know were produced in this environment. Although few relevant Indian originals survive, we also know that the later Tibetan tradition of elaborately planned symbolic iconography was first evolved in these centers of Buddhist learning, in which the founding fathers of Tibetan Buddhism were themselves trained. This link will be taken up later.

At the original Pala shrines an architectural conception developed which had been implicit in earlier Indian tradition. This is the conception of the shrine as a cosmic mountain, raised upon extensively ornamented and complex-planned terraces. Among the precedents for this type of building must be the group of remains at Lauriya Nandangarh, which once constituted a tall brick stupa raised upon multiple polygonal terraces with numerous zigzag re-entrant angles in their plan. The date is probably c. 600 AD. Somewhat similar remains are known further west, at Pawaya and Ahicchatra, perhaps also related to a certain Hindu temple pattern. But the 8th-century Pala version of this idea, at Somapura (Paharpur, Bangladesh), was probably the most magnificent. It was conceived as an integrally designed architectural *mandala* – a huge, high cruciform shrine, with icon chambers facing the cardinal directions, encircled by terraced and roofed verandas stepped down in tiers, with re-entrant angles. Around the base a vast enclosure was ringed by 177 cells. The terraces were faced with thousands of large terracotta sculptured plaques – of which over 2,000 are still *in situ*: a design technique reminiscent, for example, of Saheth-Maheth and Devnimori. And the iconography embraced, apparently, the whole field of Indian symbolism, not only Buddhist subjects. A similar site has also been recently discovered on the Mainmati ridge.

We can only speculate on the overall symbolism and architectural magnificence of these monuments. But we can be sure that such shrines, with their various Southeast Asian offshoots, were realizations in architectural form of conceptual diagrams first set out on cloth and paper in which the whole of Vajrayana's systematic Buddhist philosophy was summarized. Its scheme follows the general plan of the four directions of space around a central area, each of the five symbolizing one of the realms of human knowledge and cosmic experience, summarized by a Buddha of a particular color – yellow, green, red, blue, white – together with subsidiary figures representing his subsidiary functions, some of them terrifying in appearance. Sculpture and painting presented these dramatis personae of embodied psychic principles, defined in a text called *Sadhanamala*. Although most of the images of this form of Buddhism are known from its Nepalese and Tibetan branches, a few important sculptures survive in India, notably a twelve-armed, three-headed stone image in Patna, a deity called Hevajra with his female counterpart Shakti from Paharpur, and a few bronzes, one at Rajshahi.

In India, this art vanished utterly after Buddhism was exterminated by the Muslims in the last years of the 12th century, and the luckier monks fled to Tibet and Burma. In Southeast Asia, however, this conception had provided the basis upon which similar Buddhist temple mountains had been founded, expressing in their structures a similar embracing metaphysical image of the cosmos. For in fact the general idea of the mountain peak as emblem for the source of life and reality was indigenous among the peoples of Southeast Asia. Buddhist theory married this idea with its own cosmology in one way; Hindu in another.

Buddhist shrines in Java. The most complete Buddhist example is Borobudur in central Java, originally constructed about 800 AD by a central Javanese Shailendra king. It is one of the world's most impressive monuments, and it is unique in the state of preservation both of the structure and its colossal scheme of relief decoration, as well as for the fact that it was completed virtually as designed, without accretions, save a terrace at the foot. It lacks, unfortunately, any inscriptions. It is, however, in a consistent Javanese style, and many small associated

Palm-leaf illumination to a Buddhist Wisdom text painted in Bengal, 1112 AD; the lady Wisdom in her meditation band is worshiped by two adoring women. Victoria and Albert Museum, London.

bronze and gold icons are known; yet that style is extraordinarily close to the Pala – a fact which must have some significance not as yet fully elucidated. The structure amounts to a comprehensive expression of Mahayana Buddhist doctrine with its iconography of the Bodhisattva, and may well have provided an inspiration for some of the Hindu temple mountains of the Khmer in Cambodia. By about 1000 AD it seems to have become overgrown and neglected. Only between 1907 and 1911 was it excavated and restored by the Dutch authorities.

It stands on a large square plinth; upon this rise five square terraces diminishing in size. Each side is equally stepped out twice to a central projecting stairway, which runs steeply up to the top of the fifth terrace. On this last stand three further circular diminishing terraces, the topmost crowned by a single bell-shaped stupa containing an invisible and unfinished stone Buddha; around it on the circles are ranged 72 further stupas of open stone latticework, each containing its own large Buddha icon, partly visible. Vast quantities of decorative molding, scrollwork and fantastic symbolic figuration proliferate. The major sculptural scheme is carved around the inner faces of the square terraces, and on their high enclosing walls. To walk in *pradakshina* around each of these roofless corridors, one's attention focused by the narrowed space onto the continuous relief sculpture which lines it, is to witness the unfolding of the cardinal imagery of Buddhist compassion, power and salvation. Its central figure is a royal Bodhisattva, which suggests that the monument was meant to authenticate some ruler, either before or after his death. At each level, raised shrine niches contain larger hieratic Buddha figures facing out over the fertile country around. The unity of the carefully elaborated iconic system proclaims the truth of the full-fledged Mahayana doctrine as a comprehensive explanation both of how the cosmos unfolds from the center "out" and "down" to the lowest levels at the base and of how ultimate knowledge may be attained by progressive ascent to higher levels of inclusive understanding.

There are two other, lesser monuments, associated with Borobudur stylistically. One, Chandi Ngawan near Muntilan, is probably the earliest work of the series. Chandis Mendut and Pawon are probably about contemporary with Borobudur – Pawon, in fact, being a kind of "antechamber" on the road to Borobudur, with a carved relief iconography of wealth. Ngawan consists of a row of five shrines facing east, each containing an image of one of the five Buddha principles evolved in the Vajrayana Buddhism sponsored by the Palas in northeastern India. Together they constitute the Vajra-dhatu or "masculine realm" of total reality. The five square terraces of Borobudur most likely refer to these five. Above and within the Vajra-dhatu is the Garbha-dhatu, the feminine "womb realm" of truth, whose three principles are the central Buddha and two Bodhisattvas, Lokeshvara and Vajrapani. Colossal, peaceful, seated figures of these three are still installed in the cuboid cell chamber of Mendut, which was raised on a broad plinth and crowned with one principal stupa and smaller ones ranged on the terraced roof, and which is faced with relief sculptures of Buddhist iconography. Originally there may have been four more Buddhas within, completing the interlinked Vajra- and Garbha-dhatu scheme. In principle, therefore, Mendut and Borobudur express a similar underlying idea, the former abbreviated, the latter expanded.

Several Chandis were built by later kings of the central Javanese dynasty. Kalasan is a large, square shrine on a plinth with projecting porticoes on each face, thus generally resembling a Hindu temple-type represented in India by Deogarh. Its crowning stupa was raised on an octagonal drum whose faces were carved with Buddhist

Head of a monk carved in stone from Chandi Plaosan, Java, 9th century, which beautifully expresses the Buddhist ideal of unworldly peace and bliss.

iconic figures on a pattern slightly reminiscent of that of the Dhamekh stupa at Sarnath. Each portico was itself crowned with a quincunx of stupas – a constant grouping in a great deal of Southeast Asian architecture, Hindu as well as Buddhist. Sewu was also a cruciform shrine, surrounded by smaller temples. So too was Plaosan, whose sculpture was especially beautiful. The roofs of all these consisted of stupa terraces. Chandi Sari is more like Mendut; its cell once contained a triad of Buddha principles. But it is, mysteriously, three-storied. In the 11th century a Javanese Buddhist monastery was actually set up in the Hindu Chola kingdom of southeastern India.

It is interesting that other central Javanese shrines dedicated to Hindu deities also use stupa crowns (e.g. Lara Jonggrang). It seems that in Indonesia, as in Pala India, syncretism and some mutual tolerance prevailed. During the east Javanese period these continued (927–16th century), and many sites combine Hindu and Buddhist elements. Structures were also often reworked. The execution of colossal monuments as integrated transcendent images of whole systems seems to have declined – partly perhaps for economic reasons, partly also because a new type of cult had begun to develop. This may have treated the Buddhist shrine very much like the Hindu, as a point of entry into the actual world for the spiritual being whose image the temple housed. The great Chandi Jago

(Malang) is the paradigm. This may have been a monument to a king of the Singhasari dynasty, who died in 1268 and whose spirit was provided with both a Shiva statue at Waleri and a Buddhist one at Jago. The latter shrine was reworked later, perhaps in the 14th century, and adorned with non-Buddhist narrative sculpture in an early Wayang dance and puppet style. The square stone cell was set back on two high terraces carved with fine foliate ornament. These terraces seem to have fulfilled the same function as the courtyards standing before the sanctuaries of later east Javanese and Balinese temples, in providing a meeting place between the emerging spirit and representatives of the people. This illustrates one terminus of the centuries-old Indian cult of Buddhism as dynastic sponsor. It may also be related in some way to the very term "Chandi," which has a funeral connotation, since that word is a name of the Hindu goddess of time and death! The huge central figure at Jago was the Vajrayana Amoghapaca, a form of the Bodhisattva Avalokiteshvara; it was surrounded by a stone group of deities in exterior niches, four transcendent Buddhas and four goddesses. The style of these splendid large figures is idiosyncratic and strikingly Indonesian.

Image of the Buddhist Goddess of Wisdom from Singhasari, east Java, 13th century AD, imbued with total serenity. Rijksmuseum voor Volkendkunde, Leiden.

Much fine sculpture in a related style was made for other Buddhist shrines elsewhere in the eastern Javanese domains. Among it are an unparalleled stone image of the Buddhist goddess of wisdom from Singhasari, many fine small bronzes, and a number of icons synthesizing the figures of the Buddha and the Hindu royal gods Shiva and Vishnu. All the Buddhist aspect of this art vanished with the incursion of Islam between the 14th and 16th centuries.

Sumatra. One episode of stupa architecture which is still very insecurely dated between the 11th and 14th centuries is the ruined Maligai stupa at Mmara Takus in central Sumatra. Here an older brick stupa was enclosed in a large brick tower, surmounted by a bell-shaped stupa, and decorated with sandstone carvings. The plinth was rectangular, the base 28-sided, the body cylindrical with a 26-sided stepped-out cushion beneath the stupa crown. The structure it most nearly resembles – though not in detail – is the Dhamekh stupa at Sarnath in India, which seems otherwise to have no descendants. A fine bronze of Lokeshvara dated to the 11th century is known from Gunung Tua in Sumatra.

At Padang Lawas, however, in the Batak region of central Sumatra, about 16 monuments have been found, all but two Buddhist. But the Buddhism they represent was a form of Vajrayana which the Batak Shamanic cult of spirits and magic had thoroughly permeated. The shrines themselves, called *bairo* – vernacular for *vihara* – consist of high and narrow brick cells, crowned with a square story, an octagonal and then a circular story, the whole surmounted by a large stupa surrounded by smaller ones. Facing sculptures of monstrous beings line the lower stories; inside there were massive sculptures of Vajrayana Buddhist principles. Such shrines must have been foci of dynastic cult about which we know virtually nothing, save that they must have owed much to the Vajrayana of eastern Java, and ultimately of Pala India. There is no certainty – though it is possible – that they were also funeral monuments. Perhaps the monks who served them resembled the still mysterious Ari of Pyu Burma, against whom more conservative Buddhism in that country reacted so strongly.

The growth of Buddhism in Southeast Asia. In other regions of Southeast Asia a similar form of Vajrayana Buddhism also flourished, though it was itself eclipsed, not by a different religion, but by a more fundamentalist Buddhism in, so to speak, Buddhist reformations. We have very little archaeological evidence as yet for the earliest Buddhism in Burma, Thailand, Cambodia and Vietnam, though many sites await excavation. What there is suggests that Buddhist art there followed a pattern broadly analogous to that followed in northeast India, at first under the influence of late Gupta types, then of Pala, with Indonesian influence also playing a part in the 8th century. The very earliest stratum of Buddhist art, however, seems to have been based on patterns evolved by the Shatavahana art of the southeast of India. The Buddha from the Kamara river in Celebes has been mentioned; but elsewhere, notably in Malaya (Sungu Bujang, Kedah, 4th to 5th century) and Thailand (Pong Tuk, 5th to 6th century), Buddhist bronze icons have been found of a type related to but probably later than the Amaravati type of c. 300. Brick stupas and monasteries of a similar date there must have been, from Burma to the Celebes. We know virtually nothing of them. But it is most likely that the Buddhism they fostered was not sharply distinguished as Mahayana or Hinayana – a distinction far too readily assumed to be hard and fast by many scholars.

The earliest established dates for Buddhism and, no doubt, its monasteries are: in the Malay peninsula (Suvarnabhumi), 5th century; in Burma a few Pali inscriptions and some remains of buildings at Hmawza, c. 500 AD; in Vietnam the great Dan-Duong Buddha, probably 5th century; in Funan (Cambodia) a set of superb carved wooden Buddhas, surprisingly well preserved in swamp, of the 5th to 6th century; and in the Mon kingdoms of Dvaravati of southern Thailand and lower Burma, 6th-century texts cut on sandstone architectural fragments at Nakhon Pathom; in Thailand, some stupa remains and bronze Buddhas at Pong Tuk, sandstone "Wheels of the Law" at Pra Pathom, and early 7th-century reliefs from Pra Pathom. From this period on, all the countries of Southeast Asia knew and patronized Buddhism. Even though Funan monks were called to China, and superb stone and bronze Buddha figures came from the school of Phnom-Da, during the 7th century in Cambodia, as well as Champa, Hinduism became predominant. In Malaya, however, still scarcely investigated, there have been found, alongside Hindu relics, some of the most magnificent Buddhist bronzes ever made, probably influenced by the Shailendra styles of Java. One, a Bodhisattva from Chaiya, may be of 8th- or 9th-century date. Others, in the Taiping Museum, are in a distinctive style, strikingly reminiscent of the sculpture of Chandi Sari in central Java. The two Buddhist countries however where the faith flourished and produced major surviving monuments are Burma and Thailand.

Buddhist Burma. Burma was divided into two main spheres of influence, upper and lower Burma. In upper Burma a people called the Pyu, speaking a Tibeto-Burmese language, built huge cities whose splendor was recorded in Chinese T'ang chronicles, and which probably remain to be excavated. One such city was recorded in the 8th century as having a circumference of 50 miles, and containing 100 monasteries lavishly decorated with painting and precious metal. These people were in direct contact with the Vajrayana Buddhists of northeastern India. Among them flourished the priestly sect called the Ari, almost certainly Vajrayana, who cultivated astronomical and sacrificial magic. A few remains of their stupas survive, which have a generic resemblance to the Dhamekh stupa at Sarnath and to Vajrayana monuments of Indonesia. They were tall, solid cylindrical towers of brick on stepped circular plinths, crowned by bell-shaped stupas. One must have been over 150 feet high. There were halls on plinths, also generically resembling Indian prototypes in having four porticoes. In lower Burma, the kingdom of the western Mon people (probably affiliated to the eastern Mon kingdom of southern Thailand, called Dvaravati) produced a magnificent Hinayana Buddhist art on which was founded the later art of Burma.

The racial Burmese, who infiltrated upper Burma after 900, when the Pyu were eclipsed, and came to dominate both regions, opted for Buddhist fundamentalism, and combined it with their animist cult of the Nats. Anawrahta's 1056 decree resulted in the official adoption of Mon art as the basis of all Burmese art. Mon craftsmen were among those carried off to build and furnish the new dynastic capital on the site of Pagan, a city originally founded in 849. Here, until the coming of the Mongols in 1287, a magnificent episode of Buddhist architecture and associated art took place, a large part of which stood fairly well preserved until the earthquake in 1975. Kyanzittha, Anawrahta's successor, restored the tower at Bodhgaya, partly in Burmese taste; and a smaller copy was built at Pagan. There can be little doubt that this Buddhism was adopted as the framework for dynastic power and social cohesion.

Pagan's brick and plaster buildings must illustrate something of the vast wealth of Buddhist architecture which once stood all over Asia, but has now vanished. For Pagan's vaulting technique comes from late Gupta work in eastern India. Probably the present remains were themselves surrounded by dense building in wood, which has naturally perished. Among the many surviving structures are brick halls identified by inscription as originally royal palaces, and the fine stone library (c. 1058), square, with a roof of diminishing tiers, rising in concave silhouette to a peak, the corners and center of each tier marked by a characteristic flamboyant antefix. There are monastic halls lined with cells (So-ming-gyi) and others based on wooden types with ridge roofs.

It is the sequence of stupas and stupa *cetiyas* which are the characteristic development at Pagan. There are thousands, ranging from small heaps to mountains of brickwork. The greatest, with their interior brick-built Buddhas and their sculptured or painted terracotta wall plaques (some glazed) dealing with subjects from a limited range of Pali literary sources, notably the *Jatakas*, represent an attempt to recapture the spirit of "primitive" Buddhism without sacrificing too many of the possibilities of architectural magnificence. The evolutionary sequence of the stupa *cetiya* revealed at Pagan is broadly as follows.

The earliest, probably Pyu version, the Bupaya, is a tall dome, basically a cylinder, bulbous at the shoulder, standing on an octagonal plinth, crowned by a high concave cone which, with its molded cushion, combines into a single volume the original small square enclosure at the summit called *harmika*, and tiered umbrellas. The

Opposite: the Schwezigon (Golden) Pagoda at Pagan, Burma, a much-restored stupa of the early phase.

Opposite below: terracotta relief from the Schwezigon Pagoda, Pagan, representing a royal figure accepting reverence, 12th century (?).

Below: diagram of the Ananda temple, Pagan, 11th century. Fundamentally a stupa on a plinth which has been opened up to contain a shrine with icons (see inset).

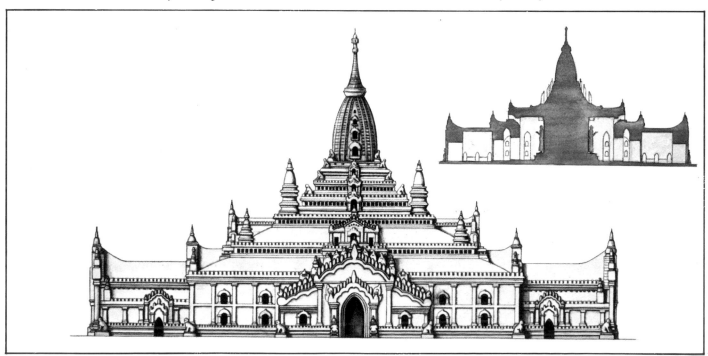

second version (e.g. Lokananda, Myin Pagan), probably of Anawrahta's time, stands on higher plinths, its bulbousness diminished and foot splayed, to give it a bell–like contour belted with shallow moldings which runs directly up into a concave cone ringed with deep moldings. Yet another version mounts an actual stupa of this shape on a "mountain" of three or five broad, diminishing square plinths, up each face of which climb stairways suggesting a simplified Borobudur. A third version, very close in shape to Pala prototypes, has the bell-like stupa heavily molded, the crowning cone also, the three square plinths emphatic, with a stupa–crown motif constructed at all of their corners.

Perhaps in imitation of lost work in contemporary India, the Burmese began to open up the interiors of these terraced plinths with wide corridors, adding porticoes and porches, deepening the lowest stories. The cylinder of the stupa dome was carried down into this undercroft to the floor, and large Buddha icons were added to its base, often four facing the cardinal directions. Thus was elaborated a *cetiya* which was at once stupa and temple. The internal rooms and corridors could be decorated with reliefs and painting. The best known of these is the great Ananda (dedicated in 1090) and still in use. Its stupa crown, however, is square in section and modeled after a Hindu northern Indian temple tower; its four entries have approach halls added to them.

After the Mongol invasion work was at first desultory and then more or less ceased at Pagan. In the other major cities such as Rangoon and Mandalay it has continued down to modern times. The people are still Buddhist; and therefore, following old custom, the major stupas have been continuously either torn down and rebuilt, or encased in ever larger shells. It is not yet possible to analyze their history. They have preserved the basic contour of the spreading bell with towering molded conical pinnacle; though other shapes, some of Khmer inspiration, are known among the smaller structures. The monks play an extremely important part in society, not least as astrologers and celebrants of spirit festivals; and much decorative art is dedicated to Buddhist uses.

Thailand. Thailand is another country where a fundamentalist Buddhism lacking the idea of the Bodhisattva and the knowledge of the great Mahayana sutras is still deeply entrenched in the life of the people. Its present-day religious art has undergone much Burmese influence. In earlier centuries, however, the Mon traditions of Dvaravati exercised a substantial influence upon the art of the Khmer, who were, at this time, dynastically Hindu. Lopburi, the greatest Mon city, was taken by the Khmer in 1002. Ultimately, like the Burmese in Burma, the Buddhist Thai coming in from the north took over both regions.

Few facts are yet established about the history of architecture during the early phase of Thai occupation.

There were many monasteries, all containing stupas and shrines of various patterns. The earliest authenticated is the Wat Buddhai Svariya at Ayutthaya (early 13th century), a towered shrine approached by a columned hall. The stupa proper, often containing relics, seems to have retained its general Mon bell shape, having a circular flanged base and a finial of onion contour. Some stupas were raised on high circular drums which could be hollowed out and converted into shrines containing images. It seems also that the Buddhist Thai royal dynasties adopted the Hindu Khmer custom of each king building for himself a shrine as a funereal monument, which accounts to some extent for the number and magnificence of surviving stupas at other Thai capital cities of Sukhodaya and Savankhalok. Some fragments of painted narrative and ornament survive in the chambers of a number of buildings. At Chiengmai in the 15th century one of Thailand's greatest kings, Tiloka, built a small version of the great Mahabodhi temple at Bodhgaya, almost certainly on advice from monks from Ceylon. Its exterior panels are sculpted with single large figures of celestial beings, perhaps intended as images of royal protectors.

The Thai attempted to purge their Buddhism, and bring it into conformity with what they conceived to be the oldest and finest doctrine. To this end they maintained contacts when they could with Ceylon, and the history of the Thai Buddha image reflects these efforts in a way which architecture cannot; for architecture was continuously overworked later. The principle behind the Buddhist icon in Thailand is common to most Buddhist countries, but is here especially clearly visible. It is that each major icon of the Buddha is a fount of magical power. Sacred images were treated as dynastic palladia, and were transported from conquered cities to a victor's own capital. If images were to contain such power, they had to be as close as possible in design to a great early original. The icon, with its periodic revisions, thus evolved according to a standard set of types, of which later copies were repeatedly made in different regions. First was the fine group of types evolved in the trade-route city of Sukhodaya in a first attempt to emulate Ceylon images, with a Mon inflection, during the 14th century. They have smooth, somewhat indefinitely rounded modeling, lacking firm planes, and dominated by sinuous linear curves, which give the figure a supernatural elegance. The Sukhodaya walking type, with its turned-back elongated fingers and "boneless" undulating body, epitomizes the idea. The second, the U Tong, first evolved in Ayutthaya in the later 14th century, shows an elegance somewhat diminished in favor of Dvaravati-Khmer firmness and squareness; it follows an idea which had its own authenticating roots in Mon antiquity. Then, in the northern kingdom, when Tiloka re-established direct links with Ceylon and images from there would have been brought over, it must have been apparent how far the earlier types of icons had departed from the "original"

Ruins of Wat Jaj Thaimongan at the great city of Ayutthaya, southern Thailand. The quincunx of towers is based on the Mahabodhi pattern. 14th century AD.

pattern preserved in Ceylon; and so the massive and simplified "lion" type was created, in an attempt to recapture the spirit of the oldest canonical archetype. The many later images of the Buddha, large and small, made either for monastic communities or in the pursuit of merit, follow one of these major types, or even a fusion of them, with a distinct bias towards that Sukhothai elegance which seems to be in some sense a "natural" Thai ideal.

Modern Thai Buddhist art at the present capital, Bangkok, shows heavy Burmese influence. The vigor of older work has been diluted with surface ornamentalism, flamboyant decoration, gilding and elegantly repetitive figure sculpture. The atmosphere of spiritual lightness and unreality this art purveys seems expressly intended to keep the imagination of monks and people in a realm removed from the taint of everyday "reality." This Buddhism is thus distinct from Chinese and Japanese Zen, which emphasizes the identity of the apparent and the transcendent. In the Hinayana countries of Burma and Thailand as well as Vietnam and later Cambodia, not to mention Ceylon, the stupa continued to play its role as center of animist and magical ceremonial, while at the same time remaining the focus of authentic Buddhist teaching and the monastic order. On many Thai Wats, for example, a version of the Chinese fertility dragon, interpreted as an Indian *naga*, is carved running down the rails of the approach stairs, thus indicating that the presence of the Wat is meant to exercise a benign influence through its "gift" of heavenly water – a transformation of the fertility and wealth-giving function of the earliest Indian stupas. The shrine with its monks is the center of, among other activities, elaborate rituals of the agricultural calendar, domestic and funeral rites. Such a social standing suggests that the Buddha, who was after all a human teacher, symbolizes a spirituality which far transcends ordinary terrestrial and celestial affairs. It is more than probable that this Theravada system, although its present customs must differ in vital details, can at least give us a clue as to the kind of role the early stupas and monasteries of Indian Asia once played in now vanished societies.

Angkor. One last Southeast Asian version of the stupa, much modified, sums up the possibilities of Buddhism as a dynastic religion. It is the colossal sacred precinct of Angkor Thom, centered on the building called the Bayon, in Cambodia. This enormous complex of building, unparalleled in scale, represents the culmination of a long series of Hindu shrines. It was built after about 1200 by Jayavarman VII, whose mission it became to reconquer the empire of the Khmers after his predecessor's domain had fallen to the Cham of Vietnam. He changed his dynastic allegiance to Buddhism, presumably for political as well as supernatural reasons. Each of the many famous towers of Angkor Thom is faced with four colossal masks of Lokeshvara, lord of the worlds and one of the two Bodhisattvas of the Garbha-dhatu, who was chosen by that king as his personal patron. These faces demonstrate at once the compassionate all-seeing power of the Bodhisattva and the king. He built a shrine to his mother as the Incarnation of Buddhist Wisdom. And since Angkor was, as we shall see, itself a huge sacred hydraulic system for propagating fertility over the surrounding terrain, Bayon and Thom demonstrate how Buddhism was able to assume the potentiating role in another guise.

The Thom is enclosed in 10 miles of moats. To build it

Collection of Buddhas inside a shrine at Angkor. Some belong to the last Bayon phase, 13th century; others are earlier, and were probably made while Hinduism was still the state religion.

Jayavarman was obliged to raze large areas of the older city and many of his predecessors' monuments. The Bayon is a temple mountain on the traditional Khmer pattern, but by far the most elaborate. Its central shrine has eight porticoes; subsidiary shrines stand on terraces as nodes of a superb complex of galleries lined with miles of figural and decorative relief. A multitude of stone and bronze images were placed in them. In the Thom strange environmental inventions were constructed, all apparently unprecedented. Among these are mile-long rows of colossal figures of gods tugging a huge serpent railing, which interprets the sacred mountain, the Bayon, as the "original" mountain used by the Hindu gods to churn out worlds from the original undifferentiated milk of being; lake-sized fountains which represent Buddhist paradises; and a huge image of a white horse above the surface of one tank representing a legend of the appearance of Avalokiteshvara (Lokeshvara) in that guise to save sailors who prayed to him from drowning. This is the last and certainly the largest effort of Buddhist Mahayana architecture in Indian Asia. After the final fall of Angkor, Cambodian Buddhism became a modest Theravada.

Tibet. Throughout Tibet, however, a different Buddhism flourished until very recently, producing a huge number of monuments and quantities of art, most of which have never been cataloged or even seen by western scholars. It is hoped that the Chinese will one day undertake the massive task of listing and publishing. Tibet's Buddhism derived directly from Pala India, and includes a range of Vajrayana systems, though both the Buddhism and the art were elaborated in specifically Tibetan ways. Many works of portable art have reached the west, notably the painted hangings (Thang-Kas) and small bronze icons. These illustrate the complete dramatis personae of transcendent Buddhist principles, whose interaction in diagrammatic relationships may realize all the psycho-cosmic phenomena of Vajrayana "reality" and enlightenment. It is more than likely that the prototypical repertoire of figures was once painted and sculpted in Pala India, although apart from a few palm-leaf manuscripts we know very little of such work.

Tibetan architecture represents an amalgam of the Pala conception of the Buddhist shrine and monastery with the rough-stone building styles developed locally, adapted to the mountainous terrain and the harsh highland climate with its constant winds. In fact the Tibetans, a creative but once very warlike people, received Buddhism late in its history. It first entered under King Srong-tsen-gampo in 640 AD, and was recognized as a state religion in 779 AD. Its greatest epoch of expansion was between the 10th and early 13th centuries; and during this time it maintained close links with the Pala universities, with many great teachers coming from Pala Bihar. Samye was the first great monastery to be founded in 715; Sakya in 1073. The earliest style of art seems to have been a version of late

Gandharan, that came via Kashmir from Fondukistan-Ushkur, modified by direct Pala influence.

Buddhism wove itself into the entire social and administrative fabric of the country, and the stone-built monasteries on their craggy knolls developed virtually into towns, which were the focus of all the activities of life, including trade. Here too the monks presided at seasonal ceremonies, births and funerals, demonstrating the benevolent power of the Buddha's teaching, and controlling, in his name, the spiritual beings with whom the Tibetans feel their awesome landscape to be populated.

All over Tibet, inside monasteries and scattered across the countryside, stupas – called *chörtens* – were built, of every size, sometimes in long rows. They fulfilled the classical Buddhist purpose of constantly reminding Buddhists of the teaching concerning reincarnation, enlightenment and Nirvana. Beside large monastic *chörtens*, shrines were built, with sculptures, painted plaster illustrations of doctrine, carved wooden beams, posts and doors inside them.

The large stupa shrine was constructed in vernacular versions of the canonical Buddhist pattern. One was the bell-shaped dome standing on up to four diminishing tiers of plinths crowned by a harmika die and tiered conical "umbrella" spire, perhaps with a stairway rising up to a Buddha image set in a niche at the base of the dome (e.g. at 11th-century Tholing), not at all unlike contemporary Pyu structures. Another, which was very common, was distinguished by a dome splayed out at the shoulder (e.g. Champaling, before the 15th century). But by far the largest and most important combined the stupa with its plinths into a shrine, in the same fashion as some examples at Pagan (also under direct Pala influence). In these the

This stupa at Bodhnath, Nepal, epitomizes the significance of the Buddhist stupa everywhere.

A *chörten*, or stupa of Tibetan type, at Namdo in Nepal. The architecturally simple exterior is painted, the interior is decorated more elaborately.

dome becomes a solid circular tower with a projecting roof; the tiered plinths are opened up to contain chambers and corridors whose projecting eaves are often molded, and through which the stupa tower descends. These interior spaces may contain icons, the larger ones often of clay and painted plaster, as well as stretches of wall painting. The outstanding characteristic of Tibetan *chörtens*, as compared with the stupas of countries with hotter climates, is the contrast between their austere and simple exteriors and the efflorescence of brilliant figurative imagery and symbolic ornament contained within.

Symbolic stupas of Nepal. The whole long history of the idea of the stupa as symbol is summed up in one powerful architectural image. In and around Katmandu in Nepal are several stupas where the general design of the structure is not at all remote from that of the earliest Indian examples: a virtual semi-dome stands on a drum and square plinth; above is a cubical *harmika* die, which is crowned by the conical "umbrella" spire. Each component is taken to symbolize one of the elements. On each face of the die is painted a pair of eyes facing out into one of the four directions of space.

In this image is expressed very clearly the archetype of which the other monuments we have surveyed are all in some sense modulations, authenticating both Buddhism as popular faith and as dynastic authority. The stupa stands as emblem both of that Nirvana into which the Buddha passed at death, by which the highest truth was realized, and also of a power more than divine to which the gods themselves submit. To know the truth was in India to become the truth. However emphatically the human Buddha himself may have rejected any suggestion that he was divine, however often he may have refused to offer any definition of the ultimate, Buddhist culture nevertheless identified him as Cosmic Being, axis of the world, source as well as goal of all reality. That is the basic meaning of every stupa.

Images of the Buddha

The Buddha was a human teacher who died c. 489 BC. He founded an order of monks to continue his teaching, which was based on the breaking of all attachments, especially to the idea of self. But Buddhist speculation over the centuries evolved an artistic iconography to convey *what* the Buddha nature was. It was not the physical body of the actual Buddha; and the truth about it was intrinsically unutterable. A symbolic body was thus developed whose physical characteristics were only emblems for aspects of Buddhist teaching and cosmology. And since the Buddha nature was not identified with any single actual body, it was accepted that in universes numberless as the Ganga sands there would naturally be an infinity of Buddhas appearing to teach the *Dharma*, or doctrine. This painting of the 6th century in Cave 2 at Ajanta illustrates the idea.

Above left: a Gandhara relief in schist of the 2nd century AD represents the birth of the Buddha-to-be from his mother's side.

Left: an icon of the meditating Buddha from Gal Vihara, Ceylon, of the 12th century. This is the conservative pattern of image which "refreshed" the Hinayana art of southeast Asia at that time.

Below: the Katra Buddha, from Mathura, is the earliest type known before the pattern was fully fledged for the symbolic body. Here the sage is shown as a great-armed hero with noble Bodhisattva attendants, probably early 2nd century AD. His head protuberance is shown like a snail-shell. Mathura Museum.

Left: before he achieved enlightenment under the Bodhi tree at Bodhgaya the Buddha experimented with severe asceticism, which he rejected as a means of discipline. This icon, cut from schist in Gandhara in the 2nd century AD, represents the ascetic experiment. Lahore Museum.

Right: meditating Buddha sitting between two Bodhisattvas in the shrine Chandi Mendut, central Java, cut c. 800 AD. This triad represents the central doctrine of esoteric Buddhism.

Below: a Kashmir ivory icon of the 7th century AD, representing the Buddha undergoing temptation by the beautiful daughters of Mara, the god of death, whom he will ultimately conquer by his discovery of the true way of enlightenment. Prince of Wales Museum, Bombay.

Right: a seated meditating transcendent Buddha from Borobudur. Its massive barely inflected forms are intended to illustrate the state of calm beyond time.

Below left: this teaching Buddha from Sarnath, in Bihar, where the Buddha preached his first sermon in the Deer Park, epitomizes the 5th-century AD Gupta style of sculpture. Sarnath Museum.

Below: in the 5th-century Cave 17 at Ajanta this triad of seated Buddha with Bodhisattvas was probably cut later. But the atmosphere of mystery and splendor reflects the strangeness of the cosmic visions contained in the Mahayana texts.

Left: this stone carving, in Khmer style, of the 12th century, from the great Thai city of Ayutthaya, represents the Buddha meditating on a magical *naga*, or snake. A legend says that a *naga* called Mucalinda raised the Buddha on his coils above a flood sent by Mara to prevent him reaching enlightenment. But the Khmer mythology of the snake saw it as emblem of cosmic fertility, and this must be part of the meaning here. Ayutthaya Museum.

Right: this standing Buddha carved at Mathura in India has the smooth and even rope-like folds which were one of the features of Gupta period images. It is cut in the characteristic pink Mathura sandstone, but would probably have been painted and gilt. 5th century A D. Mathura Museum.

Below: this huge golden Sukhodaya type of Buddha represents the symbolic body in all its glory. All Buddha images in India and elsewhere would once have been gilded with leaf like this Thai 13th-century icon.

Right: in this semi-ruined shrine, called the Prang Sam Yot, at the ancient Thai city of Lopburi a Buddha image is still worshiped. Behind is a stupa. The architecture and sculpture of Lopburi go back into Khmer and Mon times, when Mahayana Buddhism flourished.

Below: this Buddha comes from the facing of one of the great vanished stupas of Mirpur Khas, in Sind, Pakistan. It is finished in fine terracotta and painted, as once all Buddhist architectural sculpture was. 4th century A D. Victoria and Albert Museum, London.

Above: this standing Buddha from Sarnath is in early Gupta 4th-century style. British Museum.

Below left: this scene in the Shwe Dagon Pagoda, Rangoon, Burma, shows how Buddha images are revered today, and would have been in the past.

Below: a Gandhara painted stucco head of the Buddha, c. 200 AD, the hairstyle being still close to the Romano-Hellenic patterns imported from the eastern Mediterranean. Karachi Museum.

Above: this votive tablet illustrates the sweetly undulant type of walking Buddha developed at Sukhodaya in Thailand. 15th century. National Museum, Bangkok.

Above left: Buddha dying and passing into complete Nirvana; a 15th-century sculpture in the same sinuous Sukhodaya style. National Museum, Bangkok.

Left: colossal sculpture of the dying Buddha at Polonnaruwa, Ceylon, of the 12th century, cut into a rock face, perhaps a prototype of the many reclining figures in Hinayana countries.

Below: colossal bronze standing icon of the Buddha from Sultanganj in India, 9th century AD. Birmingham Museum.

5. The Hindu Temple

Simple hallows, a sacred spot of the Toda people on a hill near Ootacamund, Nilgiri hills, where divinity dwells. It is marked with red paint.

Plan, purpose and origin of the temple. The origins of the Hindu temple proper are obscure. The archaeological evidence suggests that temple building started later than stupa building, although it must be accepted that the popular worship of rustic shrines is far older than Buddhism. For early Buddhist sources describe the Buddha himself visiting with reverence local centers of worship called in the texts *cetiyas*. Hinduism, as we know it, represents an amalgam of Brahman Vedic traditions with popular cult; and at the present day virtually all the possible levels of combination coexist. The Brahman Vedic culture is exclusive, reserved to that caste, and is even more exclusive than the inner tradition of Buddhism. Now at most Hindu shrines Brahman families provide the official priests who conduct ceremonies for the benefit of the populace.

The fundamental purpose of the Hindu temple is to sustain the living presence of a god, who acts as the spiritual guardian of a community, or even of a household. He or she will confer blessings if pleased, and will need to be pacified if angry. The temple is thus the home of the god, and so it is modeled in the first place on the homes of men, made of mud, brick or wood. But the more magnificent it becomes, the more it will come to resemble the palace of a king. Its decoration will then suggest wealth, fertility and celestial bliss.

The nucleus of the temple is the hallows – a sacred object or icon in which a divine presence dwells. This is enclosed in a cell which the priest may enter, to attend the hallows and perform ritual offering (*puja*). The simplest shrines have only a porch added to the cell, where devotees may stand, to shelter from sun or rain. In larger shrines this becomes a hall (*mandapa*) and the cell may be set back from it along a short corridor so as to keep the deity more removed from the common people. The interior is usually dark; and the god who dwells in the hallows is treated as an honored guest would be in the home. The priest bathes the hallows and anoints it with butter or oil, dresses it and decks it with ornaments given by wealthier devotees. He salutes it by waving a lamp, offers choice food, perfume and flower garlands. It may be entertained with music and dancing – for which a special open pillared hall may be constructed aligned with the cell so that the deity may witness the dance. The priest emerges from the cell bearing the offerings which have been consecrated by their contact with the divine, and distributes them to the congregation. The assembly hall need not be very large, for the congregation usually stands, there is coming and going, and the priest will repeat the offering and distribution as often as necessary for fresh groups of worshipers. After the fixed time of audience (*darshan*) the doors are closed and the god sleeps.

The living temple is not only a place of worship; it is also a social center where people may sit on stone benches in the shade and discuss local affairs. Before he enters the hall a worshiper may perform *pradakshina* around his deity, a custom also adopted by the Buddhists. This may be in the open around the outside of a modest shrine, whereas a larger temple will provide a covered ambulatory. Above the cell there is usually a tower (*shikhara*)

A sculpture of the goddess Durga from a ruined medieval temple worshiped by modern villagers, daubed with pink paint, on Mandata island in the holy Narmada river, Madhya Pradesh.

which marks the holy place so that it can be seen from far off. This is the outstanding architectural feature of a fully developed temple.

The origin of the temple itself lies in the idea of the primitive hallows. This is some object in which a god has taken up residence. Every village has, and has probably had since time immemorial, at least one – often far more – hallows that is reverenced by the people without the benefit of priestly offices. Others may stand among the fields. These myriads of hallows testify to the ability of rural Indians to discern and revere spiritual presences in natural phenomena. A hallows may be an ancient, gnarled tree, the stump of an anthill, a large stone, a battered and unidentified ancient sculpture dug up from a field, a little clutch of boulders or a cluster of snake holes at the root of a tree. Usually such hallows are daubed, spotted or striped by the villagers with red paint – itself an emblem of vital sanctity. Offerings will be left before the hallows each day – consisting for example of handfuls of flowers or little balls of cooked rice. Some of the spiritual entities may be identified as male *yakshas* or female *yakshis* – capricious and dangerous, vaguely monstrous beings who may inhabit particular keyspots such as big trees – or as *nagas* or *naginis* – snake-like creatures who are guardians of wells and tanks, symbolizing fertility and fortune. These supplied some of the chief dramatis personae attending the stupa in early Buddhist decorative sculpture; and it is worth recalling that both Buddhism and Hinduism spread with particular success into regions of Southeast Asia where the people were already devoted to cults of similar nature spirits.

Brahmanism. Over this fundamental layer of aboriginal cult Brahmanical Hinduism spread. Buddhism taught detachment from the world, which leads to personal salvation, a condition higher than that of the gods. So, in a sense, any Buddhist interest in gods, the heavens and fertility was always, in the last resort, a concession to popular belief. Brahmanism, however, moved naturally into the world of aboriginal cult, adopted and adapted its deities, assimilating them to the personalities of its own greater gods. The huge Brahman encyclopedias of legend, from the *Mahabharata* on through the series of *Puranas*, represent the literary aspect of this vast, centuries-long effort of synthesis and syncretism. In them are collected stories of divine visitations, of adventures and misadventures, with their theological interpretations, from many different regions of India.

The Brahmans, as a priestly caste with their knowledge of Sanskrit and the ceremonial to which the earliest sacred Sanskrit texts are devoted, were eventually able to take complete command of the system of Indian deities and hallows. In practice they seem to have "colonized" the villages of India between about 200 BC and 700 AD. But their own ancient Vedic ceremonial seems to have required no building of a kind to leave archaeological traces. The Vedic sacrifice and fire ritual, with their attendant hymns, seem to have been performed in the open air, offered directly to the elements. Today the Brahman *homa*-altar in Kalighat temple, Calcutta, stands in the open. And even though altars of different designs were prescribed in the Vedic commentaries for different rites, no examples survive physically from early times.

There is one small shrine, Temple 40 at Sanchi, an apsidal stone plinth with stairs approaching from each side, which may have been some kind of altar; perhaps it was originally covered by a wooden superstructure; perhaps not. At Bairat the footings of a circular shrine of some sort also survive; but whether either of these was a Vedic altar is uncertain. Furthermore, the great gods of historical Hinduism have only the most tenuous relationship with the main Vedic deities. Shiva and Vishnu are the two principal impersonations of cosmic creative energy to whom the greater number of actual Hindu temples are dedicated; but neither plays much of a role in the Veda. The goddess to whom many of the others are dedicated under various more recent names – Lakshmi, Durga, Parvati, Kali – is likewise a shadowy figure in the oldest texts, appearing there under other names.

The first temples. As to who commissioned India's great temples, numerous inscriptions confirm that they were most commonly built by kings and members of their families, partly as an act of merit for their own and their ancestors' benefit in heaven, but also as an act of self-dedication to patron deities – not necessarily a single deity, sometimes several. Most temples would be built at the capital cities of dynasties; but others would be built at centers of pilgrimage and secondary cities. Land and villages would be donated to support them with their resident priests and staff. We do know, however, that ministers, merchants and guilds of artisans also erected temples. One of the ways for anybody of wealth to earn supernatural favor was to commission sculptures, gilding, subsidiary buildings, repairs, or even small subsidiary shrines, to the limit of their purses.

The artists seem to have been organized in groups under masters; and the groups may have traveled from job to job. They worked according to guild rules; these were preserved mostly by word of mouth, but in later times probably in manuscripts like some on palm-leaf recovered in Orissa. Proportional schemes for figures, iconographic designs, hand gestures, colors, plans and elevations for buildings and their detail, all seem to have been carefully defined. But it is not correct to imagine that Hindu artists were simply dedicated anonymous craftsmen. Plenty of signed works survive, giving us the names of master sculptors. Two sculptors at Belur (13th century), for example, call themselves "champion among rivals" and "tiger among sculptors." Masons and carvers nevertheless seem to have occupied a relatively humble place in society; and perhaps because of their readiness to travel, they seem to have been regarded as a rather promiscuous and unreliable class of people.

On the evidence of archaeology, it was probably under the Kushans that the first Hindu temples in the modern sense were built, in brick. The temples themselves do not survive; but some of their icons do, almost certainly among the earliest in India, carved at Mathura from the 2nd century AD on. They include stone images of Vishnu, Shiva and Surya the sun god, and testify once again to the creative importance of the Mathura school. Precisely why and how these particular deities came to the fore we may never know. But it seems probable that their rise was connected with their role as canonical patron gods of royal dynasties. The Kushans also commissioned from Mathura artists over-lifesize stone sculptures of themselves – perhaps to set in shrines near divine icons. Certainly in India, and Southeast Asia later on, images of the high gods were dedicated by members of royal families as concrete testimonials to an identification of royal person with patron deity.

In fact the few shrines we know that are earlier in date than those of the Kushans all lack icons. It seems that a normal process whereby the rustic hallows evolved into a recognized temple included the following stages: the raising of a plinth or offering table; enclosure with a railing; covering by a canopy or roof; and building of walls. It may be that the idea of dedicating a completely *new* temple on a spot not previously hallowed could only arise once the conception of the sculptured icon as a valid dwelling for the deity had evolved. For only then could a new sanctifying presence be invoked by appropriate ceremonial. The earliest known shrine with an explicit dedication, that at Beshnagar (Vidisha district, Madhya Pradesh), may date from before the dedication of the pillar by the Greek Heliodoros nearby in about 140 BC. It has the plan of an apsidal hall, like a Buddhist *chaitya*, and was dedicated to Vasudeva, who is often, but by no means certainly, identified with the Hindu god Krishna. We cannot say whether it ever contained an icon or not. Inscriptions from around Mathura dating from the 1st century BC also refer to other shrines of this deity. It seems possible that a movement of personal devotion (*bhakti*) to this personal god had by then got under way, perhaps in emulation of the Buddhist cult of the person of the Buddha. The same factor of emulation might account for the lag of about half a century between the appearance of icons of the Buddha and then icons of Hindu gods in the same region.

It has been plausibly suggested that the prototype for the full-fledged Indian structural temple is represented by a building called "the temple of the double-headed eagle" excavated at Jandial, Taxila, and dating to the 2nd century BC. This was on a Greek pattern, with Ionic pillars. It is composed of a cell (Greek *naos*), portico (*pronaos*) and walkaround (peristyle). It also has the Greek rear crypt for storing treasure (*opisthodomos*). In addition, it incorporates a plinth massive enough once to have supported a tower, which some authorities believe to have resembled a pyramid. Without the rear crypt, the other elements came to constitute the standard pattern for the Hindu temple down the centuries. The earliest surviving actual stone-built examples, however, used only the cell and a stocky-pillared portico; these are at Tigowa and Sanchi (Temple 17) and date to the early 5th century AD. They too lack their icons. There are also a few other sites in Bandelkhand and Malwa where the plans of such simple, and maybe earlier, shrines can be traced.

At Kunda (Jabalpur district) a very basic square shrine of dressed sandstone blocks – three walls and a roof with no portico – may in fact be the oldest Hindu shrine standing; for its superficial 5th-century work may be Gupta restoration. But during the 6th century shrines on the plan of cell and portico, complete with surrounding ambulatory passage, are known at Nachna and Bhumara in central India, at Baigram (Dinajpur, Bengal) and Aivalli (Bijapur). The cell, of course, was designed to contain the hallows or icon which received offerings; the rest of the structure must have been for auxiliary ceremonial.

The plan develops. There is a group of early temples which shares the basic pattern of the apsidal Buddhist *chaitya* hall. Two are known at Taxila (2nd century BC). Two other examples are of 5th-century AD date, at Ter (Hyderabad) and Kapotesvara (Krishna district). It has been suggested that these latter may have been actual Buddhist structures adapted to Hindu use. But such an assumption seems unnecessary. For the evidence suggests that the apsidal pattern may well have been a standard

Below right: relief from an Aivalli temple, illustrating Shiva and his wife Uma, with his bull and an adoring ascetic, c. 600 AD. Prince of Wales Museum, Bombay.

Below: Durga temple, at Aivalli, 6th century AD, an early type of Hindu temple, with a pillared walkaround and a later tower over the main shrine, which is apsidal.

Indian secular architectural form in wood, as well as stone, from the earliest historical times. It is possible that the apsidal pattern preceded the cell and portico, though at one important site we can study the two patterns side by side. This is Aivalli, the first capital of the Chalukyas, in the Bijapur district of the Deccan. And here the evidence still stands for the vocabulary of temple elements known in early medieval times, out of which were isolated and developed the two main lines of Hindu temple structure by combination and selection of characteristic features.

Aivalli (Bijapur district) is a small fortified town, the first capital of the Chalukyas. During the early 6th century a large number of temples were built here marking the growth of the dynasty's political power. One type (the Kontgudi group and the "Lad Khan") consists of a square hall fronted by a simple colonnade. The hallows-icon was set against the back wall; and the whole building was built and roofed with huge slabs of stone. Its structural prototypes still stand on the hill behind: megalithic chamber tombs. At Mahua and Parsora there are similar early shrines. On the Lad Khan, and on one of the Kontgudi group, appears the first hint of what was to become the standard system of accumulating the Hindu temple tower by piling up reduplicated and diminishing similar stories. In each case a small distinct chapel stands above the center of the cell roof. The sparse sculpture is relatively crude, but adumbrates later standard iconography. On the pillars of the front gallery are cut the purifying goddesses Ganga and Yamuna; the columns are decorated in relief with lotus roundels, jeweled swags and scrolls; the stone-cut lattices imitate wooden originals. On the Lad Khan, column reliefs of celestial couples actually engaged in the act of love first appear. The sculptural style is descended from that of the Shatavahana caves of the Western Ghats.

The Durga temple is a kind of inversion of the Buddhist apsidal *chaitya* hall. The latter's inner columniation becomes wall to enclose the shrine, its outer

Especially in Cave 3 (dedicated to Vishnu) the great Deccan tradition of Hindu rock sculpture comes into its own. Here the stone blossoms with imagery, from major icons to legendary scenes and bracket figures of godlings. There are also a few fragments of wall painting, Hindu versions of the late Ajanta style. Just like Buddhism in the Western Deccan, Hinduism also developed the art of cave excavation and massive rock sculpture in a series of major monuments.

Cave sites. Two of the most famous are the great Shiva caves on Elephanta island near Bombay and the Dhumar Lena at Ellora, on similar iconographic cross-plans. The Elephanta cave contains a magnificent series of grandiose sculptures. The central icon, within the rock-cut *garbhagriha* (womb house) at the center of the cross, is the Shiva *lingam*. A *lingam* is the image of Shiva's divine procreative energy, a stylized version of the erect male sexual organ, which is the central icon in all Shiva temples. This sexual image sums up much in the mythology of Shiva which relates him to the principles both of terrestrial fertility and of asceticism; for the latter emphasizes restraint and transformation of the sexual energy at the personal level. Shiva also personified Time as the agency both of creation and destruction; and the colossal triple-faced bust icon at Elephanta represents this idea. The proper left face is female, symbolizing God as generative mother; the central face expresses Shiva as immovable sustainer of the cosmos; the right shows the ferocious aspect which the god wears when he appears as destroyer and consumer. Elsewhere in the cave Puranic legends of Shiva's "life history" are illustrated in massive relief panels. A similar iconographic scheme is followed in the Dhumar Lena cave at Ellora, perhaps with slightly less vitality.

Great Trimurti, three-faced icon of Shiva, in the cave temple on the island of Elephanta, off Bombay. To the right is the female creative aspect, to the left the male destroyer. 8th century AD.

wall a surrounding colonnade. The whole is raised on a high plinth. Its sculptures were worked on until well into the 7th century, however, and vary much in style. Its modest storied tower was added later, but follows the convex outline of what became the standard north Indian tower. Such towers also crown the shrine of other temples, notably the Huchimalligudi. And in them a full version of the temple plan also appears: the cell proper extends at one end of the oblong central pillared hall; the portico stands at the other. An ambulatory surrounds the whole.

The Chalukyas moved their capital to the beautiful site of Badami in the 7th century. Here they built a superb city protected by strings of cliff forts, focused around a huge dam which sealed one end of a valley, and irrigated a large area of land. This is a fine early example of the association throughout Indian Asia of dynastic city and hydraulic engineering, which reached its apogee at Angkor. The privileges of a king were firmly based on his responsibility for the fertility of the heartland of his kingdom; and this economic fact was reflected in the concept of kingship and various forms of royal ritual. At Badami there are several architectural works of great importance. First are two temples, the Mahakuteshvara (c. 600) and the Malegitti Shivalaya (c. 700), in which was rehearsed what was to become the full Pallava type of shrine, setting the pattern for all southern India. The main nave hall and cell have relatively plain walls, punctuated by pilasters; the cell is roofed with a superimposed series of smaller shrines, crowned by a dome-like octagonal stone finial. This type was continued at the last of the Chalukya capitals, Pattadakal, in the Virupaksha temple, which was actually built by the conquering Pallavas from the east.

At Badami, however, other important work was done in the four caves excavated during the later 6th century, at the same period as the latest caves at Ajanta (1–5, 21–27).

View of veranda of cave at Badami. The icon is of Vishnu; to the right the columns show opulent striated fruit shapes, and jewel strings incised on their lower faces. 7th century AD.

Ellora is in fact a most important site. It was the capital city of the Rashtrakutas, at first governors under the Chalukyas, but later an independent dynasty. Here many Hindu caves were cut and decorated, as well as some Buddhist and some Jain, between about 640 and the early 10th century. The greatest of them is the Kailashanatha. This is a huge, multi-storied monolith, some 200 × 100 × 100 feet, cut direct from the hillside by successive kings excavating around it an immense quarry. When the quarry was deepened, the shrine gained a lower stage leaving a rock bridge to give access to the first shrine; and in the quarry walls around were cut yet other caves, some dedicated to Vishnu, notably the Dashavatara. But the main shrine evolved around a natural *lingam* in a rock cleft and so was dedicated to Shiva – a splendid example of how reverence for a natural hallows has stimulated the development of a major temple. Its sculptural style displays iconic images of cosmic energy. It too has a few remains of painting here and there. The massive pillars in the Ellora caves are usually one variant or another of one fundamental idea: the flowering vase engaged within the volume. This may be combined with other emblems of opulence – jewel strings and pleated cloths. Together these reflect the notion of celestial fertility and good fortune.

Pallava shrines. In fact the style of the two upper stories of the Kailashanatha is a version of the late Chalukya–early Pallava idea. The Pallavas were a Shaiva dynasty ruling the Tamil southeast coastal region. They seem to have

Right: relief sculpture on the Kailashanatha temple, Ellora, of a half-male, half-female deity (compare page 34), showing vestiges of the paint and plaster with which these rock sculptures were once finished.

Below: view into the quarry in which stands the great monolithic Kailashanatha temple, 8th–9th century. This was carved inside and out from a hillside around a natural *lingam*.

introduced the worship of Shiva into the area, and developed a stone architecture to replace earlier Buddhist brick and limestone stupa building. They evolved a type of shrine which derived from one of the Chalukya patterns at Aivalli. This type became itself the pattern for a number of Hindu shrines constructed in Southeast Asia. For the Pallavas sponsored an overseas colonial expansion, the chief object of which was not conquest but trade. The Indianization of Southeast Asia was probably carried out not by force of arms but by the gradual evolution of trading depots into cities and centers of culture. Local dynasties, often of mixed Indian and local stock, adopted, along with Hindu dynastic culture, Hindu patterns of shrine. Between about 690 and 800 AD these were dominated by Pallava forms. Then it seems that first Rashtrakuta and later on Chola influences played the chief role especially in the Hindu sculptural styles of Java and Cambodia.

Pallava architecture included both caves and structural buildings. The first, dated c. 600 AD, is a cave cut by Mahendravarman I at Mandagapattu (South Arcot), dedicated to the Hindu trinity, Brahma-Shiva-Vishnu. His inscription boasts that this was the first temple ever made in the Tamil country only of stone, without wood or other auxiliary materials. It was the first of a long series of several dozen Pallava caves, some dedicated to Shiva, a few others to Vishnu. They follow a single, slightly evolving pattern. This consists of a largish hall fronted by massive pillars – an expansion of the basic portico – with a

small cell cut into the rear wall to house the icon. At first this cell was shallow; later it became deeper. The pillars developed two characteristic Pallava features. The first was a massive, curvilinear bud-like sprout emerging from each of two sides of the capital. The second was a squatting lion caryatid incorporated into the lower part of the pillar.

The later caves, from c. 630 on, also incorporate an external relief of the facade of a structural temple, together with internal panels of rock-cut narrative relief in a characteristic restrained and beautiful style. Two well-known large versions of this sort of relief are the spreads of legendary scene cut onto the faces of what were sea cliffs at Mahabalipuram (Mamallapuram), the coastal capital of king Mamalla (630–68). Above one of them, and elsewhere nearby, are groups of *rathas*, small monolithic shrines, carved from rock as sculptures of a variety of different types of building: perhaps they were meant as a kind of summary testimonial at the capital to the kinds of temple in use in the Tamil country. A feature of three of the *rathas* also appears on early Cambodian shrines. This is a lintel spanning a niche or an entrance, sculptured as a *makara* monster's face, spouting festoons of foliage.

Three great temples survive following these patterns – one at Mahabalipuram, and at Kanchipuram the Kailashanatha and Vaikuntha Perumal. They each consist internally of a large hall giving onto the cell along its long axis. Externally, the cell is roofed with a pyramidal tower of repeated stories, each a compressed version of the main volume, with rows of miniature blind pavilions added.

Below right: the Shore temple at Mahabalipuram, a very early example of the south Indian type, with a pyramidal tower composed of diminishing, repeated stories; 7th century.

Below: cliff-face relief sculpture at Mahabalipuram, cut by the Pallavas in the 7th century AD, representing an episode in Hindu legend, sometimes called "Arjuna's penance."

Over the main cell rises a higher pyramid crowned by a domed octagonal monolith. The walls are punctuated by plain pilasters, and massive, curved drip-moldings run along the eaves. In addition, the whole shrine is closely surrounded by a heavy wall, into the face of which are let small cells, perhaps as shrines for now vanished icons of lesser deities. The open ambulatory space between temple and wall is conceived as a true roofless architectural volume. This architectural idea was particularly developed at Angkor, in Cambodia, during the 9th and 10th centuries. And it is possible perhaps to recognize faint traces of Pallava sculptural style in the remains of the early altars at Mi Son in the Vietnamese kingdom of Champa.

The Chola period. In the southeast of India, however, new developments took place under the Chola dynasty, who took control of the Tamil country, after the Pallavas had fallen to an early brief-lived episode of Pandya power. In the 8th century the latter cut a single smallish Shiva rock shrine, on the pattern of the Kailashanatha; this is a monolithic image of a structural temple at Kalugumalai (Tinnevelli district). The Chola period, however, is often called the golden age of Tamil culture, beginning about 866. Under Rajaraja I (985–1016) and his successors, until the reign of Kulottunga II (1133–50), the Cholas claimed control of large areas of northern Ceylon, Burma, Malaya, Sumatra and even Bengal. They also maintained trade relations with many other regions. Their power then faded, and by the early 13th century the Pandyas had reasserted themselves, and claimed the whole Tamil region, developing a range of architectural forms which had virtually no influence in Southeast Asia, where the Hindu epoch had already drawn to a close. The Cholas, therefore, were the last southeast Indian dynasty whose art styles fertilized the Southeast Asian.

Great Chola temple, the Brihadishvarasvamin at Tanjore, c. 1006 AD. Its long hall and huge pyramidal shrine contain corridors which bear the remains of early paintings.

While the Cholas were at the height of their power, the whole Tamil region was extremely prosperous. Very large numbers of shrines were built, and more than 70 temple towns were established. There were, however, five great imperial shrines which epitomize the Chola architectural image. The most important were the Brihadishvara temples, dedicated to Shiva, at Tanjore (c. 1006) and Gangaikondasholapuram (1025). The pattern of these shrines derives directly from the Pallava type, but increases vastly the size and gathers the walkaround under the roof. The crowning dome of the Tanjore temple is some 190 feet high. The whole shrine lies under a huge pyramidal tower, and stands on an elevated plinth. The tower consists of diminishing stories made up of rows of miniature false wagon-roof shrines, presenting alternately their side elevations and fan-like facades. The outer wall of the shrine level is articulated as a series of pilastered bays; in the spaces between the bays are huge stone relief icons of aspects of deity; and on either side of the doorway are carved colossal, ferocious guardians leaning on their clubs, a pattern initiated under the Pallavas. Inside, the walkaround encircles the main cell; and at Tanjore the walls of this ambulatory bear the remains of wall paintings, that represent celestial beings and female dancers.

A most important artistic activity under the Cholas was bronze casting. Many superb icons, up to about half-lifesize, are known. They were individually cast and dedicated. Once installed in a shrine as vessels of the divine they became, with increasing age and accumulating reverence, ever more sacred. Some of the finest known were dedicated as personal images by members of royal families, testifying to the sense of identity between a

queen, prince or princess, and the deity represented in the icon. Even small bronzes only a few inches high may embody the superb stylistic imagination of the Chola founders. Of course the art of bronze image making had been widespread in all parts of India before. Buddhist icons have already been mentioned. The Pallavas produced some fine examples of Hindu images. But the special sensuous beauty of Chola work is universally recognized. Perhaps the most striking type is the Shiva Tandavalak-shanam or Nataraja. It shows the god Shiva dancing the cosmic dance within an aureole of flame, four-armed, with streaming hair and one leg cocked up. This particular icon represents the form of Shiva especially sacred to the holy city of Chidambaram.

It is not easy to isolate the influence of Chola art upon the arts of Southeast Asia. For by the 10th century Hindu

Chola bronze icon of a queen as the goddess Parvati. One of the most beautiful female figures in the art of the world, this was cast probably in the 10th century AD. Freer Gallery of Art, Washington.

traditions had long been established overseas, and had developed their own styles. But it is impossible not to recognize an affinity of a general kind between the form of Chola temples and the shrines at the Lara Jonggrang complex dedicated to Shiva that stood at Prabamdanam in Java (c. 900). The relationship is not one of direct descent, but rather of community of idea.

It is not possible, however, to consider Hindu art in Southeast Asia before describing the evolution of the north Indian Hindu temple. For despite the strong links between overseas colonies and the great Tamil trading region, the inland temples of the north nevertheless made their own contribution to the evolution of the Southeast Asian shrine, especially in the conception of the cross-planned temple mountain.

The north Indian temple. In the northern part of India there once stood a vast number of temples. Time, and the ravages especially of Muslim invaders, have devastated dozens of sites where anything up to 80 or 90 temples towered above their reservoirs. The earliest dated dynastic site is at Eran where a rock shrine bears an inscription of 401 AD. It is devastated; but a number of major Vishnu icons survive, including a colossal boar incarnation, and a large standing image in a style clearly derived from Mathura. Other ruined sites of Gupta date are at Shankargarh and Mukundarrah. The finest remains, however, are on the hill at Deogarh, where the major temple is usually dated to c. 600 AD. As well as its entry portico, this shrine had porches on its three other sides, each of which sheltered a superb relief panel of Vaishnava cosmic iconography on the walls of the main shrine, with stories of Rama and Krishna, Vishnu's earthly incarnations, around its high platform. From the various stone remains it is clear that by the Gupta period northern architectural and decorative conventions had become established. These include stocky columns, whose sections are beveled from square to octagon to 16-sided, and whose massive capitals may bear fluting; cell door-frames which were richly carved with foliate scrolls and loving couples, while the center of the lintel was often occupied by a persona of the shrine's deity, with at the feet of the jambs sculptures of the two purifying goddesses of the rivers Ganga and Yamuna; and an inner ceiling of the portico often carved with a lotus, emblem of the unfolding universe.

The most important external architectural feature of any Hindu temple is usually its tower (*shikhara*). This is a tall pyramid of masonry that rises above the main cell. The shapes of their towers and the way they are integrated with the rest are what mainly distinguish the different regional architectural styles. The origin of the *shikhara* is uncertain; it certainly evolved under the Guptas. An inscription dated 437/8 AD at Mandasor refers to shrines that "tower like mountain peaks." The terracotta plaque discovered at Kumrahar, probably from western India and dated to the 2nd century AD, shows a tower very similar to that of the later Buddhist shrine at Bodhgaya. The standing version of this dated probably to the 7th century AD. And a ruined brick tower at Bhitargaon (Kaunpur district, Uttar Pradesh) was probably likewise a straight-sided pyramid – the standard southern shape – with central tiers of arched niches that contain figures running up the center of each side. Both these were built on brick vaults, a technique later abandoned in favor of corbeling, but adopted for the Buddhist architecture of Pagan in Burma. This motive also appears, as we have seen, on the earliest of the Buddhist caves in the Western Deccan; it probably thus gives the tower an essential metaphorical reference to the palaces of heaven. Gradually, however, the pyramidal form was modified as it developed a light convex curve, and the ornament of its faces, while usually retaining some vestige of the arches, was elaborated in different ways.

The fundamental idea, however, seems to have been well established by the 6th century: that the tower represents a heavenly mountain peak, extending up from the surrounding terrain into invisible regions beyond normal human perception. The usual crown, a thick stone disk with gadrooned edge, called the *amala* fruit, represents the root of the manifest world. The stone *shikhara* tower appeared on the cross-planned temple of Deogarh, mentioned above (c. 650), making it the earliest northern example of the north Indian type and the sole example of high Gupta style. Unfortunately, it is now so ruined that its exact shape remains uncertain. As we have already seen, however, the tower had appeared in the south at the Chalukya capitals of Aivalli, Badami and Pattadakal. The curvature of the northern temple tower first appears in a group of brick shrines (late 7th to 8th century) at Sirpur, Rajim and Kharod (Raipur and Bilaspur districts, Madhya Pradesh). Here too the temples have "southern" architectural features, notably the pilasters punctuating the walls of hall and shrine, and the pyramid of similar diminishing pilastered stories which compose the tower – soon to vanish in the north, though it remained in use to cover the temple hall in Orissa; the central vertical band of *chaitya*-arched niches, a non-southern feature, is also present. It seems more than probable that this northern group represents the type of temple upon which the Cambodian shrine was patterned; for the towers of Cambodia have diminishing pilastered stories, curve and niches. The date is about right, although so much has vanished in India itself that it is not possible to say that any of these actual temples were prototypes for anything in the Southeast Asian tradition.

The next stages of the evolution of the curved tower can only be traced in Saurashtra (western India), where multiple niches and miniature towers were gradually compressed into a unified design. By the 9th century, at Roda and Shamlaji (north Gujerat) and at Ghumbi, Pashtar and Miani (Saurashtra), the tall, high-shouldered, curvilinear tower of the full north Indian style had been developed. The arched niches and *amala*-crowns of small subsidiary corner towers had been incorporated as rhythmic punctuations of a single, overall, three-dimensional unit.

Development of the shrine in the 8th and 9th centuries. During the 8th and 9th centuries, all across the old Gupta empire, from Saurashtra in the west, through Rajasthan, eastwards into Bengal and down into Orissa, parallel developments of the Hindu shrine took place. The pattern remained relatively modest: a square cell surmounted by a curvilinear tower, itself crowned by an *amala* and fronted by a large *chaitya* arch, aligned with a hall, either closed with latticed windows, or open like a portico, with pillars supporting its roof. On the three exterior walls of the cell arcaded niches may bear sculptures of subsidiary deities. Varying patterns appear within the overall tower design, all of them based upon rhythmic horizontal and vertical recesses, projections and moldings. From Nareshar and Amrol (Gwalior district), Batesara (Moreva district) and Wadhwan (Gujerat) to Jagatsukh in the Himalayan Kulu valley and Barakar (Bengal) the type blossomed and multiplied. At Ambenari and especially Osia (Rajasthan) beautiful versions were created. At Osia a group of shrines raised on high plinths have elaborately sculptured niches, doorways, columns and capitals. Their sense of proportion and overall unity make this group perhaps the epitome of early medieval northern architecture. Kashmir had evolved by the 9th century a local style obviously based on wooden prototypes (Wangath, Avantipur). This had a large trefoil pillared arch, and a plain pyramidal sloping roof, in two stepped stages, with overhanging eaves. Its pillars and pilasters were lightly fluted, conveying reminiscences of the Greco-Roman prototypes in nearby Gandhara. In modern Pakistan the 9th- and 10th-century temples at Kafirkot and Bilot combine the trefoil arch with an orthodox northern tower.

In Orissa, to the east, a continuous series of stone shrines illustrate beautifully the next evolutionary phase of the northern temple. The transition from the modest early medieval shrine to the high medieval temple can be traced. This is partly because Orissa was never conquered by the Muslims, who elsewhere as they looted and ravaged spent enormous effort on destroying Hindu temples in the regions they conquered, between the 8th and 12th centuries, dismantling them and shattering the images. The temples discussed above are survivors of this whirlwind. In Orissa, however, great temple cities still stand virtually intact, their shrines dating from c. 700 to 1200 AD kept in continuous use and repair to the present day. Around the big shrines cluster smaller ones. Bhuvaneshvara is the most important archaeologically; but Puri, with its colossal 11th-century temple of Jagannatha, is one of the most important religious centers in India.

Between the 8th and 12th centuries AD the Orissan temple developed by an increase in size and height, and the addition of aligned halls and peripheral porticoes. The fundamental layout of shrine and hall remained intact, for it reflected the whole *raison d'être* of the structure. One other characteristic of medieval Hindu architecture is the disparity of scale between the relatively small inner spaces and the exterior mass. For the temple is conceived primarily as a mass of stone – approximating to the monolith – excavated on the inside, and carved on the outside. It is thus a colossal sculpture, rather than an engineered shelter like western or Muslim buildings. This quality of mass and volume is carried through into the detail of figurative and ornamental sculpture.

At Bhuvaneshvara the developing series is initiated by the Parashurameshvara (c. 700). Here the enclosed hall has doors on each side and stone latticed windows, framed with lively animal sculpture, while the whole exterior is covered with shallow relief ornament. It is quite simply roofed with a double tier of sloping stone slabs. The moldings of the tower have a horizontal emphasis. So too have they on the tower of the Vaital Deul (c. 850), though this has a transverse wagon-roof, crowned by a trio of *amalas*. There are others elsewhere in Orissa, as well as other parts of the north, the largest being the Telika Mandir at Gwalior; and the type of shrine seems commonly to have been dedicated to a goddess. At the Vaital Deul and the Parashurameshvara the hall is fully engaged with the cell-tower unit. This unit is structurally disengaged in the Mukteshvara (c. 900), and remains so in later temples; the hall forms a unit in its own right, roofed with its own tiered pyramid. There are sculptures in the outer niches. In the Rajarani (c. 1000) the size has much increased, and around the base of the tower cluster ranges of lesser

The Lingaraja temple complex at Bhuvaneshvara, Orissa, a city full of medieval temples which are still in use. This one dates from just after 1000 AD.

dancing, we may guess that the temple maintained a corps of professional dancing girls, like those described by the early European travelers in India, whose roles also included subsidiary marriage to the main god and prostitution as a sacred rite.

The last of the great Orissan temples dispenses with the dance pavilion. Its huge fundamental shrine and hall are separated from an additional hall by flights of steps. It is the so-called Black Pagoda, in fact a temple to the sun god, on the shore at Konarak, dated to the 1230s. Never finished, in all probability, and lacking most of its upper works, it was to have been on an immense scale, but is now much eroded by windblown sand. It was an extraordinarily original conception. For its high plinth bears 16 colossal sculptures carved around the plinth, which convert the chariot for the sun god, after the pattern of the huge wooden temple cars still used in India to carry sacred images in seasonal procession through their cities. Especially famous are the rows of hundreds of erotic sculptures carved around the plinth, which convert the shrine into a temple of love unparalleled even in India. And on the upper terraces still stand colossal, freestanding figures of female musicians and dancers.

To understand the religious significance of such architectural sculpture we must look to the city of Khajuraho in Bandelkhand, once the capital of the Chandella kings, who built here, between about 950 and 1150, some 80 temples, of which about 30 survive; a few are in very good condition and some have been restored. Most were foundations of the royal dynasty that vanished before the Muslim destroyers; some were built by individuals, and others by guilds of citizens. Some are Jain, their iconography being much like Hindu, save for the central icon which represents the Jina. The elements of the

Sculptured wheel from the great Black Pagoda, or Sun temple, at Konarak, Orissa, left unfinished c. 1240 AD.

towers, like foothills to the main peak of the *shikhara* – also a special feature of more westerly shrines, like some at Khajuraho. Most important, the main cell-tower unit of the Rajarani effloresces with splendid sculpture. In the niches are celestial girls called *Apsaras*, and punctuating the whole are bands of superb foliate sculpture, reflecting the ancient imagery of fertility and abundance. At another once magnificent site in Orissa, Khiching (Mayurbhanj), there once stood a series of small shrines of similar type and date. They are especially notable for the school of sculptors who worked there; the ornament resembles that on the Rajarani, but a group of superb icons of Shiva is unrivaled in medieval Hindu art.

The significance of music and dance.

At Bhuvaneshvara the next stage in evolution appears in two major temples built soon after 1000 AD: the Lingaraja and the Anantavasudeva – the former by far the larger, some 240 feet long, its tower about 160 feet high. In this type, the cell and hall, linked by their corridor, are enlarged. But aligned with them are added an open dance pavilion, its roof supported by ornate inner piers, and an extra closed hall beyond it, each with its own pyramidal tiered roof, those of the main hall and of the extra hall at the Lingaraja being crowned, like the tower, by a colossal stone-cut *amala*. The huge temple of Jagannatha at Puri is a version of this type. The presence of the dance pavilion suggests that the dance had by this time become not only a thoroughly institutional part of temple ceremonial, but also a general spectacle to be seen by a relatively large public. All over India dance pavilions were being built; and it is probable that what we now know only from south India as the Bharat Natyam had then reached a peak of development. Of course temple dancing had normally taken place in the main hall. But where there is substantial provision for

The famous temple Khandariya Mahadeva, at Khajuraho in Bandelkhand, where there were once more than 80 temples. This one, c. 1000 AD, epitomizes the image of temple as cosmic mountain.

architecture are superbly integrated as comprehensive images of the cosmic mountain, Mount Meru. From the main pinnacle centered above the shrine cell, symbolizing the supernal mountain which is the axis of the world, the clustered lesser peaks run down over roofs of hall, porch, and surrounding ambulatory with its projecting porticoes. The floor levels of all these stand on a high plinth, which has an elaborately recessed ground plan, and is approached by a long stairway. The faces of the plinth bear sculptured scenes of religious events enacted on earth, notably scenes from the epics which feature incarnations of the high gods. The interiors, with their elaborate pillars and complex ceilings, are as lavishly carved as the exteriors. Around the outside of the structure, at the level of the cell and hall, run bands of figure sculpture representing gods and celestial beings. These are the heaven bands, raised above the level of earth, slung like garlands around the cosmic mountain, a kind of outward efflorescence of the deity residing in the cell who is the Seed of Being within the womb house, fertilizing the mass of stone. Among the celestial figures are major and minor deities, musicians, dancers and the beautiful heavenly girls called *Apsaras* whom legend describes as "full of unassuageable sexual desire." The temples are carved with scenes of the erotic delights that are shared with them by sages and warriors who have gained heaven. For the Indian conception of heaven, formed in the heroic period of the epics, was as a place of joy and pleasure. From the highest religious point of view, of course, the heavens were not a final goal. But the thought that there was a higher realm, where life was vastly long, and where all the pleasures known on earth could be enjoyed to the full, unspoiled by the uncomfortable realities of life, exercised a powerful pull towards religion in the imaginations of ordinary men. It is also likely that there was a symbolic connection between the sculpted erotic images and the pleasurable activities of the actual dancing girls at the greater shrines. Certainly, as we shall see, music and dancing as human arts were considered reflections on a lower plane of ideal celestial arts. And this conception exercised an important influence upon the aesthetic theories according to which human music and dancing were developed and valued. Every king regarded it as an essential part of his royal duty and privilege to maintain a corps of musicians and dancers, whose skill contributed to his sense of divine glory. This institution, transmitted to Southeast Asia, was the origin of the great styles of music and dance of Cambodia, Java and Bali, which survive today in Indonesia, but have probably now vanished from Cambodia.

Final flowering in India. Variants of this classic high medieval northern temple type of various dates survive in many parts of western India, Rajasthan, central India, and even in the rather isolated southern state of Mysore. Western temples develop particularly complex surface decoration; elaborate recesses and moldings punctuate the

Erotic sculptures at Khajuraho represent the joys of heaven, and are carved at the level of the main shrine. The girls are *Apsaras*, celestial beauties, c. 1000 A.D.

plinths, together with relief friezes of, for example, lion heads, elephants and horsemen. Around the heaven bands small deities framed in embossed niches multiply; and narrative reliefs of popular stories, animals, birds, dwarfs, teachers and students proliferate. Inside, brackets are pierced into undulating forms. Door frames and inner pillars burgeon with small details of dance and music. Ceilings are pierced and carved into a multitude of flame, lotus and bud shapes. Perhaps the epitome of this style was the Solanki dynasty Sun temple at Modhera in Gujarat (11th century) of which the dance pavilion still stands with its encrusted pillars, above a stupendous stepped tank. At Kiradu (Marwar) the ornate pillars of another 11th-century hall still stand. At Mount Abu, in Rajasthan, a similar style of architecture and sculpture, executed in white marble, has continued down to the present day, applied principally to Jain temples.

In central India a series of temples were cut by the Paramaras of Malwa in the 11th century, the ground plans of whose plinths developed away from the rectangular towards the star-shaped. The interiors were also much elaborated. This style prompted developments further south, in the Deccan in the 12th and 13th centuries under the later western Chalukyas (Dharwar, Gadag, Haveri) and especially the Kakatiyas (Warangal, Hanamkonda, Palampet). The interiors are richly and minutely carved in hard stone, the pillars often incorporating disks deeply molded as if turned on a lathe; the figure sculpture outside is very sparse, but inside elaborate, with pierced brackets ornamented with *Apsaras*. Perhaps the most fantastic development of this mode was in Mysore, where between the 12th and 14th centuries under the Hoyshalas an extraordinary series of dark stone shrines were built, following – surprisingly – a northern type (e.g. at Belur, Halebid, Somnathpur). Here are star-shaped plans, or multiple cells dedicated to different deities sharing the same hall and plinth. But the outstanding feature of Hoyshala art is the extraordinary proliferation of deeply undercut decorative foliate ornament, all over the exterior heaven bands and the interior of the building. The somewhat puddingy figures may be so heavily loaded with ornaments that they blend with their niches. The series of epic and narrative legends carved around the plinths of some of the Hoyshala temples are the most extensive in India.

While these styles were flourishing in the Deccan, the Muslims were invading and devastating the north. The great kingdoms that had sponsored building and supported the temples were destroyed, most being replaced by warring Muslim sultanates. Only here and there did temples occasionally arise where modest Hindu dynasties or Jain communities asserted some independence. At

Detail of sculpture on a Hoyshala temple at Halebid, Mysore, 13th century. The deeply undercut elaborate ornament parallels the complexity of the temple plans, and aims at an effect of stunning exuberance.

Chitor (Rajasthan) a 15th-century Tower of Victory was erected, in a late version of an earlier style. At Ranakpur, also in the 15th century, some Jaina temples were built. But their aesthetic impetus had died, along with the necessary command of resources. Only in the far south did Hindu temple architecture continue to flourish, on an ever more grandiose scale, virtually into modern times.

Hinduism in Southeast Asia. Hinduism depends for its ritual as we have seen upon the caste of Brahmans who alone are qualified to act as priests and come into contact with the divine forces that dwell in icons of great gods. When Brahman families established themselves in the Indian trading colonies of Southeast Asia, Hinduism installed itself. There were Hindu shrines in countries which later became exclusively Buddhist during the early and still scantily documented periods of their history, for example the Mon kingdoms of lower Burma and Thailand. But there were three regions in particular where Hinduism flourished especially – Java, Cambodia and South Vietnam. Here the evolution matched almost exactly in date the flowering of Hindu architecture in India, running from relatively modest beginnings in the 6th century to its apogee in the 12th. So it is possible to see the Hindu temples of these regions as branches of the same cultural phenomenon.

Java. In Java there had been Indianized principalities since the 1st or 2nd century AD. They may have been Buddhist. But when in the 7th century a central Javanese dynasty adopted a south Indian Pallava form of script, they also adopted the worship of the chief Pallava deity, Shiva. The earliest Hindu shrines to survive in Java were the work of this dynasty, which then retreated to east Java before about 780 under pressure from a new, mainly Buddhist dynasty, the Shailendra. They built a group of shrines on the Djieng plateau, a high, volcanic region where there are sulfur springs and lakes. There seems little doubt that Shiva was identified with the indwelling spirit of the whole massif, long familiar to the people, and its volcanic activity was interpreted as the manifestation of Shiva's destructive power. There are other volcanic areas in Java also containing shrines sacred to Shiva (e.g. Mt Ungaran, Mt Sendara). Thus the normal Hindu process of giving to local powers the names and identities of the great gods was naturalized in Indonesia.

The earliest temples to survive on the Djieng plateau are normal Hindu shrines (e.g. Chandi Puntadewa), single-celled, having only a small entry porch without pillars, and roofed with only one or two diminishing stories that repeat the form of the cell. Their outstanding architectural features are: first, a characteristic hood-molding over doorways and image niches, carved with the likeness of a monster head on the lintel, that spews out foliage down both jambs which terminates at their feet in other scrolled monster shapes – certainly a fertility symbolism; second,

Hindu shrine, part of the Prambanam complex built about 900 AD in central Java by the Shailendra dynasty.

scroll-curved balustrades to the approach stairs; and third, a miniature pavilion at the top corner of each story. It is impossible to match this pattern of shrine precisely with any Indian prototype. So it is more than likely that the Javanese stone Hindu buildings we know were by no means the earliest put up in Indonesia, and that there may also have been stylistic influences passed on to them from work as yet unknown in neighboring regions of Southeast Asia.

There are, however, a few shrines of a slightly different pattern in the Djieng, for example Chandi Bima, which is far closer to Indian prototypes. This has no approach stair, but is crowned by a tall pyramidal storied tower, with vertical bands of arches running up the center of each face, and at the corner of each story engaged pillar stubs with fluted capitals that are very close in type to some at Chalukyan Badami. All these early shrines, however, share the general Indonesian custom of dispensing altogether with genuinely structural pillars.

A few iconic sculptures that survive from this earliest Javanese period are also in an idiosyncratic and highly developed style. One group of Hindu deities especially, from the ruined Chandi Banon dedicated to Shiva, shows some affinities with Pallava sculpture; but their majestically achieved forms are unequivocally Indonesian.

The Shailendra dynasty, which had taken over central Java and built the great series of Buddhist monuments described in the previous chapter, did build one colossal Hindu complex, Lara Jonggrang at Prambanan, about 900. It thus corresponds roughly in date with the rise of the Chola power in southeast India. Once 232 temples stood in the great walled courtyard. The heart of the complex is a row of three shrines dedicated to the three persons of the Hindu trinity: Shiva at the center, flanked by Vishnu and Brahma. The central Shiva shrine is some 120 feet high. It stands on a high plinth that supports a close processional pathway lined with splendid relief sculpture of Hindu legend, especially of the epic *Ramayana* which has continually supplied the main themes for Indonesian dance drama. The shrines are pyramidal; their chambers have relatively plain walls paneled by pilasters, somewhat in Chola vein. The towers, however, are completely original. Their tiers bear rows of gadrooned miniature stupas, derived of course from earlier Shailendra Buddhist architecture.

After the eclipse of the Shailendra a succession of dynasties ruled from centers in eastern Java, fundamentally Hindu, but also combining Buddhist elements into their cult. Between the 10th century and the 15th a whole series of shrines, royal rock tombs and sacred bathing places at volcanic springs were made. The shrines were square cells supported by heavy molded plinths and topped by massive pyramidal towers (e.g. Chandi Kidal, 13th century); the rock tombs sometimes have low-relief sculpture reproducing such *chandis* on their facades. The relief sculpture on the shrines becomes steadily closer in appearance to the stylized puppets still used in Wayang performances. Music, dance and puppetry survive as living arts in Java. The large iconic sculptures, once set up in the shrines and at the bathing places, preserve a splendid power. Two of the finest are the high god Vishnu riding his tempestuous bird-like vehicle, Garuda, from Belahan, perhaps a dedicatory image of King Airlangga (died c. 1049); and an elephant-headed Ganesha, god of wealth, from Blitar (13th century?), whose back is carved with an image of death.

After the arrival of Islam in the 14th century Hinduism was eliminated in Java. It survived, however, in the small island of Bali until the present; and a whole popular culture has survived with it. This includes an architecture of shrines belonging to family groups, which is based on courtyards with spirit houses and split-*chandi* gateways, elaborate seasonal ceremonies and domestic rituals, a superb tradition of dance with spiritual possession, and visual arts based upon Wayang conventions, many of them now adapted to the tourist market.

Indochina. Thus Hinduism with its monuments has survived in one part of Southeast Asia into modern times. Its greatest artistic splendor, however, coincided almost exactly in time with perhaps the greatest flowering of

Chandi Kidal, an east Javanese shrine with a massive, overhanging roof tower, of the mid-13th century.

Hindu art in the whole of Southeast Asia, under the Khmer in Indochina. There, between the 9th and the 12th centuries, a series of shrines was constructed of a splendor probably unrivaled in India itself. The basis of this art was laid during the evolution of the two successive earlier kingdoms on the Mekong river, called by Chinese historians Funan and Chen-la. It was natural that their dynasties should follow Hindu traditions, since the founder of the first kingdom of Funan was said to be a Brahman, who married a local princess; although, as we have seen, Buddhism was by no means unknown. Funan was already in existence during the 1st century AD, but its first surviving major works of art – some superb stone icons – date to the 6th century; and a series of similar sculptures continues through the Chen-la epoch into the 9th century when the Khmer took control of the region.

These stone icons were most likely housed in wooden or brick shrines; but no such structure is known to survive. However, a number of finely worked stone lintels are known, symbolically important members which probably once supported the door frames of such shrines. They are carved on their faces with lobed or arched relief designs; monsters at each end spew swags of jewels and scrolled foliage, sometimes interspersed with figures. The icons represent the main deities of Hinduism, Shiva and Vishnu, and occasionally a figure which combines the attributes of both, called Hari-Hara. There are also some icons of opulent goddesses. It is possible to discern an evolutionary sequence among them: some of the earliest resemble quite closely in style 4th- and 5th-century images from Mathura in western India; others resemble the polished style of Gupta sculpture, for example at Deogarh. It is, in fact, possible that Indian craftsmen traveled to Indochina. But the latest and finest images are in a superb sophisticated style unique to the region, which laid the foundations for the succeeding art of Khmer stone carving.

The first step towards Khmer imperial art was taken by the king known as Jayavarman, who in 802 established his capital at Phnom Kulen – a mountain. The peoples of Southeast Asia have always tended to believe that spiritual beings inhabit mountain tops, and could be approached there by intermediaries such as shamans. This king was therefore adapting local religious tradition to his state purpose. After Angkor on the river plain became the capital, during the reign of Indravarman I (877–89), all the huge temples built there by successive Khmer rulers were raised on high plinths, combining the Hindu image of the cosmic mountain at the center of the universe with the Southeast Asian mountain-spirit tradition. There was almost certainly some influence on their conception from the great Javanese site of Borobudur; for there had long been dynastic relations between the rulers of Cambodia and the Shailendra of central Java.

The city of Angkor. Angkor was not only a city. It was conceived by Indravarman's engineers as the center of a vast hydrological project which radically increased the fertility of the Cambodian plain, by catching and controlling the seasonal floods of the waters flowing into the Great Lake (Tonle-sap). Angkor was laid out on a rectangular grid of canals, moats and watercourses and included enormous artificial rectangular reservoirs. The land excavated to make these was heaped up to construct the towering temples built by successive kings. The irrigation system radiating from the reservoirs of Angkor watered an unprecedented area of rice paddy. The empire

of which it was the capital became rich and extensive, and the city was regarded with religious reverence. Its life-giving water was under the control of the king, and the king was thus in a very special sense the intermediary between heaven, source of the fertilizing waters, and earth, the producer of wealth. Records suggest that the king, as personation of his god, would ritually celebrate with his queens, as personations of the land, the marriage of heaven and earth in the shrine at the summit of his temple mountain. Popular versions of such a ceremony were carried on until recently in Indochina. It is more than likely, although the evidence is not decisive, that rites at least analogous, though perhaps more complex, were performed by Indian rulers in India, in accordance with the Indian theory of kingship. The Khmer king expected after death to be united with his patron deity, and dedicatory statues would be set up in his personal shrine to testify to this union.

The series of temples at Angkor follow a basic pattern, although they vary considerably in size and magnificence. The earliest are of brick faced with stucco, the later of stone, elaborately carved. Kings and their families often built several; and there were a few in and around the city also dedicated by important private individuals. One of these last is also perhaps the most beautiful – Banteai Srei (c. 960). Generally speaking, the later royal temples are the largest, as each king strove to surpass his predecessors. And as time went on, and available space within the city became short, earlier temples were destroyed to make room for later. The last temples of all, Angkor Wat, and the Buddhist Thom, with its Bayon, are of quite stupendous and unparalleled size.

The basic pattern is relatively simple. Within a rectangular walled enclosure at ground level the artificial mountain rises in terraces, square or rectangular in plan, often walled. Within the walls at ground level or on the terraces may be cloisters. On the topmost terrace stands either a single main shrine, or a quincunx arrangement of five, containing icons, either the *lingam* of Shiva or figure sculptures of gods. Within the enclosure or on the terraces may stand other shrines to other deities, as well as long occasional buildings such as libraries and administrative offices. The main staircase runs from the center of the eastern side up the terraces through a series of gateways towards the door of the main shrine; and there may be other staircases up the other sides. The cells themselves are usually cubical volumes, their corners sometimes vertically recessed, having either one door with an unpillared entrance porch, or one on each of the four sides. Above the lintels elaborately carved decorative pediments symbolize the rainbow bridge between heaven and earth. At the foot and eaves of the cell volume are moldings; above rises a tower, composed of tiers of diminishing compressed versions of the cell-story, running to a point. These, on the later shrines, notably the Wat, are arranged to give the whole tower a beautiful bud-like curve. Up each face runs a band of antefix arches, derived from the Indian bands of *chaitya* arches on a few temples in Madhya Pradesh. The exteriors of the shrines, and of many other structures, may carry friezes and panels of relief sculpture; always there is much scrolled foliage, often with figures of celestial beings – deities and *Apsaras* – in decorative framed niches. And on the later large stone monuments are series of relief illustrations of Hindu legend. Each temple thus becomes an image of the complete mythical Hindu cosmos.

The series of the chief known temple mountains runs from the earliest, the Preah-ko, at Roluos near Angkor, which was completed about 879. The first at Angkor itself is the Bakong (881). The Bakheng, begun in 893, had 108 tower shrines on its terraces. The series includes the Pre-Rup (dedicated 961) which was probably the first such temple meant as a dwelling for the deified spirit of a dead king. Similar in date is the beautifully ornamented Banteai Srei, which contained a superb and massive icon of Shiva seated with his wife Uma on one knee. The huge Baphuon (1050–66) was about 1450 × 425 feet but is unfortunately almost completely destroyed. It was conceptually the immediate prototype for the Wat, which was built by Suryavarman II early in the 12th century and is the culmination of the whole series.

Below right: orchestra and group of dancers in front of Balinese temple Legong Kraton. In Bali a version of Hindu culture survives entire and unified; dance and temple belong together.

Below: a late 13th-century Cham shrine, the Po Klaung Garai, a relatively complete structure.

The Wat is 1,700 × 1,550 yards. Around its outer wall runs a vast cloister. Its open colonnade on the first terrace contains over a mile of continuous narrative relief sculpture, 6 feet high, in a vivid and idiosyncratic style. The full-round figures, on the other hand, notably the guardians on the terraces, are relatively rigid and lacking in life. The architectural conception, however, with its superbly articulated and decorated inner volumes, varied roof types, moldings and stone paneling, is an unrivaled achievement. The central shrine symbolizes the hub of the universe; 4 miles of moat 590 feet wide enclose the whole. Along the great causeway which approaches it from the west (not the east, as usual) are enormous balustrades in the likeness of serpents – emblems of cosmic fertility. The elaborate western gate complex indicates that this was meant as the mortuary shrine of its builder.

Cham art in Vietnam. The colossal effort required of the people, and of the economy of the kingdom, to complete the Wat seems to have exhausted their resources. At any rate, after Suryavarman died, the Cham, of the neighboring kingdom of Champa, seized Angkor (1177) and sacked it. They were later repulsed; but no more great Hindu shrines were built in Angkor. The dynasties of the

Cham had always lived a precarious existence in Vietnam, in the shadow of the Khmer, and pressed by the Sinicized Vietnamese from the north. They had, however, developed a dynastic Hindu art of their own, which was no mere imitation of the Khmer, although it owed much to the art of Chen-la. Before 980 their sacred capital had been at Mi Son in the northern part of their kingdom. But they were then forced by the Vietnamese to retreat, to make their southern capital at Binh Dinh in 1169. At both sites they built series of modest dynastic temples, as well as other shrines in other cities. Much archaeological investigation, however, remains to be done in the Cham terrain.

The earliest Cham art so far known dates probably to the 7th century when the king was a scion of the ruling family of Chen-la. The ruins of many temples built in Mi Son, before the move, suggest that their pattern was a single cell with portico and tower. The doorways open to the west with blind arcades on the other sides. These arcades are narrowly framed in pilasters which give a strong vertical emphasis to the exterior. The roof of the tower was again of diminishing stories, with a small pavilion at the center of the side at each level. The outstanding feature of the art was the superbly carved stone altar tables which seem to have supported icons within the cells – an un-Indian feature, sometimes said to have been derived from a Chinese pattern. But the actual style of much of the ornamental carving and figure sculpture suggests strong natural affinities with the art of Chen-la. But it has a sweetness and grace unlike any other art we know well. Some superb work has been excavated, but alongside the more sophisticated creations another style existed, perhaps executed by local rather than Cambodian artists. This appears in architectural decor – ornamental lions and monster heads, for example. In the later 9th century it seems to have taken over even for major icons. This style is marked by massive, block-like figure volumes, and heavy worm-like foliage ornament in which there seems to be more than an echo of the Bronze Age Dong-son ornamental style.

The 12th-century shrines at Binh Dinh, notably those still standing called the Silver Towers, are versions of the older Cham style, with pointed horsehoe *chaitya* arches, and the formal plasticity of older architectural projections reduced to bands of molding. Some are still beautiful. But the defeat by the Khmer in 1145 had much reduced the status of the Cham kingdom. Icons lost their Indianized finesse, and became relatively crude and massive. By the later 14th century the Hindu concept of divine kingship had died in Champa, as it already had in other parts of Southeast Asia – save for Bali – and yielded its place to a fundamentalist version of Hinayana Buddhism.

One of the superb Chen-la type of iconic stone sculptures from Cambodia, the Goddess of Koh Krieng, c. 800 AD. The continuity of surface is almost total.

The City of Angkor

Angkor was for long a fascinating mystery to Europeans. This vast city, lost in the jungle of Cambodia, its ruins inhabited by a small community of monks, had once been the center of a huge empire, between c. 880 AD and the 13th century. It had been visited in the 16th century by a Portuguese missionary called Antonio de la Magdalena; but his account remained unpublished, rumor alone circulating. Then in 1860 a French naturalist, H. Mouhot, reached Angkor, and wrote about it in the press. In 1866 the Scot John Thomson photographed it, and the mystery, far from being diminished by accurate information, was only increased. For the remains at Angkor, as they were investigated by the French, turned out to be those of the largest complete complex ever created by man before modern times. Even today excavation is by no means complete. The jungle waits to reestablish its grip on the colossal stone structures, as on the gate of the Ta Som shrine here shown.

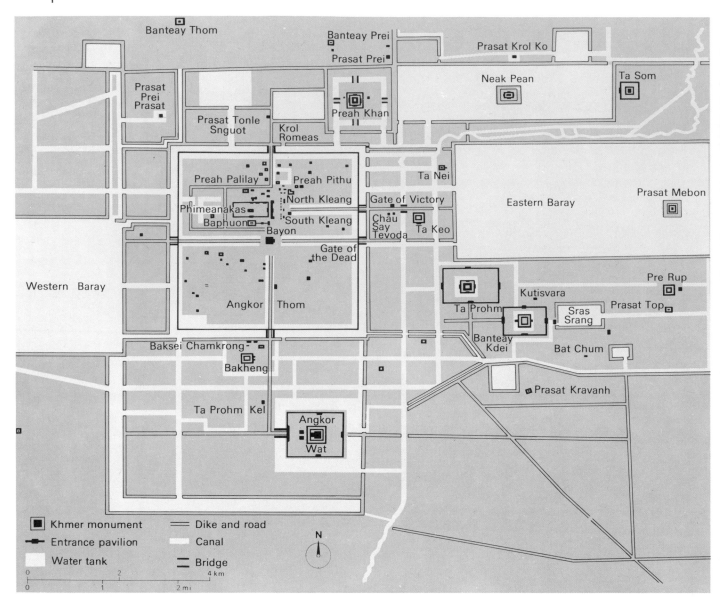

Banteay Thom

Banteay Prei
Prasat Prei

Prasat Krol Ko

Neak Pean

Ta Som

Prasat
Prei
Prasat

Prasat Tonle
Snguot

Krol
Romeas

Preah Khan

Ta Nei

Eastern Baray

Prasat Mebon

Preah Palilay

Preah Pithu

North Kleang

Phimeanakas

Gate of Victory

Baphuon

South Kleang

Bayon

Chau
Say
Tevoda

Ta Keo

Western Baray

Gate of
the Dead

Pre Rup

Ta Prohm

Kutisvara

Prasat Top

Angkor Thom

Sras
Srang

Baksei Chamkrong

Banteay
Kdei

Bakheng

Bat Chum

Ta Prohm Kel

Prasat Kravanh

Angkor
Wat

N

■ Khmer monument   ═ Dike and road

▬■ Entrance pavilion   ▢ Canal

▢ Water tank   ═ Bridge

0   2   4 km
0   1   2 mi

Above: the vast scale of Angkor will be clear from this map. Essentially the city was the sacred focus of an immense hydrological system, which controlled the seasonal flood waters by retaining them in reservoirs, called Barays, and releasing them through a network of canals and channels into the surrounding rice-growing terrain. Each ruler of the Khmer empire built his own temple mountain, which was his link with the gods, on a larger scale than his predecessors. To build the last two, the Wat, and the Thom with its Bayon, earlier parts of the city had to be destroyed. Each king would perform the required seasonal ceremonies in his own shrine, to ensure the fertility of the land. The earliest surviving temples are the Bakong (c. 881) and the Bakheng (c. 893)

which had 108 tower shrines on its terraces around the central pyramid.

Right: Banteai Srei is perhaps the most beautiful work of Khmer architecture, founded 12 miles from Angkor in the late 10th century by a Brahman of royal descent. Its many auxiliary buildings, all of sandstone, are adorned with the most profuse ornamental and figurative sculpture. It too is a terraced mountain shrine. This colossal divine monkey shows how free-standing icons were ranged on the terraces of Khmer temples; many of them have been lost, however.

Above: view of the Ta Keo, c. 1020, the chief temple built by the great emperor Suryavarman (d. 1050). It was probably the first of the great personal temple mountains in Angkor to be built entirely of stone.

Left: this is a relief from one of the gable antefixes of Banteai Srei, illustrating a Hindu legend especially associated with mountains. It represents the high god Shiva sitting with his wife Parvati on the summit of Mount Kailasha. Beneath it is the demon Ravana who shakes the mountain, but Shiva stills it with the touch of his foot.

Right: one of the celestial girls, *Apsaras*, carved on Banteai Srei, surrounded by a frame of foliage which symbolizes the fertility it is the temple's function to induce.

Above: these celestial girls, *Apsaras*, carved on a wall of the Wat, are clothed and have their hair coiffed in the height of Khmer chic. They look much as the Khmer royal dancers must have looked.

Left: Angkor Wat is the largest individual structure at Angkor. It is Suryavarman II's personal temple mountain, built in the early 12th century, the crowning achievement of Khmer architecture. It is 1,700 yards long and 1,550 yards wide, surrounded by a vast external cloister. It opens to the west along a magnificent causeway lined with balustrades in the form of colossal serpents, emblems of the fertilizing waters. The western gate complex is nearly as large as the main shrines. There are three principal enclosed terraces. *Above* is a view across the moat; *below* an aerial view into the complex of buildings.

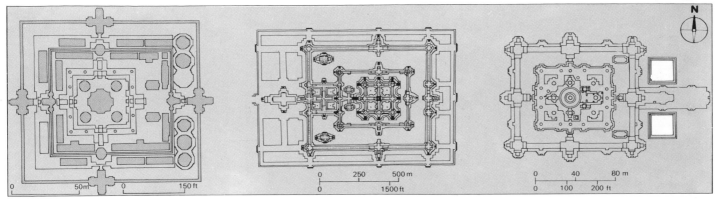

Above: this set of plans, chronologically arranged, of temple mountains shows how the conception evolved. The mountain was always felt in Southeast Asia to be the most suitable place from which to establish contact with the gods, and most shrines incorporate the idea of the mountain. The shrines are left to right the Ta Keo, c. 1020, the Wat, early 12th century, and the Bayon, c. 1200.

Right: relief sculpture representing a battle between the Khmer and the Cham. The open colonnaded gallery on the first story of the Wat contains over a mile of such relief sculpture, some 6 feet high.

Below right: this elephant terrace within the Thom was probably a ceremonial platform upon which the king would appear.

Below and left: one of the structures on the terraces of the Wat was a library. Behind it rises the main shrine. These pictures illustrate how the Wat is an architecture of open spaces as much as of enclosed volumes, a feature probably derived from southeast India.

Above: part of one of the mile-long balustrades running north and south from the Thom, which represent the gods pulling on the body of the cosmic snake, using it as a churning rope to twirl the central mountain Bayon, so churning the worlds like butter out of the originating ocean of milk.

Above left: the lake shrine of Neak Pean was one of the many symbolic buildings put up by Jayavarman VII, the last great emperor of the Khmer, whose city was the Thom, and whose temple mountain was the Bayon. He died, aged over 60, in 1219, after thirty-odd years of warfare and feverish building. He adopted Buddhism as his state religion.

Left: this gateway to the city of the Thom displays the colossal masks of the Bodhisattva, Lord of the Worlds, whom Jayavarman adopted as his patron deity. They have become the symbol of Angkor, although in fact they are work of its last, perhaps declining, phase. The Thom is surrounded by 10 miles of moats, and contains more stone – and that dressed – than all the Egyptian pyramids together.

6. The Themes of Indian Art

The monuments described in the two previous chapters were made to express certain fundamental ideas. Their architecture quite consciously sought to embody them in physical shape according to accepted symbolic formulae. Western readers, whose minds are not prepared to receive these ideas in their full depth, may well find it easiest to approach them through the avenue of representational and decorative arts. For it is in these that the fundamental ideas are worked out through the detail of human experience, which all men to some extent share.

Unity and immensity in Indian culture. There are two dominant intuitions underlying Indian culture: the first is unity, the One; the second immensity. All the manifestations of idea, in verbal and material form, represent methods for developing in detail and reconciling these two intuitions. In addition, religion, philosophy, society and art are so much reflections of each other that it is impossible to separate them in the way European thought is accustomed to doing. This effect is itself produced by the Indian urge towards unity; and all the conceptual discoveries of Indian thought, all the aesthetic achievements of Indian culture, remained devoted to its overriding vision of the cosmos and life as an interdependent whole, a unity embraced by a single self or mind, which is also the stuff out of which in their immensity the infinite cycles of the cosmos are woven. The structural patterns of Sanskrit and the Sanskritic languages, with the works composed in them; the organization of society according to what developed into the caste system; the subject matter and the structural principles of the arts – all reflect the two polar themes. The most powerful human emotions were harnessed for their realization.

Indian conceptions of society were an expression of the

Previous page: colossal head of Shiva, from Udaipur, 8th century AD, carved of black basalt with gilded hair; earrings and crest jewel contain goddesses. Victoria Hall Museum, Udaipur.

Below: pottery figures of deities at the Iyanera temple, Madras.

complementary themes. But behind them lies another conception which was always taken completely for granted in India by all her native religions and philosophies: reincarnation. This is often a stumbling block to the European in his attempts to approach Indian realities; for his own implicit faith (based, of necessity, on no evidence) is that each "life" is unique and self-contained. India accepted very early in her history, by about the 6th century BC, that if the individual life of man or any other creature was to have any meaning, in the face of the intuition of immensity, the "uniqueness" theory was inadequate. In fact the concept of reincarnation seems to be of great antiquity and to have existed widely even in archaic Europe. To this day research suggests that a surprisingly large percentage of the population of the western world believe in it, without ever having heard it taught institutionally.

The doctrine of karma. Briefly, reincarnation recognizes that a living being is not simply the animal within a single skin, whose duration is limited by the discernible span of time from its birth to its death. It sees the real being as a continuing entity whose duration includes many lives in different living forms, each one of which it wears and changes as a man changes his suits of clothes, wearing each for a time only. Precisely what the continuing entity is, is not defined. A simple causal explanation of the way one life takes up from another is offered by the doctrine of *karma*. This teaches that the residual effects of one life generate a fresh life with characteristics conditioned by the first. But the underlying idea of total unity sets all such lives in a larger perspective, identifying them as merely apparent multiplicities within worlds of time and succession that are partitions within the great whole. The vista of time embraced by the duration of any of the series of reincarnations is colossal – many tens of thousands of years. And since each such real being passes through many different life forms, every Indian is conscious in a very personal way of an intimate relationship between all the orders of living creatures.

Very early (by about the 2nd century AD) India had envisioned universes numberless as the grains of sand in the banks of the Ganga. In developing this insight into vast number and infinity she long anticipated western astronomical thought. Buddhist literature (for example the 2nd-century AD *Saddharmapundarika* and 4th-century *Avatamsakasutra*) saw these numberless universes as appearing and disappearing within the hair-pores of the transcendent Buddha principle. Hindu literature (for example the 2nd-century AD *Bhagavad-gita* or 7th-century *Markandeya Purana*) saw them succeeding each other in colossal cyclic ages, each lasting no longer on the divine time scale than one blinking of the eyelids of supernal deity. The two images, the Buddhist and the Hindu, reconcile the intuition of infinity with that of unity, and both of these with human experience of selfhood. For only

Two ascetics carrying their personal water-pots in the Gandhara schist carving of the 2nd century AD (Museo Nazionale d'Arte Orientale, Rome) match the modern ascetic, a follower of Shiva, who walks in a modern Calcutta street in front of a small city shrine.

the idea of reincarnation could set individual life into any valid relationship with such a vision of virtual infinity. And Indian religions taught that the individual self was capable of attaining such infinity as a function of its own unity. This is an extremely difficult thought to grasp, and to present. It gave to Indian society its unique fundamental premise.

This premise, from the everyday point of view, was that every living being had not one but many chances of self-fulfillment. And since each such being was, so to speak, only wearing a certain form for a period of time, then the function of society was to provide a framework within which the successive lives might be led, in a variety of forms, if possible in an ascending series. There were specific moral undertones; for the form any being happened to be wearing at any given time represented the stage the reincarnating entity had earned. And this was the product of the value of all the past deeds of that entity – its *karma*. Thus a being with a high social status embodied an entity buoyed up by a substantial backlog of good *karma*. To be born a Brahman was not "the luck of the draw" but represented the fruit of much past virtue. To be born to suffering was not intrinsically bad; for it was the swiftest way to work out evil *karma*, and so help redeem oneself towards better future births. Hence bad fortune itself could be beneficial to the incarnating entity. This is the reason why the Buddhist monk and the Bodhisattva-in-the-making were always referred to as "well born" or "of good family," implying that much good *karma* contributed to his status. The social structure was thus intimately related to an interwoven structure of implicit and explicit beliefs. The gradual consolidation of the caste system into the form recognizable today took place probably between the 2nd century BC and the 4th or 5th century AD, long after the metaphysical principles by which it was justified had been formulated. The system's integrity thus reflected the underlying Indian search for unity; it did not precede it, and it was not the only manifestation in social terms of the underlying conceptions.

The ultimate principle of unity is always invoked in every human activity, and its expression is the aim of all systematic knowledge. This gives to every Indian philosophy or science a kind of hierarchical structure. Source and goal are always the same. Hinduism was continually concerned with building pathways towards a positive intuition of the Brahman, the one reality of which all lesser realities are parts or subsidiary functions; while Buddhism devoted itself to gathering the necessary merit for, and clearing away obstacles to, enlightenment, which was identity with an unspeakable, unknowable, Buddha principle. Both religions used the arts to achieve their ends, in different ways; but they shared a common inheritance of legend and symbolic imagery. Even the Buddha was not averse to ensnaring his brother Nanda to become a monk by first arousing his desire for heaven by showing him the *Apsaras*.

Above: erotic sculpture in the heaven bands of the Khandariya Mahadeva temple, Khajuraho, executed with sensuous, softly inflated forms c. 1000 AD, illustrates blissful life in the higher realms.

Below: figure of a goddess carved on a Chola temple at Kumbakonam, in south India, c. 1100 AD.

The role of unity in art. In fact, as has been suggested, it is a mistake to believe that all art in India was overtly religious. We have seen that an enormous quantity of poetry and drama was composed for the enjoyment of courtiers, from all epochs, and of popular poetry for the people. We do not know directly, but we can infer, from literary references and the characteristics of the art that does survive, the existence of a correspondingly large quantity of secular sculpture and painting. Indeed it is probable that a medieval Indian town or city contained more visual art owned by more people than any comparable city anywhere else on earth. And yet this art, in its methods of construction and its technical resources, reflected yet again the two fundamental intuitions, which were connected, as by an umbilical cord, to the central nourishing ideas of Indian culture. Indeed, we have seen that it was probably normal for secular artists to work on religious buildings. At their best the Indian arts abound with vitality. Even though their subjects are usually derived from episodes of the great classic myths and legends, the artists strove not simply to repeat but to vitalize their work in a special way. They followed canonical patterns and ideal types, not because they were under any theological constraint to do so, but because they believed that these contained the whole justification for their art. Indian artists were not perfectionists in, say, the Muslim sense. They did not strive totally to control the hand and imagination according to immutable geometric and calligraphic forms. But they did believe that they should give constantly renewed life to real but invisible and intangible prototypes which could never be completely expressed in any one performance – or even in the lifetime's performances of one artist or a whole school of art. And these prototypes represent the principles of unity behind the multiplicity of all human visual experience.

One could call these the ideal forms which the arts sought to realize, just as all members of society attempted to live out the true patterns appropriate to their caste and social class. In architecture and sculpture, by the 6th or 7th century AD, prescriptions for the measure and layout of design had been codified and had come into use; by the 10th century they were fully evolved and certainly written down. These were schemes of overall proportion, both for different types of buildings with their detail, and for bodies of various human and superhuman beings in the figurative arts, which would authenticate each work as the reflection of the transcendent reality it was supposed to express. The measures were in all cases based upon units or modules derived from the human body, and were intelligible as proportions to the human eye. Their function was to enable art always to contain some sort of divine presence. This high aim was enough to justify what might seem at first sight a restriction.

The notion of heaven and the divine in India may seem to the western mind rather ambiguous. On the one hand, both Hindu and Buddhist traditions accept the existence of heavens as realms of splendor and enjoyment, far beyond any earthly parallel, which can be attained by the heroic and wise when they die. This seems to have been a very old conception. It appears in the epics; and very early Buddhist legend refers to the Buddha visiting the heaven of the 33 gods – a subject quite often represented in Buddhist art. Heaven is also where the Hindu gods live, surrounded by different classes of celestial beings whose task it is to make life there totally pleasurable. On the other hand, even the heavens are only one stage in the vast series of possible rebirths. Ordinary gods need to hear the Buddha preach in order to gain their own salvation. And the high gods of Hinduism, although they appeared there sometimes in the guise of mythical kings, were each thought to transcend the heavens, which were after all a world better, but no more "ultimate," than any other. For even a divine life, however colossally long by human standards, comes at last to an end; the garlands wither, the eyes begin to blink.

Metaphorically heavens were thought of as floating

Above: in this wall painting of the 5th century in Cave 17 at Ajanta a king wears an elaborate and delicately wrought jeweled crown, and a striped brocade jacket.

Left: celestial dancer from a Hoyshala temple at Belur, Mysore, 13th century; an amorous monkey seizes her scarf.

"beyond the sky." They were felt to be a repository of ideal, unblemished realities – a constant of the Indian imagination – where the patterns for all the earthly arts are generated and realized. If to attain heaven is a natural reward for virtue, it must contain all that the human heart can desire. Hence the inhabitants of heaven are beautiful, richly clothed, garlanded and jeweled; their seemingly endless pleasures are untroubled by sickness, pain or anxiety. The role of the earthly arts is to bring each living person as close as possible to heaven, through intensity of pleasurable feeling.

The function of ornament. In society, this was one role of clothing, hairdressing and jewelry. It is not known whether India had the sort of strict sumptuary laws concerning who might wear what and when, which were such a feature of Chinese and Japanese society. But it is certain that every individual in India strove as far as he could to present an elegant social persona. The figures in art represent ideal versions of divine persons (Sanskrit *deva*, from the verbal root *div* = to shine) and their ornaments. Even today the Indian tends to adorn his wife with his wealth, though nowadays he does not adorn himself as once he did. The clothes and ornaments she wears honor both him and her: him, in that they show his substance; her, in that they illustrate his perception of her inner nature. For the role of ornaments is to realize visibly the term "opulence" that has been used many times in this book. It means "displaying wealth." And this is exactly what the arts of India always set out to do: to express the body's inner feeling of wealth, fullness and fertility, raising its status towards the divine. The very techniques of sculpture, and of related painting styles, reflect this idea; for they deliberately create the bodies of their gorgeously ornamented figures out of almost total convexities, smooth and grateful to the hand. Hollows are only the meeting places of convexities. And these convex surfaces, which look as though they were gently inflated by some juice or energy from within, are linked by a continuous and sweetly undulating linear surface. All the visual arts of Southeast Asia were deeply imbued with this original Indian feeling for form.

In fact, one most ancient Indian way of honoring any revered object or person is to hang on them flower garlands, rich cloths or scarves, and strings of gems. The earliest stupa sculptures show sacred trees garlanded in this way; and the ornamental designs on the pillars of many medieval temples are stylizations of the shapes of pleated cloths, jewel strings, and flower garlands, or of a vase overflowing with flowers and foliage. This imagery is carried across into all of Southeast Asian art. It appears vividly in Khmer architecture; the figures in reliefs on Angkor Wat, for example, are set against the patterns of rich fabric. In principle, wealth and fineness of ornament imply nearness to divine status. The god, and his representative the king, are distinguished by their visible

wealth, as well as by their beauty. The heavens are made glorious as much by their "embroidered cloths" (recalling W. B. Yeats) as by the physical beauty of their inhabitants; and such beauty is a function not only of bodily shape and proportion, but of the ornaments a person owns and wears, especially his jewels. The Bodhisattva in Buddhist art wears fantastic crowns, draped strings of pearls and other gems; and one series of Buddhist texts (the *Sukhavativyuha*) describes a paradise of jewel trees growing over a transparent lapis lazuli ground beneath which extends a vast jewel net: thus was symbolized ultimate beauty.

This complex of ideas gave a powerful impulse to the invention of the decorative arts in India. We can read from sculpture and painting the extraordinarily high standard of skill and invention of weavers and dyers, of gold- and silver-smiths, and carvers of wood and ivory. A few pieces of ancient Indian silver are known. There are superb pieces of filigree jewelry from Taxila and other northwestern sites. And in Java, for example, a whole series of Buddhist silver offering trays of the 8th or 9th century has come to light, adorned with superb curvilinear floral designs resembling closely some of the patterns which appear in the decorative panels of Ajanta painting. Much recent Thai and Burmese silverware still embodies old Indian designs. As can be seen from the plates, one of the features of Indian personal ornament, especially of necklace, hip girdles, armlets and anklets, is repetition and multiplicity. This is characteristic of the Indian feeling for rhythm, which also appears in architectural moldings and profiles. Units multiplied into long series exalt the mind with their suggestion of wealth. Gold repoussé shows repeated bosses and curls. But individual stones, which included semiprecious or decorative stones, were not cut to exactly identical shapes as they would be by modern western jewelers.

Left: detail of the multiple jeweled hip girdle worn by a goddess on the railing of Barhut stupa, 2nd century BC.

Below: gold jewelry found in burial chambers in south India of the 2nd century AD, a pendant with lotus flowers and pendants of ornamental ball design. Musée Guimet, Paris.

Needless to say, no ancient Indian cloth survives. But from the painting again we can see that gorgeous designs, including stripes, diapers and curling floral forms were produced by incredibly fine gauze weaving, tie-and-dye and embroidery. By the time the Muslims and Europeans became closely acquainted with India (from the 16th century on) the Indian products they sought most eagerly were the textiles. South Indian painted cloths were in demand at the 17th-century Mughal court. But huge hangings of cotton painted with ornaments and legendary scenes are now known to have long been made for northern temples and palaces into recent times.

Devotionalism and art. Ornament is a way of attributing glory to that which is adorned. But in the Indian context it means more: to apply it is an active expression of praise and adoration. A temple, a deity or a wife deprived of ornament is unthinkable. An emotional movement towards the object or idea demands to be

Below right: ivory carving of the Bodhisattva Avalokiteshvara from Kashmir, 12th century AD, granting boons to worshipers. Prince of Wales Museum, Bombay.

Below: ornamental stone column from Khiching, Orissa, carved with a tree of fertility on a tapestry-like band, and down-turned petals. 10th century AD.

fulfilled by active expression, by giving, a giving which is not only thought of as "sacrifice" from the giver, but also as a gesture of praise. It is often not realized how important this devotional attitude is in Indian and Indianized culture. There can be little doubt that kings harnessed it to their own political ends. But it was always there to be harnessed, endemic in Indian civilization, expressed at the personal level in the lives of innumerable saints, and in thousands of hymns and poems. It is the factor which links secular and religious arts into an indissoluble unity of intent; and it is more than likely that it prompted the great upsurge of figural and iconic religious art which took place in the first centuries of the Christian era.

The Indian term for this devotional attitude which inspires all praise is *bhakti*. Its overtones of meaning run all the way from human love to sublime self-abolition in deity. Indeed these are thought to be degrees of the same function. Indian religion and art alike cultivate the positive human feelings to a quite exceptional extent. According to the doctrines of *bhakti*, it is actually through feeling that a person is able to approach most directly the infinite vastness of the One. It claims totally to transcend the austerities of yoga and the minute intellectual discriminations of philosophy.

In fact, were it not for the presence of *bhakti*, Indian

culture would wear a very different aspect. To be blunt, it would have been polarized between a grim asceticism and a spiritless indulgence. The metaphysical theories and religious teachings which lie at the basis of Indian culture – the Brahman's total abstinence, the Buddhist's rejection of all attachment – would seem at the popular level, if read literally, to make any art impossible, and to negate all joys but the ultimate bliss. For if all is a product of the One, and the way to the One is through inner realization, any outer phenomenon should not dare to claim any attention or devotion. This is the extreme monist philosophical view, which calls *bhakti* "dualist." For it is only possible to offer worship and adoration to some person or thing that can confront one as a presence to receive it. All Indians have naturally sought such presences. They found them in local spirits and hallows, in the great gods and their images, in human teachers, such as the Buddha. Even the greatest of the Hindu monist philosophers, Shankaracharya (788–828), was himself adored as a manifestation of the high god, Shiva. The dualism necessary to *bhakti* was given its own philosophical expression, notably by Ramanuja (died 1137); and the philosophical dilemma was resolved in the "qualified dualism" of Nimbarka (died 1162), who worked out the implications of the ultimate identity of adorer and adored. *Bhakti*, which had existed from at least the 2nd century BC, was thus finally accorded its Brahman philosophical canonization.

Bhakti shows its roots at the human level in secular art. To make art at all is a positive act of praise directed towards the subject matter of the art. And Indian secular art has always had a profoundly erotic flavor. The Indian imagination has sought primarily to experience thoughts and sensations of love for their own sake; and love is the human feeling which most of all requires an object. To the lover, man or woman, the object of his love appears beautiful, and the lover's aim is to enjoy the beauty of the beloved to the full through all the senses. Beauty is explicitly identified as a function of the lover's desire, existing not only in the object of love but as a reality behind and above the object, to which the object is, so to speak, transparent. Art seeks to capture and express the higher reality of the desired and loved through ideal forms, which thus claim to awaken in the spectator his own experience of desire. So secular arts aim to arouse intense sensuous response and feelings of delight. Their forms evoke them by metaphorical reference to all sorts of related pleasurable experience. A girl's breasts are like great golden cups; her skin smooth as the down of a goose; her gauzy garments ripple between her thighs like a river between its banks; a man's great arms are like plantain trees; his eyebrows shoot glances as a bow shoots piercing arrows; his chest is shaped like the face of a great bull.

Religious art accepts the same premises. But it does not come to rest in immediate sensuous responses and feelings of delight. The beauty it perceives behind and beyond its

Stone icon of Shiva standing, from Khiching, Orissa, 10th century. The river goddesses at the base of the frame offer holy water, and the frame itself bears elaborate foliage, emblem of supernatural fertility.

objects has an infinite depth. It is divine. Images of the Hindu gods, Shiva, Vishnu or the Goddess, any of the Bodhisattvas, or even of the Buddha in his *Sambhogakaya*, are made erotically charming, their physical attributes evoking no less vivid sensuous responses than secular art; but such icons are more obviously and intentionally transparent to the higher reality which they merely symbolize. And this, of course, is the real goal of the positive feeling of love, of *bhakti*; love, as its vision

Above: part of a sculpture on the base of a temple at Khajuraho, of the 10th century, representing a sexual ritual.

Right: three celestial musicians carved from a single block, on a Hoyshala temple, c. 1300, at Belur, Mysore.

deepens, changes its nature from sensuous response to spiritual absorption in the reality behind the image. Ultimately, this reality which he or she is adoring and praising comes to be perceived directly and emotionally as a function of the worshiper's own divine original self.

Indian culture, poetry, music, the visual arts and dance all find their justification in an impulse of *bhakti*, directed to some objectified image of the infinite One. The "lower" arts are imbued with a sense of the higher. For all the arts are at some level earthly representations of the heavenly archetypal arts. Every grade of response is necessary from the audience. Without the initial reaction to sensuous charm, there is nothing out of which the deeper spiritual response can be generated. It is not surprising that many Indian traditions, especially those called Tantrik, see in human sexual love an essential paradigm and prefiguring of divine union. It is also not surprising that an old saying of the Middle Ages runs: "A man who knows nothing of literature, music or art is nothing but a beast without the beast's tail and horns."

Unity in music and the dance. There is a story told in one of the *Silpa Shastra* (art treatises) of a certain king asking a learned teacher to instruct him how to make sculptures of the gods. The teacher answered that "someone who does not know the rules of painting can never understand the laws of sculpture." When the king asked to be taught painting, the teacher answered, "It is difficult to understand the rules of painting without understanding the technique of dancing." "Please instruct me in the art of dancing," the king requested. "This is difficult to understand without a thorough knowledge of the principles of instrumental music." The king then asked to be taught these; but the teacher replied, "these cannot be learned without a deep understanding of the arts of vocal music." The king bowed in acceptance. "Please reveal to me the methods of vocal music."

This story illustrates an important truth about all the Indian arts: that they are closely woven together, into a single spectrum of expression – a function of the intuition of unity. We do not know what the music of ancient and classical India was like; for it was never written out in notation. We certainly know that it existed and flourished. There are many representations of singers and musical instruments in early sculpture, including harps, flutes, drums and, by the 8th century in Rajasthan, an almost fully developed Indian *vina* with two gourd resonators – still one of the chief instruments for performing classical music. In Aryan times we know the seven-note scale was used. And the *Natyashastra* of Bharata (4th century AD) refers to more than 30 *ragas* – the special scale-like modes which are still the basis for Indian music – though hundreds are now known, of which 40-odd are in common use. Since the *Natyashastra* is, in all the other departments of art with which it deals, an unquestioned original source, even though it was amplified by later texts, there can be little doubt that music then already worked on aesthetic principles not unlike those of today. Each *raga* speaks within a specific mood; and the task of the musician is to awaken in the minds of his hearers responses specific to that mood. Each *raga* is, so to speak, a field of possible experience shared by musician and audience. The player's skill can open this up again and again, in all its breadth and depth, by wakening into resonance memory traces of emotionally charged experience, and even karmic traces from past lives, in each hearer.

Dancing follows a similar principle, working through bodily movement. But it has in addition a vocabulary of hand gestures, of eye, head and foot movements, which indicates precisely emotions, actions, objects and places; the meanings are listed and described in texts such as the *Abhinaya Darpana* ("Mirror of Gesture") of Nandik-eshvara. Thus Indian dance incorporates an extremely articulate language of mime; it is no mere ballet. To reach the heights of expression a dancer needs many years of training, so that the body and hands become amazingly supple. Elaborate costumes and make-up increase the effect. Training and equipment for dancers were provided chiefly in the troupes maintained at royal or provincial courts and at Hindu temples. The classical south Indian *Bharat Natyam*, as we know it today, has come down to us through a mere handful of temple dancers; elsewhere in India only a few fragments of tradition remain from the past. But at courts in Southeast Asia, notably in Cambodia and Thailand until recently, and still in Java and Bali, traditions of dance springing directly from imported ancient Indian court styles have survived.

The story lines of the dance were taken at first from semisecular literature, especially the epics *Mahabharata* and *Ramayana* which were held to be of divine inspiration; later from Puranic legends of the gods, especially those describing cosmic conflicts between gods and demons. There are references in old literature to princes and ladies dancing at court for enjoyment; there was also, of course, a wealth of folk dance all over India and Southeast Asia. But the high classical style was the one which was held to reflect most closely the heavenly prototypes of the dance. Many early reliefs from Bodhgaya, Mathura and Gupta shrines which illustrate life in the heavens, show scenes of music and dancing. It is these heavenly prototypes which are realized in the figurative sculptural and painted decoration on all later shrines, Buddhist and Hindu, everywhere in Indian Asia. All the figures of deities or celestial beings, even the human participants in heroic legend, are "first" conceived, so to speak, as divinely beautiful dancers in the appropriate postures, making gestures that convey the right meaning, "before" being transcribed into stone or paint. The earthly dancers of court or temple provided the immediate inspiration for this visual art. Their task was to realize as nearly as possible the transcendent timeless actuality of myth. But of course an earthly dancer needs to stand on solid ground, whereas a celestial dancer transcribed by art may float through the air in any direction. His ability to stand above the earth is one of the traditional marks of the god.

The affinity between visual arts and the dance in Indian Asia is immediately obvious. But here and there a few sets of sculptures remain on shrines which actually illustrate techniques of the dance. They belong to the end of our period, but they are immensely important, as their very existence confirms the intimate relationship between the sacred shrine and the dance. There is a virtually unpublished set on the great Shiva temple at Prambanam in Java (c. 900 AD) which matches other sets on Chola temples in the Tamil southeast of India. Indian aesthetics recognized the dance, and the other arts, as channels by which the divine manifests itself in the world. The Hindu temple had become, by the Middle Ages, a focus of all the arts. Each apparently different shrine fixes the unique Divine Center, where the Infinite One shows itself, either in the central Hindu icon or in the Buddha principle represented by stupa or image. The architecture which surrounds it is a development or exposition of the significance of the center into the physical and social environment in terms of image of courtly paradise. Art then effloresces from the temple, through the decorative forms of wealth and fertility, through the sculptured and painted figures of celestial beings who make music or love, or listen to preaching, through the actuality of ritual, when offerings are given and blessings received in return, through the performance of actual music and dance which "realizes" myth. All these different activities are meant to engage the senses and the emotions into the field of the transcendent, bringing each person's life and experience into a sacred relationship with the Infinite and the One.

Further Reading

GENERAL
Basham, A. L., *The Wonder that was India* (London, 1954).
—— (ed), *A Cultural History of India* (Oxford, 1975).

Rawlinson, H. G., *India* (London, 1948).

Singhal, D. P., *India and World Civilization* (London, 1972).

Smith, V., *Early History of India* (Oxford, 1904).

Swaan, W., *Lost Cities of Asia* (London, 1966).

GENERAL ART
Coomaraswamy, A. K., *History of Indian and Indonesian Art* (New York, 1927).

Rowland, B., *The Art and Architecture of India* [and Southeast Asia] (3rd ed., Harmondsworth, 1967).

Zimmer, H., *The Art of Indian Asia* (New York, 1955).

INDIAN ART
Barrett, D., and **Gray, B.,** *The Painting of India* (Cleveland, Ohio, 1963).

Brown, Percy, *Indian Architecture, Buddhist and Hindu* (Bombay, n.d.).

Frederic, L., *Indian Temples and Sculpture* (London, 1959).

Goetz, H., *India; Five Thousand Years of Indian Art* (Baden-Baden, 1959).

Kramrisch, S., *The Art of India* (London, 1954).

Rawson, P. S., *Indian Painting* (London, Paris, New York, 1961).

Smith, V., *History of Fine Art in India and Ceylon* (2nd ed., Oxford, 1930).

Taddei, M., *The Ancient Civilization of India* (Geneva, London, 1970).

Zimmer, H., *Myths and Symbols in Indian Art and Civilization* (New York, 1946).

SPECIAL SUBJECTS
Marshall, Sir J., *A Guide to Taxila* (Cambridge, 1960).

Wheeler, R. E. M., *Early India and Pakistan* (London, 1959).

SOUTHEAST ASIA
Bernet-Kempers, A. J., *Ancient Indonesian Art* (Cambridge, Mass., 1959).

Griswold, A. B., Kim, Ch., Pott, P.H., *Burma, Korea, Tibet* (Geneva, London, 1964).

Groslier, B. P., *Indochina* (Geneva, 1966).

—— *Indochina, Melting Pot of Races* (Baden-Baden, London, 1962).

Rawson, P. S., *The Art of Southeast Asia* (London, New York, 1967).

Wagner, F. A., *Indonesia, the Art of an Island Group* (Baden-Baden, London, 1959).

OTHER REGIONS
Belenitsky, A., *Central Asia* (Geneva, 1968).

Singh, M., *Himalayan Art* (London, 1971).

Tucci, G., *Transhimalaya* (Geneva, 1973).

Acknowledgments

Unless otherwise stated, all the illustrations on a given page are credited to the same source.

Archaeological Survey of India 13 (bottom), 133 (left), 134

Ashmolean Museum, Oxford 78

Birmingham Museums and Art Gallery, Birmingham 102 (bottom right)

Douglas Dickens, London 26 (bottom), 27 (bottom), 28, 29 (top left and bottom right), 30 (top, and bottom left), 81 (right), 96 (bottom), 107 (bottom left), 110 (top), 116, 123 (top), 124 (top left and bottom right), 125 (center, and bottom left), 126 (top left), 135 (bottom)

Elsevier Archives, Amsterdam 34 (bottom); Archaeological Survey of India 107 (top), Ewing Galloway 124 (bottom left)

Fotomass Index, London 46 (top), 47

Ray Gardner, London 43

Gulbenkian Museum of Oriental Art, University of Durham, Durham 74 (bottom)

Robert Harding Associates Ltd, London 9, 10 (left), 12, 14, 41 (top), 51, 53 (top right), 96 (top), 122 (bottom); Rainbird 31

Betty J. Harle, Oxford 68 (right)

Hans Heinz, Allschwill 98 (bottom right)

Michael Holford Photographs, Loughton 19, 39, 48, 49, 79, 88, 101 (top right), 132 (right)

Victor Kennett, London 26 (top left), 99 (bottom right), 107 (bottom), 108 (left)

Koninklijk Instituut voor de Tropen, Photografic-Archives, Amsterdam 117

Larkin Brothers, London 32, 67

Lovell Johns, Oxford 11, 15, 62

Mansell Collection, London 63

John Marshall Collection; Gulbenkian Museum of Oriental Art, University of Durham, Durham 16, 17, 42, 44, 45 (left), 46 (bottom), 52, 53 (bottom right), 54 (top, and center right), 55 (top right, center and bottom), 56 (right), 57, 58, 71 (top right and bottom), 82 (bottom)

Museo Nazionale, Naples 66

Mauro Pucciarelli, Rome 26 (top right), 27 (top), 33, 35, 100 (bottom right)

Radio Times Hulton Picture Library, London 37, 38

Rijksmuseum, Amsterdam 25

Rijksmuseum voor Volkendkunde, Leiden 90 (bottom)

Scala, Florence 21, 22, 29 (bottom left), 34 (top), 54 (bottom), 55 (top left), 56 (left), 59, 61, 64 (bottom), 68 (left), 69, 71 (top left), 72, 84 (top), 85, 97, 98 (top right), 99 (center left), 100 (top left and right), 101 (bottom right), 102, 106, 108 (right), 109 (right), 127, 129 (top), 130 (bottom), 131 (top), 133 (right)

Sejarah dan Purbakala, Jakarta 90 (top)

Graham Smith, London 92, 119 (left)

Smithsonian Institution, Freer Gallery of Art, Washington, D.C. 110 (bottom)

Spectrum Colour Library, London 18 (top)

Wolf Suschitsky, London, frontispiece, 10 (right), 64 (top), 82 (top), 89, 95, 123 (bottom right), 125 (bottom right), 126 (top right), 128, 129 (bottom)

Visual Art Productions, Oxford 53 (top left and center), 84 (bottom), 122 (top), 125 (top)

Leonard Von Matt, Buochs 120

Werner Forman Archive, London 13 (top), 24, 29 (top right), 76 (top), 99 (top)

ZEFA (U.K.) Ltd, London 18 (bottom), 20, 23, 30 (bottom right), 36, 40, 41 (bottom), 70, 73, 74 (top), 76 (bottom), 77, 81 (left), 86, 93, 94, 98 (bottom left), 99 (center right and bottom left), 100 (bottom left), 101 (top left), 102 (bottom left), 103, 104, 109 (left), 112, 113, 114, 115, 119 (right), 121, 123 (bottom left), 124 (top right), 126 (bottom), 130 (top), 131 (bottom), 135 (top)

The Publishers have attempted to observe the legal requirements with respect to the rights of the suppliers of photographic materials. Nevertheless, persons who have claims are invited to apply to the Publishers.

The author would like to acknowledge with gratitude the editorial help given by Mr Basil Gray.

Glossary

Achaemenids Dynasty ruling the Persian empire, who laid claim to provinces in NW India; founded by Achaemenes (mid-7th century BC), it was deposed by **Alexander** c. 330 BC.

Adivasis Aboriginal inhabitants of India, in isolated tribal groups, who are vestiges of early pre-Aryan populations. The word means "original dwellers."

Aesop Greek writer, famous for his classic collection of animal stories (mid-6th century BC), supposed to have been a slave in Egypt of a Thracian master.

Ajatashatru King in Magadha, son of **Bimbisara**; said to have had an interview with the Buddha c. 490 BC in which he expressed both remorse for killing his father and faith in the Buddha.

al-Biruni Great Muslim scholar (973–1048 AD) who lived in the Punjab in the train of the raiding Sultan Mahmud of Ghazni. He studied Sanskrit literature and wrote a classic book on India in Persian which is a prime historical source.

Albuquerque, A. de Founder of the Portuguese seaborne empire in Asia c. 1500 AD, based principally upon trade and piracy.

Alexander the Great Macedonian general (356–323 BC), who at the age of only 20 became emperor of the Classical world by his military skill. He entered India in 327 BC.

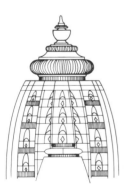

Amala at Sunak

Amala Flat, thick and heavy disk of stone which crowns the spire of the Hindu temple, its outer edge being channeled into steeply curved **gadrooning**; based on the shape of the fruit of the *Phyllanthus emblica.*

Amarnath Hindu saint after whom is named the cave in the Himalaya in which is a huge ice *lingam*; from its melt the sacred river Ganga rises. It is a famous place of pilgrimage.

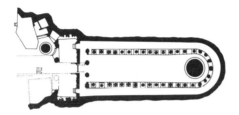

Ambulatory at Karli

Ambulatory Passage-like walkaround which encloses the apsidal end of a hall, usually covered by the same roof and separated from the hall by columns.

Antefix Raised plaque-like panel facing outwards from a building, often bearing a symbolic design, and usually placed along the edges of the roof.

Apollonius of Tyana Magician and mystic who went from Mesopotamia to NW India c. 50 AD to study under Brahman teachers.

Apsaras Celestial girl, one of the inhabitants of the Indian heaven, who is unmarried and filled with inexhaustible sexual desire. Intercourse with such girls is part of the bliss of heaven; some are dancers and musicians. Described in detail in the **Ramayana**.

Arahat Buddhist who has achieved the status of being "worthy" of enlightenment. He has cut off his outflows of will and attachment and is the type of Buddhist hero.

Aramaic Semitic language, originating in Syria and Lebanon c. 1200 BC, which became the lingua franca of western Asia, especially of the **Achaemenids**, and hence in parts of NW India; it was the language of Christ. Written in several scripts, including Syriac.

Archaeological Survey of India Organization which supervises and organizes archaeology in India, including excavation, conservation, restoration, epigraphy and some museums.

Ari Name used of a sect of Buddhists in Burma c. 9th–12th centuries AD, said to be magicians probably of the **Vajrayana**, patronized by the **Pyu**. The word may mean "enemy," which was how they were regarded by later, stricter Buddhists in Burma.

Arrian Greek author of a work called the *Periplus* (sailing around) *of the Euxine Sea* (131 AD); a major source for the ancient geography of the Indian seas. The author was prefect of the Roman province of Cappadocia under the Emperor Hadrian, and a historian.

Arthashastra Early Sanskrit text dealing with administration, civic order and morality, probably in existence by the 3rd century BC. It covers such topics as taxation, law, city planning, the army and the secret service.

Apsaras from Cambodia

Aryabhata Name of two mathematicians and astronomers. The first (c. 500 AD) was an excellent observer and worked with square and cube roots and sines; the second (c. 950) studied spherical astronomy and time reckoning.

Aryans Population group, speaking Indo-European languages, using chariots with horses, who invaded India and other countries probably from the south Russian steppes in the second millennium BC.

Ashoka Greatest emperor of the **Maurya dynasty** (d. 323 BC), who was a patron of Buddhism, and set up rock and pillar edicts which are the earliest written documents of historical India.

Asiatic Society of Bengal Founded in 1784 by a group of Englishmen including **Jones**, Colebrook and Wilkins, which began the study of Indian culture and sponsored series of publications.

Augustus (63 BC–14 AD). First Roman emperor, successor and nephew of Julius Caesar.

Aureole behind a standing Buddha

Aureole Halo, usually disk-shaped, behind the head, but sometimes a pointed frame, which represents the golden or fiery radiance emanating from a divine or sublime body.

Avatamsakasutra Huge Buddhist compilation of visionary and philosophical texts, complete before 200 AD; a main vehicle for the doctrine of the **Bodhisattva** and of total mutual interdependence among phenomena.

Bairo Shortened form of Bhairava, meaning "the Terrible," one of the names applied to the god **Shiva** in his aspect of destroying power.

Bardasanes Babylonian Gnostic teacher, who learned many facts about India from an Indian embassy to Syria in the reign of the Roman Emperor Heliogabalus (218–22 AD). His lost work is quoted by later writers.

Bernier, F. French traveler in the Mughal empire for 12 years, whose account, published in 1670–71, is a primary source of information about India then.

Bhagavadgita Summary fundamental religious text, incorporated into the epic **Mahabharata** which incorporates fundamental teachings on **yoga**, **bhakti** and **Krishna**. Date unknown, probably c. 100 BC.

Bhakti Love and adoration in the highest aspect. *Bhakti* is the positive religious attitude which requires an object, even though this object is an emblem of the Universal Self.

Bharat natyam Tradition of ancient Indian dance preserved in the southeastern region. The name means – tendentiously – "Indian dance"; in fact it is one of four principal traditions surviving in India.

Bhasa India's greatest classical poet (2nd century AD) in Sanskrit. His masterpiece is the *Dream Vasavadatta*, a vast panoramic history play.

Bimbisara (c. 519 BC). King who is supposed to have built the city of New Rajgir in Magadha, and to have patronized the Buddha. He is said to have been murdered by his son, **Ajatashatru**, incited by the Buddha's enemy, his cousin Devadatta.

Bodhisattva Buddhist figure, who incarnates the principle of universal compassion, thus passing beyond the **Arahat**. There are many named Bodhisattvas.

Brahman (1) Member of the highest **caste** in Indian society, which is devoted to religious and scholarly activities.

Brahman (2) Supreme principle recognized in Hindu theology, which embraces and generates both self and world. Union with the Brahman is the goal of Hindu religion.

Brahmanas Group of mythological commentaries on the **Veda**, composed c. 1000–600 BC in Sanskrit; an important early source for Indian philosophy, theology and legend.

Brahmi Earliest form of script used for writing Sanskrit and sub-Sanskrit languages; first known in the pillar inscriptions of **Ashoka**, later 3rd century BC.

Brahui Language of the southern Dravidian group spoken by a small isolated population on the western borders of Pakistan–Afghanistan.

Bronze Age Stage of human history when bronze rather than stone was chiefly used for tools and weapons. It began broadly about

2500 BC, and in most higher civilizations was superseded by the Iron Age, though in primitive regions it survived virtually into modern times.

Buchanan, Francis Medical man, artist and member of the Asiatic Society of Bengal, who traveled much in India and Burma, contributing descriptive and historical articles to its journal in the later 18th century.

Buddhacharita Name of a poem about the life of the Buddha by Ashvaghosha, written as a Buddhist epic, in the 2nd century AD.

Burgess, J. British scholar and architectural historian who played a major role in the Archaeological Survey of India; retired in 1889.

Camoëns Great poet of Portugal, composer of the epic *Os Lusiadas*, based on his own experiences as a member of exploratory expeditions into eastern seas, treated after the manner of Homer and Virgil.

Caravansaray Hostel for caravans to put up overnight, based upon a courtyard surrounded by rooms opening from it, and offering necessary facilities, such as water, cooking places, etc.

Caryatid Figurative shape into which part of a column or architectural support is carved, which thus appears as if carrying the weight.

Caste system Caste, from Portuguese *casta* = "pure," is a system of social stratification based originally on birth, but later upon occupation, reflecting the relative degree of theoretical "purity" of each caste according to its lifestyle.

Cave shrine Cave, generally manmade, cut as a shrine in a rock face. By its dark coolness it could provide a welcome refuge from the sun. Often elaborately sculptured.

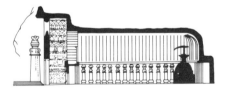

Cetiya hall at Karli

Cetiya, chaitya Two terms applied by Buddhists to the sacred object which provides the focus of their faith. They may be derived from the root *ci*, meaning "pile-up." Usually applied to **stupas**, but also to other shrines and sacred places.

Chalukyas Dynasty ruling in the Deccan in two major phases, first 6th–8th centuries, then in the western part 8th–13th centuries. During both phases they were responsible for much major art.

Cham People inhabiting what is now central and southern Vietnam, perhaps related to present inhabitants of Melanesia, who became Hindu c. 600 AD, and were eliminated as a political force by the 14th century, being supplanted by the racial Vietnamese whose culture was Chinese and Buddhist.

Chandi Name for a Hindu goddess often associated with destruction and death, adopted in Indonesia as a generic term for all ancient temples, Hindu and Buddhist, probably on the assumption that they were monuments to dead kings.

Chandragupta Founder of the **Gupta dynasty** in 320 AD.

Chandragupta Maurya King of Magadha, who founded the **Maurya dynasty** and empire in 321 BC, supposed to be the Sandrakottos who met Alexander the Great as a youth, and learned from him techniques of command and government.

Cholas Great dynasty who ruled in the south-eastern plains, the Dravidian region, 10th to 14th centuries AD.

Plan of a Tibetan chörten

Chörten Tibetan term for **stupa**.

Clement of Alexandria Father of the Church (150–218 AD) who met Buddhists in his home city and wrote an account of their religion.

Coomaraswamy, A. K. Half-British, half-Ceylonese scholar (1877–1947), author of many works on eastern art, mythology and theology, as well as comparative religion.

Corbeling Technique of making an arch by allowing higher horizontal courses of brick or stone to protrude progressively from the sides until they meet at the top; distinct from the true structured arch.

Ctesias Greek author of the 4th century BC who lived in Susa in Persia and wrote an account of India.

Cunningham, Alexander Archaeologist, numismatist, and first Director of the **Archaeological Survey of India** (1860).

Cyclopean wall Wall composed of large blocks trimmed off to meet each other at planes determined by the natural shapes of the stones, not at right angles.

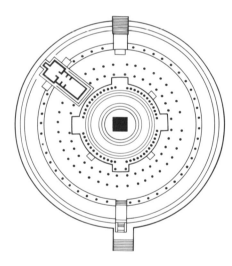

Plan and section of the Thuparama dagoba at Anuradhapura in Ceylon

Dagoba Word for **stupa** used in Ceylon and other **Hinayana** countries.

Dalai Lama Name given to each successive head of the Tibetan "Reformed" Buddhist organization, called the Yellow Hat Sect, which ruled as priest-kings until recently in Lhasa. Known in Tibet as Gyalwa Rinpoche.

Dance pavilion Columned hall aligned with the main cell of a Hindu shrine in which dancing was performed as part of the temple liturgy.

Darius the Great Achaemenid king of Persia (521–483 BC) who extended the huge Persian empire, claiming **Gandhara** and the Indus region as "satrapies," perhaps initiating a Persian influence upon Indian art.

Deva Name used of any divine being. It means "shining one" from root *div* = "shine." Particularly used of greater divinities.

Devanagari Script used for writing Sanskrit, fully fledged by the 4th century AD and still in use today.

Dharmakaya Highest of the Three Bodies of the Buddha, the unrepresentable Ultimate Identity achieved on **enlightenment**.

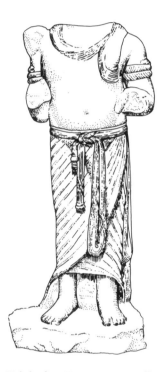

Yaksha from Patna wearing a dhoti

Dhoti Typically Indian garment made out of a single large piece of cloth to cover the lower half of the body, fastened only by folding and tucking.

Divyavadana One of the primary texts for the life and legends of the Buddha, composed in the later centuries BC.

Dravidian Group of languages in southern India, with a grammatical and lexical structure distinct from the Sanskritic languages of the north. The chief are Tamil, Telugu, Kanada and Malayalam.

Drip molding Protruding ledge running along under the eaves of a roof which allows rain to drip off away from the wall; often developed as a decorative architectural feature.

Dualist Category of theological teaching which holds that human being and deity are in some sense separate, as opposed to **monist** teaching – a necessary philosophical prerequisite for **Bhakti**. Also belief in the polarity of good and evil as metaphysically ultimate.

Dubois, Abbé French author of a very popular book on *Hindu manners, customs and ceremonies* (1817) which propagated a misleading view of India and Hinduism.

Duperron, A. French scholar of Persian, who translated in 1771 the ancient Persian classic, the *Avesta,* then published in 1801 the first translation, into mixed Latino-French, of the *Upanishads*, a book which deeply impressed Europe with admiration for Hindu philosophy.

East India Company British, Dutch and Portuguese all initiated trading companies of private shareholders who conducted trade with the east during the 16th to 18th centuries. The British Company actually came to govern large tracts of India, and its responsibilities were taken over by the crown after 1859.

Enlightenment State of inner illumination, in which the integration of the vast world of phenomena and the perceiving self becomes a fact of direct perception; explained differently by different philosophies.

Erp, Th. van (d. 1958). Dutch architect working for the Indonesian Archaeological service who recovered the major monuments of Javanese architecture, restored and published them.

Fergusson, James (1808–86). Great Scottish scholar of Indian art, especially architecture, whose role in the early days of the study of Indian archaeology was crucial; many of his publications are still primary sources.

Filigree Technique of decorative metalworking, especially pierced and convoluted designs, usually used as flat panels; it may be cut from a solid sheet, or constructed out of wire.

Finial Feature which emphasizes an end, most commonly the peak of a spire or gable in architecture, the summit of a pointed feature, e.g. a lid in metal, lacquer or terracotta wares, the tip of a pole.

Fluting Parallel concave depressions in the surface of a work of art, usually either cut in stone or hammered into metal, and usually vertical.

Fly-whisk Bunch of hair fixed into a handle, waved in the air around the head and neck to keep flies and other insects from settling; aristocratic attendants used to wield them for kings.

Gadroon Converse of **fluting**; parallel convex projections worked onto the face of an art object, usually vertical.

Gandhara Ancient name for a region embracing parts of modern Afghanistan and Pakistan to the Indus river.

Ganesha Hindu deity with a stocky human body and the head of an elephant; said to be the son of **Shiva** and his wife Parvati, and looked on as patron of wealth, fortune and beginnings.

Ganga River Ganges, regarded as sacred in India. Personified as a goddess, who purifies men of their sins, she is said to have descended from heaven leaving her trace as the Milky Way.

Garbhagriha "Womb-house," the cell at the heart of a Hindu temple which contains the principal sacred image that gives the shrine its sanctity.

Garuda Mythical being with the head, wings and beak of a bird and the body of a man, supposed to be the "enemy" of serpents, and traditionally the vehicle of the god **Vishnu.**

Gautama Personal name of the Buddha, whose clan were Shakyas; so he was also called Shakyamuni, the sage of the Shakyas.

Gnosticism Form of religion widely prevalent in the eastern Mediterranean and western Asia during the early centuries AD which cultivated "gnosis" – immediate knowledge of divine truth; often **dualist**.

Gonds Group of **Adivasis** in the Central Deccan, who speak a language of the **Dravidian** group.

Grihya sutras (c. 500 BC). Collection of maxims in Sanskrit dealing with morality, domestic and social duties, of governors and governed, according to the ideals of **Aryan** social organization.

Guadapada Hindu **monist** philosopher, 7th-century AD precursor of the greatest of them all, **Shankaracharya**.

Guimet, É. Founder of the great Musée Guimet, which is devoted to eastern art, especially that of Southeast Asia, originally in Lyons, now in Paris.

Gupta dynasty Based in **Magadha**, the Guptas forged an empire across northern India from 320 to 535 AD; under their sway a great wave of literature and art arose which is usually regarded as the high classic manifestation of Indian art.

Hackin, J. French scholar, who died in 1941 as a member of the French Resistance in World War II. He worked with the French archaeological Mission in Afghanistan, and excavated and published the important site of Begram.

Hallows Term used to denote a sacred object or image in which divine power is held to reside; a singular noun.

Han dynasty Ruled China from 206 BC to 220 AD, important for initiating the fundamental administrative systems which united the vast country.

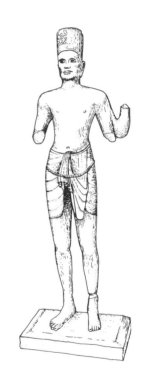

Hari-Hara figure from Cambodia

Hari-Hara Iconic figure combining the physical attributes and metaphysical symbolism of the two gods **Vishnu** (Hari) in the left half and **Shiva** (Hara) in the right half.

Harmika Small rectangular railed enclosure at the summit of the early **stupa** which later develops into a solid architectural feature.

Harsha (606–47 AD). Great emperor of Kanauj who revived the empire of the **Guptas**, introducing a period of prosperity and cultural advance; a follower of Shiva, he nevertheless patronized Buddhism. **Hsüan Chang** visited India during his reign.

Harmika at Sanchi

Hastings, Warren Greatest British Governor of Bengal (1772–74) and Governor General (1774–85) on behalf of the **East India Company.** He initiated many urgent administrative reforms and encouraged research. He was impeached on his return to Britain for shabby political reasons.

Hellenistic Term used of culture and art in the Greek cities of the eastern Mediterranean and western Asia between about 350 BC and the rise of the Roman Empire.

Herder, J. G. (1744–1803). German author who proclaimed his belief that India was the source of humane wisdom. He studied Indian literature, lectured and taught, and influenced the German Romantic movement.

Herodotus (c. 480–425 BC). Greek historian whose accounts of exotic regions, though to some extent mythical, are nevertheless very important sources of information about Oriental countries and customs.

Hinayana Name used of the southern tradition of Buddhism, whose literature is in Pali. Meaning "lesser vehicle," it was a derogatory term applied by followers of the **Mahayana.**

Hippalos Greek sailor who is said to have discovered, about 45 AD, the technique of sailing across the Indian Ocean on the monsoon winds from south Arabia to the Indian peninsula, thus cutting short the long coastal voyage hugging the shore.

Homa-altar Vedic sacrificial altar upon which offerings to the gods were burned and so ascended to heaven with the fire.

Hsüan Chang Chinese pilgrim who visited India under **Harsha** (630–45 AD) and left a detailed record in Chinese, of his experiences in Central Asia and India, called "Records of Western Countries" (*Hsi-yu chi*).

Hunas People of Central Asian origin who penetrated through the northwestern passes into the western part of the **Gupta** empire, and may have destroyed monasteries in **Gandhara.**

Iamblichus (d. c. 330 AD). Neoplatonist philosopher who wrote many important mystical texts, and a biography of the greatest master of the school, **Plotinus.**

Indus valley civilization Civilization that flourished between c. 2850 and 1350 BC, building large cities and trading with contemporary civilizations in Mesopotamia. Its culture was the heir to earlier bronze-age cultures of eastern Iran and Afghanistan.

Ionic capital from Taxila

Ionic pillar One of the three orders of Greek architectural type. The capital has a pair of lateral volutes, appearing as spirals when seen from the front.

Iron Age Archaeological epoch which succeeds, in theory, the **Bronze Age**, and during which iron comes to be used for weapons; it has no absolute dates.

Ishanavarman I Great king under whom the art of Chen-la first took shape. He ruled from Sambor Preikuk in Cambodia (611 or 616–635 AD), initiating the **Khmer** dynasty.

Ithyphallic Having an erect or swollen male sexual organ.

Jains Followers of the teacher **Mahavira** (d. 527 BC), who taught that the spirit should be disentangled from matter by means of avoiding all injury to living beings to the uttermost (i.e. ultimate) suicide.

Jataka Story dealing with a previous incarnation of the Buddha, during which he performs one of the many acts of that total self-abnegation which qualifies him for ultimate **Nirvana.**

Jones, Sir William (1746–94). Great British scholar who came to India in 1783, translated Sanskrit works into English and wrote many fundamental articles. He was the moving spirit in the formation of the **Asiatic Society of Bengal.** His work generated great enthusiasm for Indian culture throughout Europe.

Kalidasa Great poet and dramatist under the **Guptas** whose play *Shakuntala* and poem *The Cloud-Messenger* were translated into English by Sir William **Jones**, and later into other languages, taking Europe by storm.

Kamasutra Text compiled by the author Vatsyayana (c. 200 BC?) from earlier material, which deals with the techniques of pleasure, including sex, and with the life of the city-dweller of his time.

Kanishka from Mathura

Kanishka Great king of the **Kushan** dynasty, under whom the third Buddhist council was held, but whose reign-date is still uncertain, estimates ranging from 78 to 142 AD.

Kant (1712–1804). Great German philosopher, proposing the concept especially of synthetic *a priori* conditions for experience, who lectured on Indian culture and whose ideas are said to have been influenced by Indian ones.

Kanvas Dynasty ruling in Bihar c. 80 AD, of which little is known.

Kapila (c. 800 BC) Sage who founded the branch of Hindu philosophy called **Sankhya.** None of his work survives but its fundamental concepts are accepted as part of most later philosophical systems.

Karma "Action," in the sense of that which directly affects a person's subsequent spiritual life, and his physical life in succeeding reincarnations; it may be good or bad, ensuring a higher or lower rebirth.

Khan, Genghis (d. 1227 AD). Great military leader of the **Mongols**, who conquered vast tracts of Asia and eastern Europe. His family produced the Yüan dynasty of China.

Kharoshthi Script used (c. 300 BC–400 AD) in **Gandhara** and in parts of Central Asia, to write the local languages.

Khmer People of **Mon** descent inhabiting Cambodia and adjacent parts of Thailand, whose dynasty established the Khmer empire (616) and its capital Angkor (802–1215 AD).

Dancing Krishna, Chola dynasty

Krishna Personal name of one of the incarnations of the high Hindu god **Vishnu**. Born at Brindaban on the Yamuna river according to his legend, he was the object of a cult of passionate personal devotion.

Kshatriyas Second highest social stratum in the Hindu **caste system** after the **Brahmans**; technically the aristocratic warriors.

Kumarajiva (344–412 AD). Great Indian Buddhist teacher who migrated to China and at the capital supervised the translation into Chinese of 106 **Mahayana** texts.

Kural Great anthology of early **Tamil** literature, known as the **Veda** of the Tamils, compiled probably in the 6th century AD. It is more secular than religious and a classic on which much later Tamil writing is based.

Kushans Dynasty and people who originated (2nd century BC) on the borders of China. They migrated into northwestern India by the 1st century AD, there to found a major empire; it faded by the 5th century.

Kuvera Pot-bellied god of wealth, who often appears in art holding a sack from which coins spill, or a mongoose. In Gandharan art he has a wife Hariti, patron of motherhood and children.

Lalitavistara Seminal Sanskrit Buddhist text, describing the Buddha's life and many related legends, perhaps 1st–2nd century AD. It includes reference to the colossal number 10^{53}.

Lattice Panel of pierced openwork, often set into a window to exclude harsh sunlight but allow free passage to the air.

Lingam Stylized emblem of the male penis, used as **hallows** in the majority of Hindu temples, to symbolize creative power. It may be made of any material, and small versions may be used for private devotions.

Linschoten, J. H. van Dutch author of the first book (1596) in Europe fully to describe the Portuguese discoveries and trading ventures in the east which had hitherto been a closely guarded secret.

Lokeshvara Bodhisattva whose name means "lord of the world," hence he was a suitable patron deity adapted by Buddhist kings.

Lokeshvara from Cambodia

Lotus sutra English name for the Sanskrit *Saddharmapundarika,* one of the greatest **Mahayana** texts, which presents the Buddha as preaching his doctrine to vast, metacosmic assemblies of Bodhisattvas, Buddhas and deities; composed by the 2nd century AD.

Madhyamika School of Buddhist philosophy, founded by the great teacher Nagarjuna in the 2nd century AD, in which the doctrine of the invalidity of both negative and positive propositions is developed.

Magadha Region of Bihar around the **Ganga** river, home of a kingdom which was the center of many empires and cultural developments in ancient times.

Magadhi Language spoken in Magadha, a derivative of **Sanskrit**.

Mahabharata Earlier of the two great epics of India, compiled c. 400 BC–200 AD, whose heroes are the Pandava brothers and their joint wife, and of which the **Bhagavadgita** forms part.

Mahavira (d. 527 BC). Founder of the **Jain** religion. He taught that only complete abstention from injuring living creatures could lead to release from reincarnation; the religion still flourishes.

Mahayana Form of Buddhism followed in northern countries, whose texts are in Sanskrit, and which especially cultivates the **Bodhisattva** as an elaborate positive imagery for Buddhist ideas.

Mahmud of Ghazni Muslim ruler in Afghanistan (early 11th century AD) who invaded and looted northwestern and western India, destroying temples; **al-Biruni** followed in his train.

Makara Mythical water-monster with curled snout, often used to symbolize the river Yamuna, or the magical source of fertility.

Mandala Circular design used to relate a group of subfunctions to their center; in India most commonly to relate subsidiary psychological principles, personified as deities, to the central unifying reality or Supreme Self.

Mandapa Hall aligned with the main cell of a Hindu shrine; there may be two or three, each devoted to a different function.

Manusmriti Classic Sanskrit text (the title means "the Laws of Manu"), dealing with custom, law and morality, probably composed 500–300 BC.

Markendeya Purana One of the encyclopedic Hindu Sanskrit texts composed during the Middle Ages to collect and co-ordinate the vast number of myths developed in India.

Marshall, Sir John Director general of the **Archaeological Survey of India** (1902–31), under whom the sites of the **Indus valley civilization** were first excavated.

Maurya dynasty First great imperial dynasty of India (321–185 BC), founded by **Chandragupta**, its greatest ruler being **Ashoka**.

Megasthenes Greek ambassador from the Greek king **Seleucus** of Bactria to the court of **Chandragupta** Maurya; his account of life in India in the 3rd century BC has always been the most important documentation of the period.

Milarepa (b. 1052?). Tibetan poet saint, whose poems are widely known in Tibet, and whose biography was written by a pupil and is a Buddhist classic.

Mon Population and language group first inhabitating the lower reaches of the great rivers and coastal plains of Burma, Thailand and Cambodia, before the infiltration of other peoples from the north.

Mongols Central Asian horse-breeding nomad peoples, who were periodically united under great Khans. They conquered large tracts of territory both east and west, and formed a dynasty in China known as Yüan (1278–1368 AD).

Monist Type of philosophy which holds that all phenomena are essentially of one nature with the supreme principle, the **Brahman**, and that only ignorance makes them seem otherwise.

Monolith Single unbroken stone, usually of enormous size.

Monsoon Wind which blows diagonally across the Indian Ocean and Bay of Bengal, especially from the southwest in India, during late June to October bringing heavy rain, which is virtually the only rainfall most of India receives.

Mughals Turkic Muslim dynasty which took control of much of northern India after 1526, surviving, much diminished, until the 19th century. The greatest Mughal was Akbar (1556–1605).

Naga Snake in its magical aspect. Nagas were worshiped all over India as the patrons of water and treasure, and were represented often with five or seven heads, and with partly human bodies.

Nagas Tribal peoples inhabiting the densely forested uplands of the eastern Himalaya and Assam.

Nanda Handsome cousin-brother of the Buddha, who was induced to join the Buddhist order of monks by a trick. His story is told in a poem *Saundarananda* by Ashvaghosha.

Naos Name used for the inner cell or sanctuary in a Greek temple.

Nats Nature spirits propitiated and worshiped by the Burmese.

Natyashastra Classical Sanskrit text on the performance of dance-drama, the training of dancers and aesthetic theory; it was composed before 400 AD, and was attributed to Bharata.

Neolithic Archaeological epoch preceding the **Bronze Age**, when finely made stone tools were predominant; it has no absolute dates.

Nimbarka (d. 1162). Great Hindu philosopher, whose life's work was the reconciliation of the **Monist Veda** with the dualism implicit in **Bhakti.**

Nirmanakaya Body in which the Buddha as reincarnating being made his last appearance in the world.

Nirvana Ultimate Buddhist condition, when all **karma** is extinct and rebirth will happen no more; the Buddha entered that condition provisionally at his **enlightenment**, finally at his death.

Northern Black Polished ware Type of pottery characteristic of the early city sites of the Ganges valley, finely potted, fired in a reducing atmosphere.

Opisthodomos Rear chamber of a Greek temple, often used as a treasury or storeroom for sacred paraphernalia.

Ouranos/Varuna Ouranos is the ancient Greek name for the early sky god; Varuna is the Vedic Sanskrit counterpart, the two names being etymologically cognate.

Pagoda Term used in Burma for the evolved Burmese form of the **stupa** and sometimes applied by extension to a whole Buddhist monastery, or any of its towers.

Palas Dynasty ruling in northeastern India from the later 8th century to 1196 AD. The last king was killed by invading Muslims. They patronized the great Buddhist universities of Bihar and northern Orissa.

Pali Language derived from Sanskrit, probably spoken in western India during the last few centuries BC, in which the texts of **Hinayana** Buddhism are recorded.

Palimpsest Reworked artistic surface; older work is wholly or partly obliterated and new is painted or carved over it.

Palladium Sacred object or emblem, in which the power of a dynasty or the metaphysical safety of a state is supposed to reside.

Pallavas First Hindu dynasty of southeastern India (4th–10th centuries AD), worshipers mainly of Shiva. Some of their kings were considerable poets.

Panchatantra Largest known collection of Sanskrit fables, finely written, and probably designed to portray exemplary patterns of

conduct for kings. It survives in several versions.

Pandyas Dynasty ruling in the southeast of India (flourished in the 13th century) under whom the expansion of earlier Hindu temples took place.

Panini (c. 450 BC). Great grammarian of Sanskrit, founder of the science of philology.

Parthians Nomadic steppe people who occupied north Iran and other parts of western Asia as a kingdom from the 2nd century BC to the 3rd century AD.

Patanjali (c. 150 BC). Great grammarian of Sanskrit and yoga scholar who describes dramatic literature and contemporary customs.

Pediment Triangular space appearing on the front gable of a building (usually Classical), often decorated with sculpture.

Peristyle Row of columns supporting architrave and roof around a shrine, temple or courtyard; or the area so covered.

Pharmacopoeia Standard list of drugs, giving their sources and methods of preparation and use.

Plato (c. 427–348 BC). Great Athenian philosopher, proponent of the Theory of Ideas. He used Socrates as protagonist in his literary dialogues. An important school of mystical philosophy (Neoplatonism) based itself on his works.

Pliny the elder Roman orator and author. His *Natural History* is a mine of information on Classical culture and art. He perished in the eruption of Vesuvius (79 AD) which destroyed Pompeii.

Plotinus (b. c. 205 AD). Greatest Neoplatonist philosopher whose Greek *Enneads*, brief essays, are the chief source of western mystical doctrine and owe some debt to Indian ideas.

Pradakshina Ritual of walking around a revered object, place or person, keeping it on one's right hand, to pay extreme respect.

Prakrit Language derived by simplification from **Sanskrit**. There were many Prakrits spoken and written in India, which later developed into the modern regional languages.

Prinsep, J. Secretary of the Asiatic Society of Bengal, who first deciphered the **Brahmi** alphabet in 1837 – an epoch-making event in the history of Indian studies, enabling Europeans to read the inscriptions of **Ashoka.**

Pronaos Hall or space in front of the principal cell of a Greek temple, usually enclosed by columns bearing a roof.

Ptolemaic Period during which Egypt was ruled by a Macedonian Greek dynasty, the Ptolemies, from the death of Alexander the Great (323 BC) to Cleopatra VII (died 30 BC).

Puja Ceremonial offering performed by Hindus, at least once a day at home, in a shrine at other times.

Puranas Encyclopedic Sanskrit texts in which the myths and legends of India were collected by Brahman scholars; most of them are medieval.

Putti Figures of plump children appearing especially in Roman and later Italian art in an ornamental or humorous capacity; sometimes identified as Cupids, or as emblems of the unfallen soul.

Pythagoras (b. c. 580 BC). Early Greek philosopher and mathematician, regarded both as a mystic and father of western science; said to have traveled in Egypt and the east.

Pyu People inhabiting upper Burma during the early Middle Ages (from c. 450 AD) who built large and splendid cities known to the Chinese, but which no longer exist. They were overcome by the racial Burmese by the 10th century.

Quincunx Group of five things, one in the center, one at each of the four corners.

Raffles, Sir T. S. Englishman who founded Singapore as a trading colony in 1819, and as trade representative in Java between 1811 and 1816 did much archaeological research, discovered Borobudur and wrote a *History of Java*.

Raga Indian musical mode or scale, in which an entire composition is played. Many are used, each with its own characteristic mode of feeling and appropriate time of day.

Rama Hero of the classical Sanskrit epic *Ramayana* (2nd century BC–2nd century AD), looked on as an incarnation of the high god **Vishnu.** The story of the loss of his wife Sita, and her recovery with the help of the monkey king Hanuman, provides the chief themes of Southeast Asian dance-drama.

Ramanuja (1037–1137). Hindu philosopher who first successfully qualified the **monist** doctrines of **Vedanta** with the acceptance of a modified dualism as necessary for any true devotional religion.

Ramayana See **Rama.**

Ratha Modest shrine; also used of a wooden shrine on wheels or temple car.

Reliquary Box or jar meant to contain the bodily relics of a saint, often finely crafted.

Repoussé Metal plate which has been beaten into a design from the back.

Rishi Inspired sage of Brahmanical tradition, often endowed with insight into past and future, and magical powers.

Rouletted ware. Type of pottery, characteristically Roman, decorated with simple patterns impressed in the wet clay with a notched wheel or roulette, dating to the years just post-BC.

Roundel Circular framed panel, usually ornamented.

Saddharmapundarika ("Lotus of the good law"). See **Lotus Sutra.**

Sadhanamala Buddhist Sanskrit text consisting of a collection of detailed descriptions of **Vajrayana** deities as an aid to invoking them and realizing their presence. Composed probably by the 8th century AD.

Sambhogakaya Intermediate golden symbolic body in which the Buddha nature may be visualized, as distinct from the **Nirmanakaya.** It is the body represented in most icons of the Buddha.

Sankhya system Earliest of the orthodox systems of Hindu philosophy, whose concepts were used in many others. It envisages two irreducible principles, spirit and matter, the aim of release being attained by the liberation of spirit from matter. Its founder was reputed to be **Kapila** and its earliest surviving text is the *Sankhyakarika* by Ishvara Krishna (3rd century AD).

Sanskrit Language of the Indo-European group, highly inflected, originally spoken by the **Aryans**; in it were composed the **Veda** and its associated literature before 600 BC. Later it was simplified into spoken **Prakrits,** but a literary version has remained current as the language of poetry, drama and philosophy to the present day.

Santali Language spoken by the **Adivasi** group, the Santals.

Saptashataka Most important work in **Prakrit,** a collection of beautiful poetic stanzas of great brevity, wit and erotic skill; supposedly written by a **Shatavahana** king (1st century AD) but many are probably later.

Sasanians Persian dynasty which aimed to regain command of the ancient **Achaemenid** empire, ruling regions adjacent to western India (226–651 AD).

Sasetti, Filippo Florentine merchant who lived in Goa for five years (1583–88) and sent home letters describing his experiences in vivid detail; they are an important source of information on the India of his time.

Schist Dark gray crystalline rock, containing mica, whose crystals lie parallel; out of it many of the buildings and sculptures of **Gandhara** were carved during the 2nd to 4th centuries AD.

Schopenhauer, F. (1788–1860). Great German philosopher who assimilated Indian ideas fully into his own philosophy, naturalizing them into the European Idealist tradition.

Seleucus General of Alexander the Great, left in charge of the Bactrian province, in modern Afghanistan, who founded his own dynasty after Alexander's death; it controlled **Gandhara** for a time.

Shailendra dynasty Family ruling in Java (775–864) who were probably responsible for building the greatest central Javanese monuments.

Shaiva Follower of **Shiva.**

Shakas Name given to people of foreign (perhaps Scythian) descent, who infiltrated the west of India during the late centuries BC.

Shakuntala Title of a Sanskrit play by **Kalidasa** (4th century AD?). It was the first great Indian poetical work translated into English by Sir William **Jones** and it took Europe by storm.

Shamanism Form of primitive religious practice, in which specially gifted men or women, called shamans, visit the spirit world, aided by music, dance and trance, in order to help their people, for example by foreseeing the future or curing disease.

Shankaracharya (788–828 AD) Greatest Hindu philosopher, looked on by many as an incarnation of the god **Shiva.** His philosophy was an extreme form of **monism,** called **Vedanta,** which taught that every phenomenon is mere illusion, the **Brahman** alone being real. He wrote a vast body of work much of it in the form of commentaries on Vedic and other early sacred texts.

Shatavahana dynasty Ruled in the Deccan (2nd century BC to 5th century AD) and patronized Buddhism extensively. They may have been **Shakas.** One of their kings is reputed to have been a Prakrit poet (see **Saptashataka**).

Shikhara at Bhuvaneshvara

Shikhara Pyramidal tower which crowns the main cell of the Hindu temple; it symbolizes the cosmic mountain Meru.

Shiva Major god of historical Hinduism, around whom a vast body of legend and literature has collected. More Indian temples are dedicated to him than to any other deity; the **lingam** is his emblem. He is often represented in a ferocious form as Rudra; also as a dancer. His role in the Hindu trinity is that of the Destroyer. In his icons he wears a pile of tangled hair and carries a trident; he may also be accompanied by a bull.

Shiva from Tanjore

Shudras Lowest of the four **varnas**, later the lowest members of the **caste system** in Indian society who lacked any status or value, and were considered of no account; to them, numerous as they were, were delegated all the unpleasant jobs the higher castes refused to do.

Shungas Dynasty ruling in Magadha, after the fall of the **Mauryas** (c. 70–50 BC). The stupa of Barhut was built in their dominions.

Silpa shastra Group of medieval texts in Sanskrit containing technical formulae for producing architecture and art.

Société Asiatique French society for the study of Asia, founded in 1822, particularly for the development of Sanskrit scholarship.

Sri Old Indian goddess of fertility and good fortune, usually represented as a woman clad in lavish jewels, often standing on a lotus, and being watered by two elephants with their trunks, symbolizing the monsoon rain.

Stein, Sir Aurel (1862–1943). British explorer who in 1906–09 investigated the trade routes to China across the desert basin of the Tarim river; he excavated many desert sites and brought back material now in the British Museum and the Central Asian Museum, New Delhi.

Stela Standing stone, trimmed and carved with imagery or script.

Stevens, Thomas English member of the Jesuit order, who reached Goa in 1579, and there studied Marathi and other languages seriously.

Stucco Plaster made of fat, slaked lime (calcium hydroxide) and sand, which hardens by absorbing carbon dioxide from the atmosphere, the lime becoming calcium carbonate. The fine lime for Indian stucco was often made by calcining seashells.

Stupa Central monument of the Buddhist faith; originally a **tumulus** containing relics of the Buddha or Buddhist saints, it became purely emblematic, a towering structure, circular, retaining vestiges of the basic dome. It symbolizes **Nirvana**, and may be of any size.

Sung dynasty Chinese dynasty (960–1279 AD) under which much Buddhist art was made.

Surya Old Aryan sun god, taken as patron by many Hindu dynasties of kings. He is represented as a charioteer, like Apollo.

Sutra Sanskrit text which consists of teaching and philosophical explanation; it may be Buddhist or Hindu.

Swag Architectural term for an ornamental feature representing a heavy garland of vegetation, fixed at both ends, hanging between them in a drooping curve.

Tamil Language totally distinct from Sanskrit, spoken by a population in the southeast of India, who are also called Tamils.

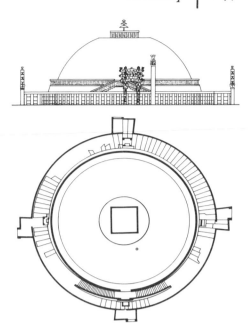

Plan and section of the stupa at Sanchi

There is an ancient and extensive Tamil literature.

T'ang dynasty Chinese dynasty (618–906 AD) under whom Buddhism flourished especially.

Tank Artifical reservoir, lake or pond used primarily for irrigation; but Hindu temples also have tanks of sacred water in which visitors bathe to purify themselves.

Tantra ("Thread" or tradition). Usually applied to a corpus of teaching contained in texts called Tantras, which embody rites that extend beyond the pale of Vedic orthodoxy; especially centered upon the feminine principle of creative energy, called Shakti, whence the term Shaktas for certain of the large body of Hindus who follow Tantra.

Tavernier, J. B. French jewel merchant who visited India five times between 1641 and 1688, traveling widely. He wrote an account of what he saw, a valuable source of information on the India of his time.

Terracotta Clay, fired at lowish temperature, to become hard; usually buff or reddish in color.

Theravada "Way of the elders" by which southern or **Hinayana** Buddhism is known, especially to its followers.

Tiloka (1441–87) King of Lan-na in northern Thailand, who is looked on as a saint. He ensured the complete triumph of Buddhism over the still-potent animist religion of nature spirits. He sent missions to Ceylon to import monks and art.

Toga Garment worn by Roman citizens – their proud mark – consisting of a single large piece of heavy cloth – wool was traditionally preferred – which was worn draped over the left shoulder, leaving the right arm free.

Trefoil Architectural term for a three-lobed shape, used in ornamental design.

Tumulus Circular mound of stones and earth used by **Neolithic** and **Bronze Age** people to cover and mark the burial place either of a chieftain or of the whole community.

Uma Name of the goddess who was wife of **Shiva** in a number of the legends connected with that god.

Undercroft Subterranean or base level of a building which supports the main floor-level.

Upanishads Set of summary texts in **Sanskrit** in which the essential mystical and religious doctrines of Vedic Brahmanism are condensed. They were meant to be studied by high-caste people who had withdrawn from worldly affairs; but now they are widely read throughout the world.

Vajrayana Form of Buddhism which developed by the 6th century AD in which psychological stages of Buddhist meditation are personified as deities, and rituals, spells and magical processes are used.

Vakatakas Deccan dynasty (c. 300–500 AD) who intermarried with the imperial **Guptas** and probably patronized the cave temple at Ajanta. They were successors in the Deccan to the **Shatavahanas**.

Varna ("color," from which caste originally developed). The four *varnas* were the earliest social strata recognized in **Aryan** society in the second millennium BC. They were the Brahmans, the Kshatriyas, the Vish and the Shudras.

Veda Ancient fourfold collection of hymns, preserved in complex archaic Sanskrit, composed probably during the second millennium BC, which are the nucleus of Brahmanical Hinduism. Most are addressed to named gods, and were used in sacrificial rituals. All later Brahmanical philosophy derives from them.

Vedanta ("consummation of the **Veda**"). Terms applied to the extreme **monist** philosophy of **Shankaracharya**.

Vihara ("living quarters"). Specifically of a Buddhist monastery.

Vina Traditional Indian stringed musical instrument, with resonating bodies, usually of hollowed gourds, attached beneath the hollow finger-board, most commonly one at each end; its strings are struck with a plectrum, and the frets, defining the degrees of the scale or **raga**, are raised to allow the tension of the string to be increased by the stopping finger, to raise the pitch of the note as it sounds. The *vina* is the emblem of the Goddess of Wisdom.

Vish Third of the **varnas**, the stratum of early Aryan society which came to embrace many castes whose occupations ranged from farming to the crafts and trade.

7th-century bronze Vishnu

Vishnu High god of Hinduism, around whom many legends have gathered; he is said to have appeared on earth in ten incarnations, among which are **Rama** and **Krishna**. As one of the Hindu trinity, he represents the principle of sustained being. In his icons he wears a full cylindrical miter and carries a club, discus and conch shell.

Vishnupurana Sanskrit **purana** in which legends especially relating to **Vishnu** were collected in the early Middle Ages.

Wagon-roof Roof composed of a single structural unit, the axis of the pointed vault of which runs transverse to the main axis of the building.

Wat Term used in Cambodia and Thailand for a major shrine, Buddhist or Hindu.

Wei dynasty Rulers of Turkic (To-pa) stock who ruled northern China 386–550 AD. They adopted Buddhism, and patronized the great series of early cave shrines at Yun-Kang.

Wheeler, Sir Mortimer (1890–1976). British museum director and archaeologist, for four years (1944–48) Director General of the Archaeological Survey of India, initiating new techniques and major reforms.

Woolley, Sir Leonard (1880–1960). Distinguished British archaeologist who excavated the royal tombs of Ur in Iraq and was brought to India as adviser to the Archaeological Survey in 1938.

Xavier, St Francis (1506–52). Roman Catholic saint, of Spanish birth, who traveled in the east with the Portuguese adventurers, making many converts and setting up Christian communities, notably in Goa and Macao. He is buried in Shang-chuan Tao.

Railing pillar with yakshi

Yaksha (male), Yakshi (female) Terms applied to nature spirits in India. They live particularly in trees, and need to be propitiated if they are to act benevolently. Some early sculptures may represent them.

Yamuna Sacred river, tributary to the **Ganga**, also personified as a goddess, sometimes called Jumna by Europeans.

Yoga Term, meaning "effort" or "union," applied to a variety of physical and meditative techniques which are designed to eliminate agitation and suffering, and lead to personal union with the supreme principle of reality.

Yüeh-chi Name by which the **Kushans** were known to the Chinese.

Zen Japanese way of pronouncing the Chinese *Ch'an*, in turn the Chinese way of pronouncing the Sanskrit word *dhyana*, meaning "meditation"; used as the name for a reforming movement within Chinese Buddhism that taught sudden illumination and opposed the use of elaborate scriptures.

Zeus/Dyaus-Pitar Zeus is the Greek father god, whose name is philologically cognate with the Sanskrit term Dyaus-Pitar, meaning "heaven-father."

Index